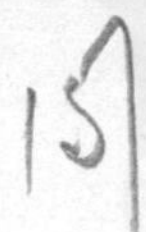

REASON
AND
EXPERIENCE

REASON
AND
EXPERIENCE

BY

W. H. WALSH

FELLOW AND TUTOR OF MERTON COLLEGE

OXFORD
AT THE CLARENDON PRESS
1947

Oxford University Press, Amen House, London E.C. 4
EDINBURGH GLASGOW NEW YORK TORONTO MELBOURNE
WELLINGTON BOMBAY CALCUTTA MADRAS CAPE TOWN
Geoffrey Cumberlege, Publisher to the University

PRINTED IN GREAT BRITAIN

PREFACE

THE work which follows can be taken, at the discretion of the reader, either as an introduction to theory of knowledge in general, or as a discussion of some leading features of the type of epistemological theory advocated by Kant. It answers in some way to both descriptions. It is a Kantian study in so far as it arose out of a detailed examination of the *Critique of Pure Reason*, originally undertaken with a view to the production of a more technical work than this, and in so far as the problems Kant raised (and to a great extent, too, the solutions he offered of them) determine the general shape of the book. But it aims at being something more than a Kantian commentary in the narrow sense. I have tried to occupy myself not only with questions of interpretation, but also with questions of truth; and to that end have attempted to see the problems I examine against the background of the general development of modern philosophy, and on occasion even of that of ancient philosophy too. As a result, I have been led in places into an extensive discussion of the views of both the predecessors and the successors of Kant, in particular those of Hume and Hegel. My excuse for casting my net so wide (a procedure which I hope will not meet with universal condemnation) is that I do not see that any discussion of the problems of knowledge, whatever the level of sophistication on which it proceeds, can avoid consideration of the types of view represented by these three writers. Certainly those questions which I myself find most difficult in the subject—the problems of the origin and status of *a priori* concepts, and of the comparative value of alternative sets of such concepts—spring directly from the topics with which Hume, Kant, and Hegel are mainly concerned.

I have tried throughout to write in a simple way, which will be (or ought to be) intelligible even to elementary students. But I must emphasize, for the sake of the unwary, that my book, though designed to throw light on a number of leading philosophical texts, should in no way be regarded as a substitute for them. I do not profess to summarize arguments and theories except for the purpose in hand; and I should certainly not claim to have expounded even Kant's theories in detail (for instance, I say virtually nothing of his views of space and time).

It is a pleasure to be able to thank those who have helped me in the production of the book. My first, and, in some ways, greatest, obligation is to Professor H. H. Price, who not only encouraged me to write, but commented at most generous length on what I wrote, enabling me to remove many imperfections both of argument and language, and pointing out others which I have not been able to remove. Mr. G. R. G. Mure, now Warden of Merton, who was my original tutor in philosophy, also read the book in typescript; and I have made changes to meet his criticisms, too, though not (I fear) such extensive changes as he would have liked. I find it the more difficult to acknowledge my debt to Mr. Mure because his thinking has affected mine at every stage of my philosophical development; I can only say that I count myself fortunate to have been the pupil of one whose conception of philosophy was at once so comprehensive and so exacting. I am also under a general obligation to Professor H. J. Paton, who, though not directly associated with the present book, has taken a continuous interest in my Kantian studies, and from whose writings on Kant I have learnt a very great deal; and to my friend Mr. H. W. Cassirer, now of the University of Glasgow, with whom I have discussed many of the problems of theory of knowledge, always with profit to myself.

I must acknowledge with thanks the permission of the Editors of *Mind* and *Philosophy* to reproduce the argument and, in places, the actual wording of papers of mine which have appeared in those periodicals.

Lastly, I have to record my gratitude for help of a different nature: to the Warden and Fellows of Merton College, Oxford, who by electing me to a research fellowship gave me the opportunity not only to learn something about my subject, but also to enjoy the benefits in the way of a liberal education which membership of such a society involves; and to my wife, who, besides giving me much general encouragement, bore more or less patiently with the distressing fact that writing a philosophical work does not necessarily conduce to the display of a temper which is philosophical in the accepted sense of the word. For what it is worth, I should like to dedicate the book to her.

W. H. W.

UNIVERSITY COLLEGE, DUNDEE

29 May 1947

CONTENTS

I. THE SCOPE OF THEORY OF KNOWLEDGE . . . 1
II. RATIONALISM AND EMPIRICISM . . . 12
III. TWO PRELIMINARY DISTINCTIONS . . . 30
IV. INTELLECTUAL INTUITION . . . 52
V. INTELLECTUAL INTUITION: TWO FURTHER THEORIES . . . 77
VI. REASON AND EXPERIENCE . . . 106
VII. SUBSTANCE, CAUSE, AND THINGHOOD . . . 140
VIII. REASON AND IMAGINATION . . . 163
IX. SELF-KNOWLEDGE . . . 190
X. EXPERIENCE AND METAPHYSICS . . . 221
INDEX . . . 253

I

THE SCOPE OF THEORY OF KNOWLEDGE

§ 1. THE questions dealt with in this book belong to the branch of philosophy known as theory of knowledge or epistemology; and it will be advisable to begin with a brief discussion of the scope and function of that study. Unfortunately this is by no means an easy subject. Before we take it up we must face the preliminary problem of whether any department of philosophy can be treated satisfactorily in isolation from the rest. It is a disconcertingly common experience that the raising of one set of philosophical questions (for example, those of ethics) frequently provokes others of a quite different nature (for example, problems of logic or metaphysics) and cannot be proceeded with effectively unless these are answered first. It is notorious, too, that the great philosophers of the past have combined, sometimes at least without appearing to be aware of it, speculations of very different kinds in works alleged to be devoted to single problems or groups of problems. Locke's *Essay*, for instance, a book whose aim is stated (in a way which itself confuses theory of knowledge with psychology) to be 'to enquire into the original, certainty and extent of human knowledge, together with the grounds and degrees of belief, opinion and assent',[1] contains many discussions which would be more properly described as psychological, metaphysical, or logical than epistemological; and the same is true of other celebrated treatises. No doubt some of this confusion is to be ascribed to the carelessness of authors; but in part, too, it seems to be due to the nature of the problems studied: the different branches of philosophy have an untidy habit of spilling over into each other at the least provocation. And if this is so we may reasonably ask whether it is profitable to treat them as if they could always be kept neatly within bounds.

Two ways of meeting this difficulty are perhaps worth a brief consideration.

(A) We may claim first that the philosophical sciences are, in fact, self-contained disciplines whose respective fields and subject-matter we can indicate with some precision, but that they are not all co-ordinate studies. The answer to the problem of the overlap of philosophical questions is to be found, according to

[1] Bk. I, chap. i, § 2.

this account, in the idea of a hierarchy of branches of knowledge, an idea which goes back at least to Aristotle. Aristotle believed that in every group of studies an architectonic or master science could be found, the principles of which were presupposed in the remaining sciences, which could be arranged in order of logical priority on a scale. Applying this to philosophy to-day we might hold, for instance, that theory of knowledge presupposes logic and is presupposed by ethics, which is in turn the master science of political theory. Obviously this way of thinking is a promising one, but we get into difficulties when we try to decide the precise details of the hierarchy. Thus, according to some philosophers, logic is presupposed in all other branches of philosophy; according to others the treatment of logic leads on irresistibly to that of metaphysics, and only in a metaphysical context can its problems be solved. It is true that the difference of opinion here does not affect the principle of a hierarchy of philosophical sciences directly, but it does suggest that the easy solution promised by its supporters may not be forthcoming.

(B) The alternative is to say that philosophy should not and cannot be treated as a series of departmental studies. The different branches of the science are so closely interwoven that their separate pursuit is impossible. Philosophy is one in the sense that the solution of one philosophical problem involves and is involved in the solution of all other philosophical problems. Logic, theory of knowledge, and the rest may conveniently designate groups of questions which have been traditionally treated together; but to assume that they are the names of genuinely independent disciplines is a gross error. There are no philosophical sciences; only philosophy.

The difficulty about this is to see how, if it were true, we could ever begin to philosophize. It looks as if we must assume the legitimacy of departmental thinking, at least as a provisional measure, in philosophy as elsewhere if we are to make any progress in solving our problems. No doubt those who advocate the theory we are discussing would admit this if sufficient emphasis were put on 'provisional'; but the very fact that they are willing to go so far shows the impossibility of their view in its strict interpretation. And, in fact, it is not true that the different branches of philosophy contain problems arbitrarily grouped together: their internal relations are certainly closer than their external. If philosophy is one its unity is more like that of the British Empire than that of the Third Reich.

To say this is not, however, to claim that everything discussed by the classical writers on, e.g., theory of knowledge really belongs to that, or indeed any, part of philosophy. And here perhaps we can find an immediate if not an ultimately satisfactory solution of our difficulty. That philosophical problems do in fact fall into reasonably well-defined groups capable of independent treatment must be assumed if we are ever to begin their solution; but that existing groups must be accepted as they stand is quite another matter. Our first task in discussing theory of knowledge must accordingly be to tabulate some of the main questions philosophers have in fact asked in the subject, in order to determine, if possible, what does and what does not belong to it.

§ 2. Among the questions about knowledge actually asked by philosophers are these: (1) What ultimately different kinds of thing and what ultimately different kinds of truth do we know? (2) How do we know such things and truths, i.e. in virtue of possessing what faculties? (3) From our having this knowledge what can be inferred about (*a*) ourselves; (*b*) the objects of knowledge and their relations to one another; (*c*) the relations of (*a*) and (*b*)? (4) How are our claims to knowledge to be tested? What justification have we for saying that we know what we know? (5) How is knowing to be differentiated from analogous states of mind such as believing and taking for granted? (6) What are the conditions of the organization and communication of knowledge? Can we devise a system of symbols which will express what we know in an unambiguous and truly reliable manner?

Now if we reflect on these specimen questions we see that they can be divided into fairly well-defined groups. Thus (1), (2), and (4) appear to be closely connected, and there are certain affinities between (5) and (6). (3), by way of contrast, stands by itself, though it is a natural enough question for anyone interested in knowledge to ask. And it is a curious fact that questions (3), (5), and (6), though undoubtedly raised by writers on theory of knowledge, are also of direct interest to specialists in other branches of philosophy, whilst the same does not seem to be true of (1), (2), and (4). Thus question (3), about the nature of the objects of knowledge and the knowing self, is one which is asked in the first instance in metaphysics, when that is taken to be an inquiry into the general nature of reality and man's place in the universe; and it may be agreed that it is more properly classified as metaphysical than epistemological. Question (6), again, has been asked in different ways by both logicians and psychologists (to say nothing of writers with purely linguistic interests), and the same is true of (5): both appear to be complex, and perhaps belong properly to other branches of learning than theory of knowledge. Questions (1), (2), and (4), by way of contrast, do seem to be peculiar to epistemology, and not to be of direct interest to any other science, philosophical or otherwise. They are, in fact, the main questions which students in the theory of knowledge hope to answer.

The business of epistemology, if these indications are correct, would seem to be to determine the nature, extent, and validity of human knowledge. And its method is purely reflective: it starts from the pronouncements of natural scientists, historians, and others, and examines these from its own peculiar point of view, considering in particular such matters as their certainty or probability, the kind of insight or evidence on which they are said to rest, and the light they throw on the possibility of gaining further knowledge. Epistemology is thus a study which cannot claim, as can physics or history, to add to the sum of direct or first-order knowledge available to human beings; its pretensions, as Locke saw long ago, must be far more modest than that. Locke declared that in an age which produced the great Huygens and the incomparable Mr. Newton it was ambition enough for him to be employed in clearing the ground and removing the rubbish which lay in the way to knowledge.[1] The relation implied here between the philosopher and the scientist still holds good. It is the business of scientists and historians to make all the exciting discoveries, to reveal the secrets of Nature, and re-enact the pageant of the past. The task of theory of knowledge, at least, is of quite a different order: it is to reflect on the knowledge gained and consider some of its general properties.

Epistemology as thus described can be seen to be a study closely analogous in status to logic. For logic, too, is not a special science to be ranged alongside empirical disciplines: no new set of particular facts is discovered when philosophers engage in logical inquiries. The pronouncements of logicians are of a quite different nature from those of special scientists: their interest is general, and they apply not to particular pieces of thinking but to thinking as such. Logical knowledge is second-order knowledge, derived from reflection on the formal relations of thought. Aristotle, the

[1] *Essay on Human Understanding*, 'Epistle to the Reader' (ed. Fraser, i. 14).

founder of logic, described its nature correctly when he said that it stood to other branches of learning as a propaedeutic study. And what is true of logic in this respect is also true of theory of knowledge. Indeed some philosophers have gone so far as to identify the two, though in fact the identification appears to lead only to confusion and misunderstanding.[1]

§ 3. At this point we must consider an obvious objection. Theory of knowledge as here described, it may be argued, is a possible branch of inquiry but also a useless one. Why, after all, do we engage in epistemological studies? I have been at pains to point out in the preceding section the fact that these studies do not themselves aim at increasing the sum of factual knowledge; and it may be felt that the results they do produce are of an otiose character. For does anyone suggest that, for instance, the physicist or the mathematician is helped in his special field by knowing about theory of knowledge? Can saying what knowledge is forward its direct pursuit? Or, to put the matter another way, does knowing what types of thing we can know enable us actually to know them? The answer to all these questions is plainly negative. Theory of knowledge, in fact, is here once again in a position substantially identical with that of logic. No one suggests that a study of the formal relations of thought improves our thinking, except in an incidental way; and there are many able thinkers who have never reflected on logical problems.

The objection can be answered in a variety of ways.

1. There is first of all the line taken by Hegel[2] when confronted with a similar objection to logic. Hegel pointed out that men apparently thought it worth while to classify and examine the several species of parrot and veronica, and asked why they should not classify and examine the several species of syllogism. The

[1] The impulse to identify logic and theory of knowledge comes from the dissatisfaction some logicians have felt with the conception of logic as concerned only with formal validity: such a logic of validity, it is said, needs to be supplemented by a logic of truth. The next step is to say that the latter is the true and eventually the only logic. But the enormous progress made by formal logic in the last fifty years cannot be ignored by an impartial observer, and in fact the so-called logic of truth turns out to consist of topics belonging properly to theory of knowledge or (in one sense of the term) metaphysics.

Historically the amalgamation of logic and epistemology in modern philosophy derives from Kant's conception of Transcendental Logic. The term 'logic' need not, however, be pressed in that title any more than 'aesthetic' in Transcendental Aesthetic. It is best interpreted in a literal sense as doctrine of concepts.

[2] Quoted on this point by Bosanquet, *Logic*, vol. i, p. 1.

forms of thinking and (we may add) the nature and extent of knowledge are at least as worthy objects of study as many things whose investigation is considered quite unobjectionable. The argument is not wholly convincing, since parrots and veronicas are objects not of reflective but of first-order study, and it is the justification of the former which is in question. Hegel's answer has, nevertheless, a certain force *ad hominem*, suggesting as it does the perfectly true reflection that not even all first-order knowledge can be justified as useful.

2. But the utility test itself is of dubious validity. By what right do we demand that every branch of learning should be shown to have useful results or be abandoned? We could only do that if we could prove that anything entitled to the name of knowledge must serve some directly useful purpose. But while it is doubtless true as a matter of historical fact that the earliest efforts to acquire knowledge both of the human race generally and of individual men are responses to practical needs, it is by no means so clear that civilized and adult human beings are in the same position. The phrase 'knowledge for knowledge's sake' may be out of fashion now, but it remains true that the acquisition of knowledge brings a certain pleasure of its own and spurs the mind to efforts which no practical necessity can justify. And if that is so we may find a defence for theory of knowledge even if we cannot show it to be useful; for, as Hume says, 'were there no advantage to be reaped from these studies, beyond the gratification of an innocent curiosity, yet ought not even this to be despised; as being one accession to those few safe and harmless pleasures, which are bestowed on human race'.[1]

3. It is, however, possible to make a different reply to the objection and maintain that the study of theory of knowledge is, after all, a useful and even necessary undertaking. The arguments for this point of view are put with some force by both Hume (in the opening chapter of his *Enquiry*) and Kant (in the *Critique of Pure Reason* and again in the *Prolegomena*). Both philosophers argue that a study of the powers of the human mind is an indispensable preliminary to the eliminating of obscurities into which men are all too prone to fall. The obscurities of which they are thinking arise from the claims to knowledge made, not by natural scientists or historians, but by philosophers. In the history of philosophy a great many bold assertions have been made: that the world in

[1] *Enquiry concerning Human Understanding*, p. 11 (ed. Selby-Bigge).

which we live is the creation of a wise and beneficent God; that it displays an intelligible and purposeful order; and that human beings have a specially privileged place in that order, as possessing free wills and immortal souls. Other philosophers have maintained, in the same general strain, that the material world is not and cannot be true reality, but is best interpreted as the appearance of something which lies beyond it, accessible not to the senses but to other cognitive faculties; and have gone on to claim that the possession of such faculties argues a special kinship between men and the ultimately real. These positions have been supported by a diversity of arguments; and by the persistency and frequency with which they have been maintained might be thought to be well established. Unfortunately for our comfort this is not the case. The distressing thing is that equally convincing arguments can be produced against the positions mentioned as in their favour, with the result that some have been prepared to assert their exact opposite and maintain, e.g., that the world is ruled by blind chance and that man has no specially privileged place in it; or again, that the material world is the only reality and consciousness merely 'epiphenomenal'. Hence arises the unhappy state which Kant calls an Antinomy, a situation in which equally plausible reasons can be produced on behalf both of a given proposition and of its contradictory; and we may well believe that when this situation arises something has gone radically wrong with our thinking. If Kant is to be believed the error lies neither in the logic of our arguments nor in the falsity of their premisses but simply in the fact that we are attempting to assert the type of conclusion we do. We are trying, in making these *metaphysical* assertions, to maintain a series of speculative propositions which could be defended on scientific grounds only if we had different cognitive faculties from those we actually possess. The way to escape from our difficulties is accordingly to review our cognitive powers and establish their limits and legitimate use. As Hume put it in one of his Kantian passages: 'The only method of freeing learning, at once, from these abstruse questions, is to enquire seriously into the nature of human understanding, and show, from an exact analysis of its powers and capacity, that it is by no means fitted for such remote and abstruse subjects.'[1] Whether we agree

[1] *Enquiry*, p. 12, ed. Selby-Bigge. It should be mentioned that Hume and Kant do not quite see eye to eye over this matter. Hume is willing to commit to the flames any volume of 'divinity or school metaphysics' which contains neither

or not with the conclusions Hume and Kant maintain about knowledge, we should at least be prepared to admit that the facts call for some such inquiry as they desiderate; and that is to admit the need for theory of knowledge in the sense sketched in this chapter.

Theory of knowledge, then, is not only a possible but also a necessary science, at least if we are to avoid the difficulties into which philosophers are constantly falling. And in case anyone thinks this justification is of a purely domestic character, I would remind the reader that the assertion of metaphysical propositions (in this sense of the term) is by no means confined to professional metaphysicians. To say nothing of philosophizing scientists, we may note that the everyday beliefs of the so-called plain man are undoubtedly influenced, though in a remote way and usually after a time-lag, by the opinions which prevail among the learned; and while it would be folly to think that single philosophical arguments, however impressive, could shake the convictions of the general public, there can be no doubt that those convictions do respond to changes in the whole climate of philosophical opinion. Thus the materialism of the eighteenth and nineteenth centuries has borne fruit in the widespread scepticism of the present era, a scepticism which determines not only men's beliefs but their actions too. It would obviously be absurd to suppose that academic discussions of the kind carried on by epistemologists could have any immediate effect on this situation; yet it is perhaps not too much to hope that it could be influenced in the long run if we could show that scientists have nothing to say on these matters and philosophers nothing positive.[1] The attempt to solve these problems would thus seem to be worth making if only because of the obvious interest of the results.

§ 4. I do not propose to say any more here either in justification of the study of theory of knowledge or in explanation of its main problems. Instead, I shall conclude the chapter with a brief consideration of two objections to epistemology understood as a science dealing with the nature, extent, and validity of knowledge.

mathematical nor experimental reasoning. He has, in fact, no use for metaphysical assertions of the type mentioned in the text. But Kant, though he agrees that it has been a mistake to attempt to support these assertions by speculative arguments, nevertheless thinks a certain set of them unquestionably true. He says, however, that our attitude to them should be one not of knowledge but of faith.

[1] The reader is referred to the concluding chapter for some qualification of this necessarily dogmatic description.

The first of these may appear to some rather trivial. It was a commonplace of the school of Cook Wilson that the very phrase 'theory of knowledge' contained an absurdity. As Professor Prichard put it in his book on Kant, written to expose the confusions of any such undertaking as Kant made: 'Knowledge is *sui generis*, and therefore a "theory" of it is impossible. Knowledge is simply knowledge, and any attempt to state it in terms of something else must end in describing something which is not knowledge.'[1] Cook Wilson himself, discussing the same point in his logic lectures, said: 'There are some things which cannot be made matter of question. . . . Our experience of knowing being the presupposition of any inquiry we can undertake, we cannot make knowing itself a subject of inquiry in the sense of asking what knowing is. We can make knowing a subject of inquiry but not of that kind of inquiry. We can, for instance, inquire how we come to know in general, or in any department of knowledge.'[2]

The answer to this contention is surely that, so far from abolishing theory of knowledge, Cook Wilson and Prichard are themselves contributing to it. They do, in fact, have an account of knowledge to offer: they say that it is a unique and indefinable state known to us by acquaintance only. To Professor Prichard this account appears to be self-evidently true;[3] but it is by no means universally accepted. Indeed, a little reflection will show it to be, at the very least, somewhat unplausible; for if knowledge is as it is described by this school it will be difficult to avoid the conclusion that neither the natural sciences nor history contain any knowledge. The truth is that the Cook Wilsonian theory is derived, like the Aristotelian and Cartesian doctrines which it closely resembles, from a study of one type of thinking only, namely, that of mathematics. As a prima facie account of that very special form of reasoning it has some plausibility; but it has not been found possible to apply it successfully to any other sphere, and even in mathematics it is not finally adequate, as I hope to show later. The suggestion that theory of knowledge should be abandoned to comply with so doubtful a doctrine can in consequence scarcely be accepted.[4]

The second objection is more serious. Hegel, who developed his philosophy in opposition to that of Kant, argued that the latter's

[1] *Kant's Theory of Knowledge*, p. 245; cf. pp. 124 and 238.
[2] *Statement and Inference*, vol. i, pp. 39–40. [3] Prichard, op. cit., p. 124 n.
[4] For a further discussion of some aspects of this theory see Chapter V below.

attempt to determine the sphere within which human cognition is valid, and thus to fix the limits of possible knowledge, was doomed to failure from the first. He supported this thesis, in the slightly paradoxical manner which was typical of his thinking, by saying that to fix a limit is already to have transcended it. To claim that there is a sphere which we are incapable of knowing is self-contradictory, for the obvious reason that there is one statement at least which we think we can make about such a sphere, namely, that it is unknowable. Hegel was thinking, of course, of the celebrated thing in itself, the bogy of the Kantian philosophy, without which, as Jacobi said in his famous epigram, there is no entry into the Kantian system and with which there is no remaining inside it. Kant had declared firmly that we cannot know things as they are in themselves, and had yet presupposed throughout his system that there are such things. His efforts to restrict human knowledge thus seemed peculiarly abortive, since he assumed as a premiss a proposition he denied in his conclusion. But Hegel did not confine his criticism of the Kantian type of philosophy to the Kantian formulation of it. He went on to say that the whole idea of instituting an inquiry into the extent of human knowledge was unsound. This was because we could not, as it were, stand back and survey the field of human knowledge without *ipso facto* re-entering it. To determine the limits of knowledge one must be in a state of knowledge, at least about epistemological questions; and that seemed to Hegel a fatal objection to the whole undertaking. He was probably thinking about Kant here, too, and in particular of his famous injunction in the *Prolegomena*:[1] 'All metaphysicians are hereby solemnly suspended from their office until they have given a satisfactory answer to the question, how are synthetic *a priori* cognitions possible.' In Hegel's view the question was metaphysical in itself.

Hegel thus had two arguments against theory of knowledge as we understand it. (1) He urged that to try to fix a limit to knowledge was self-contradictory, since to fix a limit is already to have transcended it. And (2) he thought that the existence of *philosophical* knowledge itself invalidated any such undertaking as Hume and Kant favoured. Now it is not difficult to show that the first argument, despite its apparent plausibility, is verbal only. Certainly if we say that there are some things which we are capable of knowing and others which from the nature of our

[1] § 5 (Berlin Academy edition, iv. 278).

faculties we never can, we are falling into self-contradiction; but there is no reason at all why we should formulate our position in this way. It is perfectly possible to hold that human knowledge is limited without asserting the existence of a vast sphere which lies beyond it. The most we need to make our meaning clear is to say that *if* there were any entities with such-and-such characteristics, then we could not know them; but this is a very different thing from saying that there are such entities. Thus, if we are empiricists and believe that all knowledge must be based on sense-experience, we shall hold it to be limited by that fact; but to make the assertion we do not need to believe in the existence of a supersensible world which, fortunately or unfortunately, lies beyond our powers of cognition. We perhaps need the *idea* of supersensible objects to understand a position like Kant's, but we certainly do not need to believe that such objects literally exist.[1]

Hegel's second and wider argument depends on his special conception of philosophy. He would have said that philosophy is both a rational and a positive science—rational in so far as there is no part of his object which the philosopher cannot comprehend, at least in principle, positive in so far as it leads to new truths about the world. The tenability of this view of philosophy is a matter which we shall have to discuss at a later stage in this book. For our immediate purposes, however, it will be sufficient to note that even if philosophy does have the speculative function here assigned to it, it must be considered as a reflective discipline too; and that the existence of the former side will not rule out the latter, though it will of course radically affect its content. Moreover, to argue from the asking of questions such as are posed by theory of knowledge (e.g., Kant's question 'How are synthetic *a priori* judgements possible?') to the legitimacy of the claim that philosophy is also a speculative science is clearly fallacious. The whole matter must be left in a rather unsatisfactory state at this stage, but it does not appear that Hegel has produced any decisive objection to theory of knowledge. I shall therefore proceed to the main part of my inquiry without further ado.

[1] This is not to say that Hegel was wrong in attacking the doctrine of the thing in itself as Kant himself formulated it. Kant's language at least is objectionable. His assumption of the thing in itself follows from his (obviously crucial) view of the discursivity of the human intellect, and perhaps cannot be discarded without wrecking the latter (and incidentally his moral philosophy too). But he would have been wiser to say that nothing could be said about the thing in itself than to say it was by nature unknowable. See below, pp. 69 ff.

II

RATIONALISM AND EMPIRICISM

§ 1. In the history of philosophy the main questions of epistemology have received two sharply different types of answer. It is the aim of the present chapter to sketch these answers in a provisional way, to indicate the chief points of difference between the two schools which put them forward, and to mention some of the issues on which each has been attacked. The chapter is thus intended as a general introduction to the problems discussed in the rest of the book.

The first set of answers is that given by empiricist philosophers. The essential contentions of empiricism can be put very simply: they amount to the claims (*a*) that all knowledge (or at least all knowledge about matters of fact) is based on the data of the several senses (including 'inner' sense or introspection), and (*b*) that the boundaries of possible sense-experience are the boundaries of possible knowledge. Empiricists do not always agree about the precise way in which knowledge is based on sensation, and there have been some of them (Locke is the most notorious) who have been willing to allow the possibility of inference from the sensible to the supersensible. Nevertheless, most members of the school would have no difficulty in subscribing to the two principles here stated. And in consequence they would argue that the test of a truth lies in its being (in some way) sensibly verifiable.

The alternative position favoured by rationalists can also be stated quite shortly. Rationalists begin by arguing, first, that the intellect is a source of knowledge in itself. They go on next to contend that because of this we are able to grasp truths of quite a different kind from those established on the basis of sense-experience. These truths may be called 'truths of reason', and the rationalist contention is that they are superior to any truths grounded in sensation. They owe this superiority, it is argued, to their necessary character. Truths of reason can be seen not merely to be true but, further, to be necessarily true; their certainty, as some philosophers put it, is apodeictic. And the test of a truth, according to those who support this account, is just that we should be brought to see this apodeictic or self-evident character in it. The test of a truth, to use the language of Descartes, lies in the clarity with which it can be conceived.[1]

[1] It should be remembered that the above is intended as a preliminary and

To fill out the contrast, let us proceed to consider the rival accounts in more detail. Empiricists, as we have seen, say that knowledge rests on sensation. Now the most striking feature of sensation is its passivity. I do not mean to suggest, as some old-fashioned philosophers did, that the mind is purely passive in sense-perception,[1] or that in it we simply apprehend objects without contributing in any way to the character of what we apprehend: what I do wish to do is to call attention to the fact, admitted in their different ways by all writers on theory of knowledge, that what predominates in sensible experience is the given. There is something positive and ineluctable in what we sense: in its main features, at least, it is what it is irrespective of any choice of ours. We have simply to take it for what it is, accept it as 'brute' fact. And this is in some ways a highly unsatisfactory situation. For the main feature of 'brute' fact is just that we cannot understand it: we cannot see any reason why it should be what it is, but must accept it without explanation and indeed as ultimately inexplicable. If what we know in sensation is 'brute' fact, it follows that sensible knowledge must always be lacking in intelligibility.

Two consequences follow immediately from this position. In the first place we must agree that the sensible world cannot contain any necessity in the rationalist sense. When rationalists speak of necessary truths they mean truths which are in some way self-guaranteeing or self-evident. This notion of necessity is, as we shall see in the next chapter, a somewhat confused one; but it is clear that however we interpret it, whether as dependent on the laws of logic or based on a supposed insight into real connexions between facts, it is foreign to the world of the strict empiricist. For the empiricist bases knowledge on sensation, and the results of sensation are neither logically unimpeachable nor rationally intelligible. The empiricist must accordingly hold either that there are no necessary truths or that they have no direct reference to the actual world.

The second consequence is that we must accept what is usually called the descriptive theory of science. Philosophers have always said (sometimes without any very careful analysis of their own

general account only. The last point, for example, would certainly not be accepted by Hegel. See below, pp. 82 ff.

[1] Though it might be plausibly argued that sensation is the passive element in sense-perception.

statements) that it is the business of scientists to understand the workings of Nature. What does 'understand' mean in this context? In a famous dictum Aristotle said 'we know (i.e. we understand) when we know the cause'; and most philosophers would agree to that. But it must be made clear that by 'cause' Aristotle meant the intelligible reason: the business of science, according to him, was to explain *why* things were what they were. Hence the celebrated distinction between the ὅτι and the διότι, the fact and the reasoned fact; hence, too, the elaborate apparatus of formal, final, and efficient causes, with the aid of which Aristotle clearly hoped to construct sciences made up of necessary and intelligible truths.[1] It was this aim which modern scientists repudiated when they broke with Aristotle in the sixteenth century. In abandoning the formal and final cause altogether and changing the efficient cause almost beyond recognition, until it became nothing more than the invariable antecedent of the event to be explained, they were in effect saying that science must cease to attempt to demonstrate why things happen and concentrate instead on showing how. And the empiricist doctrine of causation, formulated by Hume, is simply the formal expression of this new point of view. What the empiricist does is to attempt to show that any such ideal as Aristotle's is doomed to failure, just because scientific knowledge is based on sensation. For so long as we are bound to sense, the truths we are capable of knowing are all contingent or (as is sometimes said) 'positive': strictly speaking, we can neither see nor hope to see why they are what they are. And that is to say that science cannot explain the world but only describe it.

To turn now to rationalism, the point on which we must concentrate is clearly the rationalist doctrine of necessary truths. We must try to determine in particular the sphere to which those truths refer and their relationship to judgements based on sensation. For it seems clear that there are at least two possible courses which rationalists might take. (A) They might argue first that the descriptive theory of science cannot be a finally satisfactory account of our knowledge of Nature. We set out to *understand* Nature, they may point out, and ought not to let ourselves be put

[1] Aristotle, a rationalist in his conception of knowledge and inference if not in some other features of his philosophy, was, like so many rationalists, deeply (indeed too much) impressed by the example of mathematics. His ideal of scientific knowledge is set out in the *Posterior Analytics*, with which Descartes's *Regulae* can be profitably compared. See below, pp. 58–60 and Chapter V.

off with ultimate inexplicabilities. If sense-perception cannot afford us insight into why things happen we must have recourse to a different kind of knowledge. In this full-blooded version of the rationalist theory, reason is clearly conceived as an intuitive faculty, a primary source of knowledge whose final aim must be to replace the inferior faculty of sensation. (B) But this ideal, attractive as it has proved to philosophers, is obviously difficult to square with the actual course of scientific development. The alternative is therefore more often followed. This is to accept the existence of scientific knowledge of the kind described by empiricists and say that, just because of its evident short-comings, it must be supplemented by a more adequate form of knowing, viz. philosophy. This second point of view finds expression in the common rationalist theory according to which the world of sense is a world of appearance only. It is precisely the fact that the sensible world is opaque to reason that leads to its condemnation by rationalists. They assume, in Plato's phrase,[1] that the fully real must be fully intelligible; and conversely that what is not fully intelligible cannot be fully real. Hence the persistent *metaphysical* tendency manifested by rationalists, where metaphysics is the science or pretended science of what lies behind or beyond sensible appearance. The very possibility of metaphysics in this sense is denied by empiricists: to some rationalists at least it is beyond doubt the most important of all inquiries.

The full difference between the two schools, together with their main internal variations, can perhaps be brought out best if we elaborate a well-known distinction made by Leibniz. Leibniz, as all students of philosophy know, said there were two sorts of truth, truths of fact and truths of reason. Truths of fact are all contingent, in the sense that their certainty is not guaranteed by any logical principle; they are expressed in judgements which, in language to be explained later, Kant was to call a synthetic *a posteriori*. Truths of reason, by way of contrast, are necessary propositions, and their certainty depends (or so Leibniz says) on the principle of contradiction.[2] The suggestion is apparently that we know truths of reason in so far as we are purely intellectual beings, truths of fact in so far as our intellection is contaminated by the obscurities of sense. Now the question arises whether the

[1] *Republic*, 477^{a} 3.

[2] This is not true of some of the truths of reason Leibniz suggests, e.g. the general principle of causality and the proposition that God exists.

distinction between the two types of truth is ultimate or not; and this is a point on which Leibniz himself seems to have wavered. True, he holds (i) that the senses and the intellect are not strictly separate, but that sensing is only confused thinking, from which it might be inferred that truths of fact are only confused or unclear truths of reason; and (ii) that truths of fact have a principle of their own, the principle of sufficient reason, and indeed are rational just because of that.[1] But the real point at issue is obviously whether the principle of sufficient reason is itself reducible to the principle of contradiction; whether it is itself a necessary truth in the sense in which truths of reason are. If it is, truths of fact may be expected to disappear in the last analysis, to be replaced by corresponding truths of reason; if not, they can lay claim to independent validity. It is perhaps to the credit of Leibniz' good sense, if not of his logic, that this is a puzzle which he does not clearly resolve. But his followers, and in particular the 'illustrious' Wolff, had no such hesitations. Wolff held that the principle of sufficient reason can be deduced from the law of contradiction, and even attempted to supply the steps of the deduction. He was thus paving the way for the final disappearance of truths of fact as such.

The issue between empiricism and rationalism can be stated baldly in the questions: (1) Are there truths of fact *and* truths of reason? and (2) if so, are truths of fact *reducible to* truths of reason?

(1) The proper course for empiricists of the strict school to follow would be to deny truths of reason altogether and maintain that the only genuine truths are truths of fact, based upon sense-experience. This is the line taken by J. S. Mill, who attempted to show in accordance with it that many truths recognized by Leibniz as truths of reason were in fact nothing but very familiar empirical generalizations. He applied this analysis to geometry and arithmetic, and again to the law of universal causation; and it looks as if he would have applied it to logical principles, too, though his view of these is not wholly clear.[2] Mill is certainly not alone in

[1] The principle of sufficient reason is the principle that whatever exists does so because it fits into God's general plan of producing the best of all possible worlds. It is to God's choice of the best that we must look in seeking the reason for any particular happening. The question whether the principle is autonomous is the theological question whether God could choose anything but the best of all available possibilities.

[2] He seems undecided as to whether logical laws are empirical generalizations or tautologies in the old-fashioned sense, purely verbal propositions. Compare his *Logic*, Bk. II, chap. vii, § 5.

his extreme empiricism, but he is perhaps the only philosopher of importance who has made a serious attempt to work it out. Most empiricists would admit that their case breaks down if pushed to its furthest limits, and so are prepared to agree that there are some truths of reason. What they are anxious to maintain, however, is that these do not afford significant knowledge in the same way as truths of fact; a view which the most modern proponents of empiricism express (rather misleadingly) by calling them 'tautologies'. Tautologies are propositions which say nothing about sensible fact and are valid without regard to its particular nature; they have nevertheless a most important part to play in the structure of knowledge. This modified and (as we shall see reason to think it) improved form of empiricism was first sketched out by Hume;[1] its modern formulation undoubtedly owes something to the study of Leibniz himself.

(II) The term 'rationalist' is a good deal wider and looser than 'empiricist', and while rationalist philosophers are often agreed in what they deny they are by no means united in what they affirm. It is easy enough to see, however, that the most extreme form of rationalism would be that of Wolff, which in effect aims at getting rid of truths of fact altogether. All truths, according to this view, would be truths of reason; and that is to say that they could be known independently of any appeal to experience. This is the rationalist ideal *par excellence*, and it is illustrated most clearly in the writings of Descartes, who aimed at constructing a universal science based entirely on rational intuition, a science in which no reliance was to be placed on the senses and the imagination.[2] It is a form of rationalism which has been primarily[3] influenced by mathematics; and its plausibility will clearly vary greatly according to the view we take of the status of mathematical propositions. But it should be noticed at once that it is by no means the only form of rationalism. For rationalists can hold, as

[1] In his distinction between our knowledge of 'relations of ideas' and our knowledge of 'matters of fact': *Enquiry*, section iv, part 1.

[2] For an excellent account of Descartes' programme and its failure see L. Roth's *Descartes' Discourse on Method*. It should be said that Descartes was himself quite aware of this failure, as the last section of the *Discourse* shows, and indeed that he had a lively sense of the need to collect 'experiences' as an essential preliminary to scientific advance. Compare *Regulae* V (Adam and Tannery edition, x. 380) on philosophers who think they can produce truth out of their heads, without recourse to experience.

[3] But not exclusively. Hegel too is a supporter of this type of rationalism, and his method of approach is very different: see below, pp. 19–20.

Kant did, that there are truths of reason which are not adequately described as tautologies, but that truths of fact are still not in any way reducible to them. On this theory truths of reason will be on an altogether different plane from truths of fact: they will be expressed (to use language I shall explain later) in prescriptive rather than factual judgements. It is this type of rationalism which will be advocated in the present book.

It would obviously be convenient to have suitable labels for the four groups of philosophers here distinguished. For the want of anything better I shall use the terms 'extreme' and 'moderate', with the proviso that in philosophy moderation is not necessarily a virtue nor extremity a vice. Extreme empiricists (who might also be called sensationalists) I take to be exemplified by J. S. Mill, moderate empiricists by Hume and the twentieth-century logical positivists. Moderate rationalism may be represented by Kant, extreme rationalism by Descartes and Wolff and, in a different form, by Hegel. I need hardly emphasize that not all writers on theory of knowledge will fit easily into the categories here distinguished. There are inconsistencies in the works of most philosophers, and they are not necessarily the worse because of that.

It should not be difficult to see that both the philosophical and (to some extent) non-philosophical interests of empiricists and rationalists alike will be determined to an appreciable extent by their views on knowledge. Thus the main interests of empiricists lie in the sphere of sense-perception. Holding as they do that all knowledge is based on sense-experience, they are committed to giving an account of this basing; and that in its turn involves them in theories of the relation of sense-data or impressions to the material objects presupposed in everyday language and scientific thinking. It is in this field that empiricists have done their best work: the writings of Locke, Berkeley, and Hume are classical instances, while in the present century the empiricist tradition has been well carried on by writers like Mr. Russell and Professor Price.[1] Their exploration of the problems of perception and of the external world leads with most empiricists to a close study of both the results and the methodology of the sciences, particularly the physical sciences, and they tend to regard these as being the only reliable source of knowledge. About the other main fields of human achievement, the arts, history, religion, and morality,

[1] Kant is another major contributor to this field, his interest in which marks the extent of his separation from other rationalists.

empiricists generally show far less curiosity. It is true that both Hume[1] and Mill in different ways have as their professed aim the understanding not of the external world but of human nature; but their programme amounts to nothing more than (in the words of the sub-title of Hume's *Treatise*) 'an attempt to introduce the experimental method of reasoning into moral subjects'. They are not interested in Man as opposed to Nature, or as something other than a natural phenomenon. The Science of Man is to be a natural science like any other, and its founders see no reason why it should not be treated as such.

The interests of rationalists are less easy to describe, if only because of an obvious division in their ranks. They fall into two main groups, which we may designate conveniently, though without complete accuracy, as pre-Kantian and post-Kantian. The former approached philosophy with a mathematical bias, and they aimed at two things: the construction of a rational science of Nature, and the solution of certain metaphysical problems—questions of the general structure of the world, of the relations of mind and body, of immortality, &c. Since they thought that the method of philosophy should be the same as that of mathematics, and its ideal to reach demonstrated truth from self-evident premisses, they had no more use for history and the arts than their empiricist opponents. In practice they tended to occupy themselves increasingly with purely metaphysical questions, disdaining the empirical as unworthy of the attention of a philosopher. Now, as everybody knows, this type of rationalism was most trenchantly criticized by Kant; and it became necessary after his time to restate the whole doctrine on a new basis. The task was accomplished by Hegel. It is true that in Hegel many of the preoccupations of pre-Kantian rationalists remain: there is the same desire to construct a rational science of Nature, the same interest in metaphysics, the same conviction that the way of the intellect is the road to true knowledge. But though reason is still thought of as the supreme cognitive faculty, it is no longer held that its exercise should be confined to a single sphere or a single type of knowing. On the contrary, it is regarded as being applicable to fields hitherto neglected by philosophers, such as politics,

[1] Hume's interests were, of course, remarkably wide: not only natural science, but history, politics, and morals, all attracted his attention. But he remains the exception among empiricists, rather than the rule, though it should be said that Mr. Russell has followed him, here as elsewhere.

history, art, and religion; and, indeed, as being able to reach specially valuable conclusions in those fields. Hence the attention paid by post-Kantian rationalists to humane as opposed to purely scientific studies. German philosophers in particular singled out history as a branch of learning whose concreteness contrasted favourably with the abstractness of natural science, and made much of the concept of *Geisteswissenschaften* (humane studies). History cut less ice in Great Britain, where Bosanquet dismissed it brusquely as 'a tissue of mere conjunctions'; but in Italy Croce and Gentile, at the beginning of the present century, came to regard it as a universal type of knowing, to be identified with philosophy itself. The contrast between this view and that of, say, Descartes or Spinoza could scarcely be more complete.

§ 2. The above must suffice as a description in general terms of the two philosophies with which we shall be dealing in the rest of this book. As will be obvious, many statements about them are liable to be wrong, if only because of the internal divergences within each school. Nevertheless, there clearly is a sense in which it is correct to speak of a single empiricist and a single rationalist theory, for there are some important propositions which all empiricists would accept and all rationalists deny, and others of which the opposite would be true. We shall therefore continue to use the terms 'rationalism' and 'empiricism' without apology.

To bring this introductory sketch of the rival theories of knowledge to an end, I propose now to discuss briefly some of the stock objections brought against each of them. This should serve to bring out some of the main points to be borne in mind in subsequent chapters. I begin, as before, with empiricism.

Empiricism and the self. One of the commonest criticisms of philosophies of the empiricist type is that they fail to give an adequate account of self-knowledge. We know ourselves, it is said by these critics, in a way fundamentally different from that in which we know external objects. Knowledge of the self is immediate or direct, whereas physical things are known to us only mediately, through the impressions they make on our senses. A theory of knowledge which sees in sensation the basis of all true statements of fact is accordingly mistaken from the start.

Probably the best way of approaching this objection is to summarize the history of the problem. The main lines of the rationalist view of the self, as given above, were laid down by

Descartes. It will be remembered that Descartes, searching for an absolutely certain premiss on which to base the whole structure of knowledge, found it in the dictum *cogito ergo sum.* The fact of thinking (which I cannot doubt) implies the reality of the self that thinks. And there are certain truths about this self which we can affirm without further ado: that it is a simple substance continuing identical through its diverse states, a thinking and not an extended thing, free of the corruptibility which attends physical objects and therefore immortal. These propositions constituted the elements of what was later to be known as rational psychology.

The empiricist answer to all this came from Hume. Hume argued that if the facts were as Descartes described them, we ought to be able to look into ourselves and apprehend the simple, unextended, self-identical substance of which the Cartesians spoke. But 'when I enter most intimately into what I call *myself,* I always stumble on some particular perception or other, of heat or cold, light or shade, love or hatred, pain or pleasure. I can never catch *myself* at any time without a perception, and never can observe anything but the perception.'[1] In other words, the inference from the fact of thinking to the propositions of rational psychology is without justification. The self is to be known by introspection only, and introspection is a faculty precisely parallel to the external senses. Its data are fragmentary and disconnected in just the same way as external sense-data are, and the problem of the unity of the self is the same sort of problem as that of the unity of external objects. Psychology thus raises no special problems for empiricism.

As usual with Hume, the answer clearly demolishes the position it criticizes without producing conviction in the mind of the reader. For there is one point which it conspicuously fails to cover. Introspection itself seems to require two factors or aspects in the self: a self which is introspected and a self which introspects. Assuming the truth of the empiricist account of the former, what are we to say about the latter? We owe the clear formulation of this problem to Kant, who saw that though rational psychology is a baseless science, the fallacies on which it rests are more complicated than Hume had supposed.[2] Kant argued that experience, external and internal alike, does presuppose a unitary subject self.

[1] *Treatise,* p. 252, ed. Selby-Bigge.

[2] *Critique of Pure Reason,* especially 'Transcendental Deduction' and 'On the Paralogisms of Pure Reason'.

Unless I could relate all the data of the senses in some sort of unitary consciousness I could not describe them as mine.[1] But I can find no such unitary consciousness in introspection: 'Consciousness of self . . . in inner perception is simply empirical and continuously changing; it can produce no fixed and abiding self in the flow of inner representations'.[2] The subject self must accordingly be a presupposition of experience rather than something we know in experience. But if that is so, what can we say about it? Kant's answer is clear: I do not know myself as subject, for that would require a faculty of intuition over and above sense-intuition; I know only that there is such an aspect of myself. The transcendental unity of apperception, the presupposition of all experience, is in fact not a substantial entity, as the rationalists thought, but a point without content of its own.

The doctrine has not found universal acceptance, and, indeed, some would say that it sets as many problems as it solves. Kant's philosophy requires the existence of two selves: an empirical self we know in introspection, and a real self which manifests itself in moral action. But we are told that we can have no direct acquaintance with the latter, pure apperception being our sole point of contact with it. The trouble about this is that it appears to leave the whole theory in the air in a disconcerting way; for unless we know our real selves how can we formulate such a philosophy? It was considerations like this which led, in the revived rationalism of Hegel, to the denial that introspection can properly be treated as on a parallel with the outer senses. Self-knowledge was, as Descartes had seen, a higher form of awareness, and self-consciousness gave access to a more real object than external sensation.

The plausibility of these conflicting views will be discussed in a later chapter,[3] the intention of the above summary being simply to put the problem of the self in its relation to rationalism and empiricism before the reader. What we can claim to have learnt from this preliminary survey is to concentrate on two questions: (1) What is the status of introspection *vis-à-vis* external sensation? and (2) Is knowledge of the self exhausted in what we know in introspection? If introspection really is no more than, as Locke first suggested, a kind of inner sense, and provides the only form

[1] *Critique of Pure Reason*, B 132.
[2] Op. cit., A 107.
[3] Chapter IX below.

of self-knowledge, the empiricist view may yet be defensible. But that remains to be determined later.

The meaning of 'experience'. A second criticism of empiricism has been referred to already, the charge that empiricists narrow the meaning of the word 'experience' unduly. Claiming that all knowledge is based on experience, they proceed to equate it with sense-experience; and this, we are told, is highly arbitrary. For are there not other forms of experience than sensing, and may not these, too, be primary sources of knowledge? Among these other forms of experience have been suggested (1) the experience of the mystics, (2) the experience of the artist, (3) moral experience, and (4) historical experience.

It is not by any means obvious at first sight that this objection, even if sustained, could be used in favour of rationalism; yet its acceptance would clearly play havoc with empiricism as we have stated it. The main attraction of that doctrine, one may venture to suggest, is its clear-cut, matter-of-fact character: by confining knowledge to what can (or could if physical conditions allowed) be sensed, it sweeps away all the phantasmagoria of metaphysics, the real essences, intelligible forms, and supersensible things in themselves which philosophers have been so prone to postulate. But all these ghostly entities threaten to return to haunt us if the basis of experience is widened in the way here suggested. This is especially clear if the validity of mystical experience is allowed: who knows what extravagances will follow such an admission? The excesses of philosophies of art, again, are notorious: witness the theories of Schelling and others. One cannot suppose that these developments would be welcome to empiricists, with their horror of *Schwärmerei* of any kind. Indeed, the empiricists' only consolation would be that they could scarcely be welcome to rationalists either. For rationalists, after all, are mainly concerned to forward the cognitive claims of the intellect, and they cannot think their case helped by insistence on the validity of non-intellectual intuition as advocated by mystics and romantic philosophers.[1]

It is, however, undeniable that rationalists of the post-Kantian type have laid great stress on this argument about the different forms of experience, and the reason must now be stated. It is to be found in their belief that thought can be shown to be

[1] Hegel's violent antipathy to the philosophies of 'feeling' prevalent in his time is instructive here.

presupposed in these other forms of experience more readily than it can in sense-perception. I will try to explain this difficult idea. Rationalists, of course, hold that even sense-perception presupposes thought, and one of the characteristic doctrines of extreme (though not of moderate) rationalism is that it takes sensing and thinking to be in the last analysis not separate at all. Nevertheless, this school has never been very happy about sense-perception, and has shown its uneasiness by denouncing the kind of thinking it involves as inferior or 'abstract'. The kind of thinking involved in sense-perception, its members say, is that of understanding rather than reason, and the highest categories do not function in it. But in morality, art, and religion, we are told, the case is very different. There the march of reason is far more obvious, and that opaque element which baffles thought in the sphere of sense-perception has far more nearly disappeared. Morality, art, and religion involve, according to Hegel who is the prime exponent of this view, a series of categories which can be shown to be logically higher than the categories of understanding. Hegel is not saying that these spheres are fully rational: he thinks they have obvious imperfections, or, in his own language, involve obvious contradictions, and that for this reason they must be supplemented by a higher form of experience to which they point forward: the thinking of philosophy. Nevertheless, his assertion of their superiority to sense-experience in point of rationality is not in doubt.

There are, then, two ways of interpreting this objection to empiricism. According to both, empiricism is false because it is too narrowly based; but while the one party is content simply to call attention to this fact, the other attempts to interpret it in favour of rationalism. Hence arise two questions in theory of knowledge: (1) Are there forms of experience (or primary sources of knowledge) which are not reducible to sensing? and (2) If there are, is reason involved in them in any special way? These are questions which I propose to take up later in the book.[1]

Sense and sense-experience. The last objection to empiricism we need consider at present concerns an alleged ambiguity in its fundamental principle. The empiricist thesis as we have stated it is that all knowledge of matters of fact is based on sensation or introspection, or, again, is derived from sense-experience. Now it may be argued that these apparently similar expressions conceal an important diversity of view. Sensation results in the appre-

[1] See Chapter X below.

hension of sense-data, but it is quite wrong to identify such apprehension with sense-experience or sense-perception. For in the latter an active intellectual element is involved as well as passive sensation. Sense-experience aims at bringing sense-data under concepts, and results in judgements about the sensible world; and concepts and judgements are things of the mind. Sense-experience is thus a resultant of two components, sense and thought. And empiricism is only plausible so long as it suppresses, or conveniently overlooks, the intellectual factor which even sense-knowledge involves.

This line of argument will be considered at length in the next chapter. Here I confine myself to noting that it is one to which both empiricists and rationalists have in fact attached importance, though in my view quite wrongly. It is possible, I shall argue, for empiricists to grant the indispensability of an intellectual component in knowledge without surrendering or compromising their main principle; nor do they need to prove that intellection is ultimately reducible to sensation to establish their point. What they do need to prove is that sensation and introspection are the sole *primary* sources of knowledge, and that the part which the intellect plays in knowledge is strictly subsidiary. It is on this contention that the plausibility of empiricism ultimately turns.

Rationalism and sensation. So much for the weaknesses of empiricism. The main crux of rationalism, to which we now turn, arises over the interpretation given to sensation in that theory. I have mentioned already the tendency of rationalists of the extreme school to say that sensing must ultimately be reducible to thinking; the parallel tendency to subsume truths of fact under truths of reason has also been referred to. Despite the highly paradoxical character of such steps as these, it remains true that rationalists are driven to them by the logic of their case. For while one of the prime aims of these philosophers is to show that what is real is rational and can be comprehended by reason, the most striking feature of knowledge based on sensation is just that it cannot be comprehended in this way.[1] The given element in sense-perception is an ultimate which we have no choice but to acquiesce in; there is simply no sense in asking why it is what it is. If he accepts sensation at its face value the rationalist philosopher is accordingly forced to admit a final unintelligibility in things. And this he is naturally very unwilling to do.

[1] See above, p. 13.

The remedy is to say that sensation should not be taken at its face value, but should be interpreted in such a manner that it is shown to be a form of thinking. This has been attempted in different ways. It was tried, for instance, by Leibniz in his theory of distinct and confused knowledge. According to Leibniz, the distinguishing mark of sensation is its confused character, while that of intellection is its clarity. Thus in one passage in the *Nouveaux Essais* we read: 'Ideas which come from the senses are confused, and the truths which depend on them are so also, at least in part; whereas intellectual ideas and the truths which depend on them are distinct, and neither have their origin in the senses.'[1] Sense-perception as so described gives us knowledge of phenomena only; to know reality we must have recourse to the intellect. The suggestion with Leibniz, however (and this is the important point), is that there is no absolute gulf between these two spheres. With the growth of science, intellectual insight can replace sense-knowledge on an increasing scale, and the confusions of sense be removed. Sensing and thinking are activities which are continuous with one another, and the former gradually shades off into the latter. Sensing is thus properly described as immature or imperfect thinking, and the unintelligibilities to which it gives rise are not to be taken as ultimate.

This theory of the relation of sense and thought was one of the parts of the philosophy of Leibniz to be attacked most vigorously by Kant in the *Critique of Pure Reason*. Kant argued that it was just not true that a continuous transition from sensing to thinking was possible. Sense intuition introduced peculiarities of its own, which no amount of intellectual analysis could resolve. A prominent example of this was to be found in the problem of incongruous counterparts, first put forward by Kant in his short essay on space in 1768. A left-hand glove seen in a mirror looks right-handed, yet there is no *intelligible* difference between image and original. We can only account for the difference by recognizing an original idea of space, known to us by a species of sensible knowledge. To deny this is to confuse the spheres of logic (pure thought) and real existence. Kant went on to apply this analysis to most of the leading doctrines of Leibniz, showing how the latter's views were

[1] Taken from Russell's *Philosophy of Leibniz*, appendix of translated passages, pp. 279–80. For Leibniz's views on different types of idea see his paper 'Thoughts on Knowledge, Truth and Ideas' (1684), translated in Duncan's *Philosophical Works of Leibniz*, pp. 28–33. (I have assumed that there is no important distinction between clear and distinct knowledge in Leibniz.)

only plausible if the specific contribution of sensibility to knowledge was in each case ignored. Sense and understanding, he concluded, were apparently wholly separate faculties, and concepts and intuitions were certainly not related as clear and confused.[1]

Kant's conclusion here drew support from the continued failure of rationalists to implement their ideal and show that the obscurities of the given could be eliminated by the power of thought. Descartes's universal science, already mentioned, broke down for lack of suitable 'experiences': despite its avowed method, it could not make progress without regard to sensation. Leibniz himself would probably have said that actual instances of the refinement of sensibility were available, for instance, in the reduction of colours to light frequencies, but he was, of course, quite unable to explain in detail how, e.g., our perception of a table was to be resolved into the rational apprehension of an assembly of monads, entities apprehensible by reason alone. Yet the problem of sensation remained, and remains, a most serious one for the rationalist school. I will mention one more attempt to deal with it, that of Hegel. Hegel began by arguing that a view like Kant's, which postulated a radical separation between sensation and thought, could not be tolerated. One consequence of it was the self-contradictory doctrine of the thing in itself;[2] another, that knowledge became a standing miracle, since if sense and thought were taken as initially separate there was no guarantee that they would co-operate as Kant said they must. Having assured himself by these arguments of the impossibility of the Kantian solution, Hegel set about refashioning the battered rationalist theory. He claimed first that his predecessors had erred in limiting thought to the discursive thinking met with in the natural sciences. This thinking of understanding, as he called it, is the very antithesis of the intuition of sense; and to suppose that the latter could be reduced to the former is evidently absurd. But the position was vastly altered if we recognized a faculty of reason over and above the faculty of understanding. The thinking of reason, which

[1] Kant's criticism of Leibniz is most fully set out in the section 'On the Amphiboly of Concepts of Reflection', *Critique of Pure Reason*, B 316 = A 260 ff. It should be mentioned that his views on clear and confused knowledge were coloured by his philosophy of mathematics: he thought mathematical ideas especially clear, yet derived from a special form of sense-experience. This view is almost certainly wrong, but his main criticism can stand without it.

[2] See above, pp. 10–11 and below, pp. 69–72 on the question whether this doctrine is really self-contradictory.

Hegel thought best exemplified in philosophy, had an immediate or intuitive character very similar to that met with in sensation; its concepts were not abstract like those of understanding, but were concrete universals. To suppose there could be a transition from sensation to this kind of thinking was not unplausible. Hegel's official account was that sensation was not separate from thought but its 'other': to speak roughly, sensation, discursive thought, and the thinking of reason formed a dialectical series in which the first was thesis, the second antithesis, and the third synthesis. reason thus included within itself elements which corresponded both to the particularity of sense and the universality of the thinking of understanding, and because of this was not alien to either.[1]

Hegel was arguing, in effect, for the existence in human beings of a faculty of intellectual intuition which, ideally at least, was not merely to supplement but to replace the faculty of sense-perception. His doctrine of the relation of sense and thought committed him to that view; and indeed it was only with such a premiss that he could hope to justify his famous contention that the real is the rational. The main test of the theory comes over Hegel's attitude to experience. He believed in the possibility of philosophy of Nature over and above the natural sciences and of philosophy of Spirit over and above history and its associated studies, and he should have held that in principle these disciplines were not merely methodological or reflective but capable of providing first-order knowledge. In fact, however, he seems to have conceived the actual function of philosophy of Nature and Spirit as being to re-present the facts which the departmental sciences established, reconstructing them in such a way that their true intelligibility shone forth. Philosophy was thus dependent for its material on the empirical sciences, and though the philosopher might aim at elevating the results of the latter to the rank of 'necessary truth',[2] he could at no point dispense with them

[1] It is illuminating to compare Hegel's view here with that of Bradley, described by many as an English Hegelian. Bradley believes thought to be necessarily discursive and to contrast at once with a feeling below the level of relations (= sensation) and with a feeling above the level of relations. This latter is roughly the equivalent of Hegel's reason, but Bradley refuses to give it the name of thought. Since he believes discursive thought to be self-contradictory and self-defeating in much the same way as Hegel, Bradley is thus developing the Hegelian position in the interests of a non-rationalist or, as he would have preferred to say himself, a non-intellectualist philosophy. Although he has been called a neo-Kantian, his final view would have seemed almost as alien to Kant as Hegel's own.

[2] *Encyclopaedia*, § 12.

altogether. And this suggests that sense-perception, even in the Hegelian scheme of things, is not satisfactorily disposed of. Hegel has no more rid himself of sensation than had Leibniz. The bogy of the thing in itself, the inexplicable datum from which knowledge must start, remained to haunt him for all his efforts to exorcise it, and it is still the principal problem for rationalists.[1]

Of course, there are philosophers who are prepared to accept the empiricist account of sensation and would yet call themselves rationalists, because they believe that reason or intelligence is the source of important truths which bear directly on the world of fact, though they are not derived from a study of its details. But it is worth noting that even this moderate version of the rationalist doctrine is not free from difficulties. These philosophers say that the propositions which reason knows *a priori* are not facts of experience but its presuppositions. They hold that the human mind goes about its work of ordering and interpreting the data of sense with certain primary principles which are not so much derived from experience as read into it. According to Kant, the classical exponent of this theory, these principles have their seat in the very nature of the human intelligence; they proceed from reason itself. But the question can be asked whether this derivation is justified. Would it not be possible to say, as Hume sometimes seems to suggest, that the truth of the matter is just that we are so constituted that we approach experience in this and no other way? Our primary principles, on that interpretation, would derive not so much from the intelligence as from the imagination; and it would be a contingent fact about human nature that it used them. Given different conditions, they might on this theory themselves be different; or again, they could be altered arbitrarily. There are philosophers who say that they can.[2] It is easy enough to see from this that moderate rationalism of the Kantian type is by no means a stable doctrine: given half a chance it ceases to be a rationalist theory at all. Thus, if extreme rationalism is not exempt from hazards, moderate rationalism has its pitfalls too. But then a philosophical theory entirely free from difficulties has yet to be invented.

[1] For a further discussion of these views of Hegel's see pp. 64 ff. below, and for the whole question of intellectual intuition see Chapters IV and V.

[2] Cf. *Mind and the World Order*, by C. I. Lewis; *An Essay on Metaphysics*, by R. G. Collingwood. And for further discussion of the point see Chapter VIII below.

III

TWO PRELIMINARY DISTINCTIONS

§ 1. In the first chapter of this book it was argued that the aim of theory of knowledge is to determine the nature and extent of knowledge and to deal with questions about its validity. In the second chapter a preliminary sketch was offered of the chief doctrines of the two main schools of philosophers who have attempted to solve these problems. To try to choose between the conflicting claims of these two groups of philosophers and thus decide the issue between rationalism and empiricism will be our principal purpose in the rest of the book.

Before we can decide an issue, however, we must specify it; and this we cannot yet claim to have done in the present case. All we can be said to have learnt so far is that the solution of the problems of knowledge turns on the true relations of reason and experience. We have seen that rationalists put their trust in the former, empiricists in the latter; but we have not yet indicated how their conflicting contentions are to be brought to judgement. The chief weaknesses and internal divisions of the two schools have been pointed out, and some of the major points of controversy should be clear; but we still lack any satisfactory formulation of the main questions to be settled. We obviously must formulate these questions if we are to make any progress in our inquiry.

To meet this need I propose to introduce in the present chapter two distinctions which, in my view at least, are of decisive importance in theory of knowledge. Both distinctions were originally made by Kant, and while the first is largely unknown, the second is familiar to most students of philosophy. It is, however, no part of my intention to confine my exposition of these distinctions to their Kantian form; I shall attempt to state them independently, referring to Kant's text only when this is likely to help the reader.

§ 2. To introduce the first distinction it will probably be best to refer back to Chapter II. Among the objections to empiricism mentioned there was that based on the contention that it fails to do justice to the part played in knowledge by intellectual activities. Empiricism, it is alleged, cannot be true because knowing cannot be reduced to sensing without remainder. All knowledge involves thinking; and this we can see by considering the simplest judgement of sense. If I sense a coloured patch and recognize it as red I am already supplementing sensation by an intellectual activity; for red is a universal of an elementary kind, and to use it as a predicate is to perform an intellectual act. But if it is true of the basic judgements of experience that perception and conception go thus together, how much more is this the case with the highly refined judgements of science. Science, as Aristotle said, is 'of the universal', and the scientist is not a man with particularly keen senses but a man with a particularly keen mind. Science may arise out of sensation, but it is most certainly not confined to it.

Now all this seems the simplest common sense; but unfortunately the situation has been much misunderstood. Both rationalists and empiricists are to blame for the misunderstanding. Rationalists are to blame because they have imagined that the facts above described constitute a complete refutation of empiricism and establish their own claims. To reach this position they take two unwarranted steps, first identifying empiricism with sensationalism and then expanding the thinking which necessarily accompanies sensing until it becomes a source of knowledge on its own account. Actually there is no reason why empiricism and sensationalism should be identified; all our knowledge of matters of fact might quite well be based on sensation even if it also contained an intellectual element. But to show that it does contain such an element is not to establish the validity of intellectual intuition. This is indeed so clear that it would be difficult to suppose that any philosopher could make the mistake if we could not mention actual examples. Aristotle and (I suspect) Leibniz are cases in point.[1]

Empiricists are to blame in this situation for failing to observe the fallacious character of their opponents' arguments and for attempting to refute them by attacking their quite unimpeachable premisses. This has led to two major mistakes. The first of these was made when empiricists tried to play down the difference between sensing and the thinking which accompanies it by arguing that there is no difference of kind between sense-impressions and universals. They were helped to this extraordinary conclusion by

[1] For Aristotle's account of the genesis of the universal in sense-perception see *Posterior Analytics*, II. xix. Once he is granted that awareness of universals is involved in knowledge he thinks the case for intellectual intuition complete, because universals (according to him) exist *in re*. For this see Chapter V below. Leibniz's view is not so clear, but his theory of the relation of sensing and thinking is fundamentally the same as Aristotle's.

using the word 'idea' to cover both indiscriminately. For Locke, who must perhaps bear prime responsibility for the confusion involved, an idea is whatsoever the mind has before it when it thinks.[1] Whatever falls within consciousness is an idea, and Locke uses the term primarily to cover the impressions of sensation and reflection, the twin sources of all knowledge in his view. But universals also fall within consciousness, and Locke is bound to apply the term 'idea' to them also, adding the qualifications 'abstract' and 'general' to mark them off from the concrete and particular impressions of sense. As usual in these matters, Locke's practice is better than his principles: the very inconsequence of his thinking preserved him from the gravest errors. For these we must turn to the more logical Berkeley. In the opening pages of his *Principles of Human Knowledge* Berkeley holds up to ridicule Locke's theory of abstract ideas, asking how we can imagine a triangle which is 'neither oblique nor rectangle, equilateral, equicrural nor scalenon, but all and none of these at once'.[2] Of course, we can *imagine* nothing of the sort, and Berkeley concludes in consequence that there are no abstract ideas in Locke's sense. He failed to see that it is not a question of what we can imagine but of what we can think. In this error he was followed by Hume, who, though he improved the presentation of the empiricist case by distinguishing impressions from ideas, nevertheless employed the latter term to cover images and concepts alike, and explicitly repeated Berkeley's teaching about abstract ideas. Hume says that an idea is simply a less vivid impression, a view which is plausible enough when applied to images but quite worthless as an account of universals.[3] It would probably be wrong to say that he failed to distinguish the two senses of 'idea' altogether, but he certainly blurred it more often than he should.[4]

[1] *Essay*, Bk. I, chap. i, § 8.

[2] Op cit., Introduction, § 13. Berkeley is quoting from Locke. On the latter's theory of universals see R. I. Aaron, *John Locke*, pp. 192–206.

[3] Neither Hume nor Berkeley in the first edition of the *Principles* considers the possibility that universals might be concepts, things altogether different in kind from sense-particulars. If pressed they might have rejected any such view by the use of Occam's razor, since they thought that the function of the universal could be discharged by one particular standing for others like it. This was, for Hume, 'one of the greatest and most valuable discoveries that has been made of late years in the republic of letters' (*Treatise*, p. 17, ed. Selby-Bigge). In the second edition of the *Principles* Berkeley, however, approached the conceptualist view with his doctrine of notions.

[4] It is a striking tribute to the influence of Locke and Hume on British philosophy that Bradley in the first chapter of his *Logic*, published in 1883, should

The first mistake made by empiricists in their attempt to refute rationalist claims was thus the production of a nominalist theory of universals. The second, closely connected with the first, was to deny that perception is necessarily accompanied by conception. Empiricists were helped to this conclusion by their conviction that while the senses mirror the facts faithfully, thought distorts them, and by their desire to attain to truths not subject to doubt, a desire stimulated in recent years by the paradoxes of the supporters of the Coherence Theory of Truth. But it is not difficult to see that their case was a hopeless one from the start. For if sensation is passive, or, if we like, purely intuitive in character, sense-perception undoubtedly involves an active element. Every judgement of sense, as I have already shown, requires at least one universal: in recognizing the facts for what they are we necessarily classify them and thus bring thought into play. That, indeed, is the whole difference between sensation and sense-perception: the former is bare apprehension, the latter apprehension accompanied by an activity of thought. Nor is it true to suggest that the occurrence of this activity of thought necessarily distorts what we apprehend. The idea of a fully formed reality already existent and merely waiting for us to sense it is, at the least estimate, seriously misleading. Reality is to an important extent constructed by the mind which knows it; and would accordingly appear quite differently to creatures of different mental constitution from ourselves. And even if there is a reality independently existent (a conclusion which may in a certain sense be unavoidable), we could not know it in sensation, since our sensing is of its nature piecemeal and fragmentary. This is one of the reasons why Kant declares that the thing in itself is beyond human knowledge.[1]

The remedy for all these errors, rationalist and empiricist alike, is to recognize a clear distinction between the thinking which is a necessary accompaniment of sensation and the thinking (if there

have been at such pains to distinguish idea = psychical content from idea = logical content. Such a confusion might not even occur to one brought up in a different tradition.

[1] The term 'reality' is an ambiguous one. We may use it to cover (*a*) the familiar world of everyday experience, assumed by common sense to be what it is independently of the fact that anyone knows it; (*b*) what would be left of that world if we could abstract from our way of knowing it; (*a*) is the real as we know it in sense-perception and involves an element of construction; (*b*) is the Kantian thing in itself, which alone can claim to be independently real. As we shall see later, 'fact' and 'experience' are similarly ambiguous.

is any) which is an independent source of knowledge. This is the distinction Kant makes when he speaks of two different 'uses' of the intellect, 'logical' and 'real'.

I will first of all give the distinction as it appears in Kant's inaugural *Dissertation* of 1770, where it is stated clearly and forcefully, and afterwards develop it in more modern phraseology. 'It is, above all, to be clearly remarked', Kant says,[1]

> 'that the use of the intellect, that is, of the superior faculty of the mind, is double. By the first use, the very concepts of objects or of relations are *given*, and this is the *real use*; by the second use concepts, whencesoever given, are only *subordinated* to one another, the lower to the higher (the common marks), and compared with one another according to the principle of contradiction; and this is called the *logical use*. The logical use of the intellect is common to all sciences, but not the real use. . . . Sensitive cognitions being given, the cognitions are subordinated by the logical use of the intellect to other sensitive cognitions as to common concepts, and as phenomena to more general laws of phenomena. But here it is of the greatest moment to note that these cognitions, no matter to what extent the logical use of the intellect has been exercised upon them, are still to be considered sensitive. For they are called sensitive on account of their origin, not on account of any comparison as to identity or difference. Hence the most *general* empirical laws are none the less sensual. . . . In things sensual and in phenomena, that which precedes the logical use of intellect is called appearance, and the reflective cognition which arises from the intellectual comparison of a number of appearances is called experience. Thus the only path from appearance to experience is by reflection according to the logical use of the intellect. The common concepts of experience are called empirical, and its objects phenomena; the laws of experience, and of all sensitive knowledge in general, are called laws of phenomena. Thus empirical concepts do not become intellectual *in the real sense* by being brought to a greater universality, and so pass out of the class of sensitive knowledge. However high they ascend by way of abstraction, they always remain sensitive. When we come to the objects of intelligence which are strictly such, in which the use of the intellect is *real*, the concepts involved, whether of objects or relations, are given through the very nature of the intellect, not abstracted from any use of the senses, and do not contain any form of sensitive cognition as such.'

The context of all this, as the reader will gather, is an attack on the Leibnizian conception of the relation between sensing and thinking. I do not propose, however, to comment on it for its

[1] Op. cit., §§ 5 and 6, quoted in J. Handyside's translation (Open Court Publishing Company).

own sake here, but rather to discuss its relevance to the problems of theory of knowledge. To this end I shall now restate the distinction in more modern terms.

In its 'logical' use the function of the intellect is to intellectualize the data of sense or, in language Kant was to make familiar later, 'bring them to concepts'. Among the constituent parts of this process are (i) the formation of universals; (ii) their application to the given in judgement; (iii) the subordinating of logically inferior to logically superior universals and judgements; (iv) the drawing of formal inferences. These activities are clearly indispensable for there to be organized knowledge of any kind: unless we interpret and relate the raw material of the senses we can derive no significance[1] from it. Let us be quite clear that sensation cannot in itself afford us any knowledge whatsoever. Sensation provides the data out of which empirical knowledge is built up and is thus a primary source of cognition; but it needs to be complemented by thought if its product is to acquire meaning. As Kant said in a famous phrase, the intuitions of sense are 'blind' until they have been conceptualized. But it should be equally clear that the thought which here supplements sensation is not in any way originative. It is not, that is to say, a source of knowledge on its own account. Its concepts are formed after reflection on the data of sense and are empty of significance except when referred to these. The part which the intellect plays in its 'logical' capacity is thus a secondary and subordinate, though none the less a very important, one.

By contrast the 'real' use of the intellect is one in which that faculty acts independently of any other. The function of the intellect in this aspect is not the mere conceptualization of the given, but the production of knowledge on its own account. I shall not attempt at this stage to indicate the precise way in which Kant himself thought the claim to fulfil this sort of function could be justified; it will suffice to mention some less complicated forms of the same general view. Thus most theories of intellectual intuition imply that the intellect has a 'real' use. According to Aristotle, for instance, the primary premisses on which demonstra-

[1] This application of the term 'significance' (cf. 'meaning' just below) to experiences or concepts follows a usage of Kant's. Professor Price objected to it very strongly in reading the book in typescript, on the ground that only symbols can be said to have significance or meaning in the proper sense. But I have decided to maintain the text here and elsewhere as it is, largely through inability to find a convenient alternative way of putting what I want to say.

tion is based must be grasped intellectually: we must be brought, by a process which Aristotle calls 'induction',[1] to 'see' their necessity. The mind is here an independent source of knowledge and has, in Kantian terminology, a 'real' function. In the similar theory of Descartes, to give a second example, progress in the sciences depends on the mind's ability to discover necessary truths and intuit the relations between them. Plato's theory of Forms, again, rests on an explicit claim that reason itself can, by 'dialectic power',[2] attain knowledge of reality. All these philosophers are denying that the mind's only legitimate exercise is in co-operation with the senses; and Plato at least goes so far to the other extreme as to suggest that sensation can never be a primary source of knowledge. But of course it is not necessary to take any such view to accept the general position that the intellect has a 'real' use.

Let us now restate the conclusions argued for in the last few pages in the light of this Kantian distinction. If I am right, empiricists and rationalists should agree that the intellect has a 'logical' capacity, and the main issue between them should be whether it also has a 'real' use. The 'logical' use of the intellect is one whose existence should not be in doubt, and its recognition should neither depress empiricists nor unduly encourage their opponents. It can be accepted by the former entirely without prejudice to their main principle; for, as we have seen, the intellect in its 'logical' capacity plays a secondary role and remains throughout dependent on the given. Even if sense-data need to be intellectualized in the way we have said they do, they can none the less constitute the sole primary source of knowledge; and that they do must be the main claim of empiricism. Stated in terms of this theory, empiricism is the doctrine (1) that all knowledge arises out of sensation or introspection, and (2) that the sole legitimate use of the intellect is 'logical'. Rationalism denies both these propositions in asserting that the intellect has a 'real' use. But it should be clear from the foregoing discussion that this assertion cannot be based, as some philosophers seem to have thought, on facts which show that the mind has a '*logical*' capacity. The existence of such intellectual activities as the formation of universals and the formulation of judgements has nothing to do with the question

[1] To be identified with the 'intuitive induction' of Mr. W. E. Johnson, not with the induction of J. S. Mill.

[2] *Republic*, 511^{b} 4.

whether the intellect has a 'real' use. To establish that point quite different arguments must be brought to bear; as we shall see, we must either show that human beings are in some way endowed with intellectual intuition or, like Kant, argue that experience involves concepts and principles of which sensation could not conceivably be the ground.

It may be mentioned that the making of this distinction enables us to formulate the empiricist position in a far more plausible way than that in which it is traditionally stated. The confusion of empiricism and sensationalism, referred to above, is not to be ascribed entirely to wilful blindness on the part of rationalists: empiricists themselves have lent much colour to this misinterpretation of their position. I have mentioned already the classical instance of Hume's account of universals; and this may be taken as typical of the empiricist shyness of all intellectual activities. Indeed, it may be questioned whether even now philosophers of this school are fully aware that they can give the intellect a good deal of rope without fear of being hanged by it. The contemporary logical positivists have greatly improved the empiricist case by their accounts of the propositions of logic and mathematics; but they have not matched their boldness here by recognizing the 'logical' use of the intellect for the innocuous thing that it is, and in consequence they still hanker after basic propositions which picture the facts exactly, perception free of the contagion of thought and other naïvetés. Yet all this, if the argument of the present chapter is correct, is quite unnecessary. The only form of empiricism with which acceptance of the 'logical' use of the intellect is inconsistent is sensationalism such as Mill supported; and in view of the inherent unplausibility of that doctrine probably no one will grieve if we give it up.

§ 3. So much for the first of the two distinctions spoken of above. The second, developed effectively by the same writer, is closely analogous to it and indeed springs from what is fundamentally the same philosophical analysis of the facts. It is, however, sufficiently different from the first to make a separate statement profitable.

According to Kant,[1] all propositions or judgements are either analytic or synthetic. An analytic judgement is one in which the predicate concept is contained, though covertly, in the subject

[1] *Critique of Pure Reason*, B 10 = A 6.

concept; a synthetic judgement one where it is not so contained. The relation of subject to predicate in an analytic judgement is, Kant says, 'thought through identity', and the principle of such judgements is accordingly declared to be the principle of contradiction.[1] If this is right it follows that the truth or falsity of any suggested analytic judgement should be obvious to direct inspection: we have only to see if the predicate concept is in fact contained within the subject concept to make our decision. Putting this in Kant's language, we may say that all analytic judgements are *a priori*, in the sense that the determination of their truth or falsehood in no way depends on experience. If I know (by definition) that a subject x is *a*, *b*, *c* . . . , &c., then I can affirm that it is, e.g., *b* without knowing any particular facts. Indeed I do not even need to know that x exists to judge of the truth of the proposition.

With synthetic judgements the case is very different. There the predicate concept is not contained within the subject concept, and the relation between the two is other than that of identity. The principle of contradiction is accordingly of no value in the determination of their truth. But we cannot say, just because of that, that no synthetic judgements are *a priori*. True, most synthetic judgements clearly rest on experience: many of the propositions of everyday discourse and all those judgements which express the results of the natural sciences and of history are of this character. But the possibility remains that there are other synthetic judgements whose truth depends on some special type of insight into fact or some special relation to experience; and it may be possible to argue that there is a sense in which these are *a priori*. In actual fact Kant thinks we make synthetic *a priori* judgements in mathematics and presuppose them in scientific thinking; and he points out that many traditional metaphysical propositions at least seem to be of this type. But he recognizes that the whole notion of a synthetic *a priori* judgement is a paradoxical one, and the most urgent problem in philosophy, according to him, is to determine the conditions under which judgements of this kind are valid.

Such, in its barest outlines, is Kant's statement of this important distinction. Before relating it to the main problems we are concerned with, it will be profitable to discuss certain criticisms which have been made of it.

[1] Op. cit., B 190 = A 151.

1. One criticism I shall pass over with little more than a mention. It has been alleged (more particularly by Kant's idealist successors) that the whole distinction is misconceived because every judgement is analytic and synthetic at once. Judgement is a process by which we break up a vaguely differentiated continuum of feeling; and it is therefore analytic. But it is synthetic, too, because we make the analysis only to relate the parts together and so reconstitute a more satisfactory whole. Now this application of the terms 'analytic' and 'synthetic' to judgement, whatever its merits, has nothing to do with the sense in which they are used in the distinction we are considering. Judgement may be just what the idealists say, and Kant himself would probably have agreed to some such account; but it can still be true that, in a different sense, every judgement is either analytic or synthetic but not both. The objection, in fact, depends on a simple misunderstanding of language.[1]

2. A more serious difficulty is raised on logical grounds. As will be obvious, Kant's statement of the distinction assumes that every judgement is of the subject-predicate type. Now we are told by modern formal logicians that, though this assumption was commonly made from the time of Aristotle to the nineteenth century, it is none the less indefensible. Neither relational nor existential judgements can be subsumed under this head; and in fact we must recognize a number of fundamentally different types of proposition, no one of which can claim superiority over the rest. Any distinction which ignores these facts is bound to be seriously wrong. And so indeed it is if we accept, as I think we must, the modern account of the matter. But the question is whether or not the particular distinction in which we are interested is irretrievably ruined by the admission; and this would seem more difficult to establish. We can argue that the essential thing about Kant's theory is not what he says about subject and predicate concepts but what he says about the principle of contradiction, and so proceed to a corresponding redefinition of analytic and

[1] Note that Bradley's 'analytic judgement of sense' (*Logic*, vol. i, p. 56) is synthetic in Kant's sense. It must be admitted here that the misunderstanding is not all on one side. Cook Wilson and other critics of Bradley failed to appreciate what might be called his constructive or constitutive sense of judgement: they thought he meant by the term the taking up of a peculiar attitude to a proposition. And since they could not discover that attitude in themselves they concluded that the whole theory was muddled. Cf. Cook Wilson's *Statement and Inference*, especially vol. i, p. 87.

synthetic judgements. An analytic judgement, according to this, would be any judgement whose truth or falsehood could be determined solely by reference to the principle of contradiction, a synthetic judgement one for whose validity a further test was required. It should not be hard to see that this restatement constitutes a considerable improvement on the original definition. Not only does it enable us to apply the distinction to all[1] judgements irrespective of their form; it further allows us to see that analytic judgements are not, as Kant's account perhaps suggests, trivial or unimportant. The question whether a predicate is contained within a subject concept—whether we can think one without the other—has a psychological twist[2] in it which is equally out of place in logic and theory of knowledge; and to reaffirm in a predicate something already asserted in a subject does not seem very significant. The first of these objections vanishes, and the second loses its force, if the distinction is emended as suggested here.

3. But there are some who will not be satisfied with the distinction even in its emended form. In their revolt against the Aristotelian logic modern writers have attacked not only the dogma that in every judgement a predicate is ascribed to a subject, but also the view that the three so-called laws of thought—the principles of identity and contradiction, and the law of the excluded middle—are in any way paramount among logical laws. They have not normally wished to deny the validity of these principles;[3] what they have challenged is the suggestion that they are in a class by themselves, beyond all manner of doubt. Aristotle imagined that the three laws of thought were uniquely certain because the very attempt to deny them presupposes them.[4] What he failed to see, according to recent critics, is that the same can be said of *all* the leading principles of *any* logical system, so long

[1] Existential judgements are, of course, all synthetic. But relational judgements can perfectly well be analytic on this definition: e.g. the compound judgement 'if Dundee is north of Edinburgh, and Edinburgh is north of London, then Dundee is north of London'. (The simple relational judgement 'Dundee is north of Edinburgh' is, of course, synthetic.)

[2] Cf. A. J. Ayer, *Language, Truth and Logic* (first edition), pp. 101 ff., for the criticism that Kant produces a dual criterion, psychological and logical, of analytic propositions.

[3] Some have, however, attempted to dispense with the law of the excluded middle: see Chapter V, § 5 below.

[4] Compare *Metaphysics* 1005^b 35 ff. on the principle of contradiction; 1011^b 23 ff. on the law of excluded middle.

as we remain within that system. The three laws of thought are neither more certain nor more fundamental than any other logical laws.[1] To those who take this view the statement given in the last paragraph of the distinction between analytic and synthetic judgements will naturally give offence; but it is fortunately possible to emend it to avoid the difficulty. If we say that an analytic judgement is one true in virtue of logical laws alone, a synthetic judgement one for whose validity further grounds must be sought, we preserve the spirit of Kant's thought and at the same time avoid controversies which are scarcely in place in the present context.

§ 4. We have now arrived at a formulation of the distinction between analytic and synthetic judgements which may be expected to give general satisfaction. There is, however, one further difficulty in connexion with it which should be discussed at this point. The difficulty concerns the use of the term *a priori*. It was pointed out above that analytic judgements are all *a priori* in the sense that our knowledge of them does not depend on our having had any particular experience. Since the validity of analytic judgements rests, according to the argument we have outlined, on logical laws alone, this should be obvious enough. But we have seen also that Kant wished to say that some synthetic judgements were *a priori*, and indeed was interested in these above all others; and it remains to ask whether he was consistent in this.

Synthetic *a priori* judgements, in Kant's view, cannot rest for their validity on sense-experience, since they claim a necessity and universality which no amount of experiencing could justify. We become familiar with truths of this sort in experience, but a little reflection shows that experience cannot be their ground. And so far they are not unlike analytic judgements. But they differ from the latter in having no special connexion with the laws of logic; and that is indeed the most striking fact about them. No amount of thinking will enable us to establish the validity of such a principle as the general law of causality, just as no amount of experiencing will. Can we say, then, that the term *a priori* is applied to them in the same sense as it is to judgements which are analytically true?

There does seem to be a certain equivocation in Kant's use of this rather unfamiliar notion. *A priori* means for him (*a*) necessary, and (*b*) independent of sense-experience. Now (*b*) can be applied to

[1] For a short discussion of the plausibility of these assertions see pp. 95 ff. below.

analytic truths and those principles Kant describes as synthetic *a priori* with equal propriety. It may be, of course, that, as empiricists would say, there are no genuine synthetic *a priori* judgements; but even if this is correct, we may agree that one of the marks of suggested judgements of this kind is just their independence of sense-experience. But (*a*) cannot be applied to synthetic and analytic judgements in the same sense. The necessity of analytic judgements is *logical*: they are necessarily true because to deny them would be to flout the laws of logic and thus render all thinking chaotic. But obviously no synthetic proposition could be necessary in that sense, since the very definition of a synthetic judgement is one for whose validity some further test than appeal to the laws of logic must be sought. Any synthetic propositions which are necessary must have a necessity of a different sort, and that indeed is the burden of Kant's argument in the *Critique of Pure Reason*. The necessity of principles such as the general law of causality is not logical but 'transcendental' or, as Kant sometimes calls it, 'real'. We take them as universally valid because they are the basic principles upon which experience is built up. So far from being grounded in experience they themselves make experience possible.[1]

In view of the main object of our study it may be worth digressing at this point to consider the whole question of necessity and its different types. At the beginning of Chapter II, I mentioned the stress which rationalists lay on the idea of necessary truths, the existence of which is held to validate the epistemological claims of reason. In fact, however, the term 'necessary truth' is a highly ambiguous one, and differs in its meaning from philosopher to philosopher. This will become clear if we investigate some of the types of necessity which philosophers have recognized.

1. There is first of all *logical* necessity. That which is logically necessary is guaranteed by the laws of logic, i.e. it is analytic in the Kantian sense. Examples of this sort of necessity are not hard to come by: it is illustrated in such everyday judgements as 'either it will rain or not rain to-morrow'. What is of interest from our point of view, however, is the attitude taken by pre-Kantian rationalists towards logical necessity. These philosophers held (*a*) that it was the sole valid form of necessity, and (*b*) that it characterized judgements of the highest speculative interest—for

[1] 'Experience' is here used equivocally: compare above, p. 33 n. and Chapter VI below.

example, propositions about God, or again, propositions asserting the basic principles of the physical universe. Thus Leibniz maintained, as we have seen, that the law of contradiction was the rationale of all truths of reason, asserting in doing so that such truths were logically necessary. And truths of reason were, in the Leibnizian scheme, both the most important and the most certain of all the truths we know. Nor was Leibniz's view here essentially different from that of his predecessors, Descartes and Spinoza. Both understood by 'necessary' logically necessary, and would have said that necessary truths could not be denied without falling into logical absurdity.[1]

A short answer to this form of rationalism was given by Hume. If necessary means logically necessary, he said, we must recognize first of all that it can have no place in the sphere of fact. The contrary of every matter of fact is always possible, and no *logical* law is broken if we assert it. Hence there cannot be, as the rationalists hoped to show there was, any rational insight into the workings of Nature: we must rely there entirely on what experience establishes. Necessity is confined to the sphere of ideas. But the power of reason to apprehend necessary connexions even in that sphere is strictly limited: we find that it is, in fact, confined to the ideas of quantity and number. Hence the famous peroration with which Hume concluded his *Enquiry*: 'When we run over libraries, persuaded of these principles, what havoc must we make? If we take in our hand any volume; of divinity or school metaphysics, for instance; let us ask, *Does it contain any abstract reasoning concerning quantity or number?* No. *Does it contain any experimental reasoning concerning matter of fact and existence?* No. Commit it then to the flames: for it can contain nothing but sophistry and illusion.'

The most remarkable thing about this refutation is that in making it Hume stood on precisely the same ground as his opponents. He acknowledged both that some truths are logically necessary and that there is a faculty of reason of exactly the

[1] Leibniz's views on necessity were complicated by two factors: first, his doctrine that in every true proposition the predicate is inherent in the subject, and second, his wish to avoid ethical determinism. The first of these should have led him to say that *all* true judgements are logically necessary; but he shied from both the ethical and epistemological consequences of this and recognized a separate sphere of truths of fact, determined not by the principle of contradiction but by that of sufficient reason. Whether he intended the separation to be ultimate is another question. Spinoza had no such scruples as these, and thought true knowledge consisted entirely of logically necessary propositions.

kind that rationalists had postulated. But he maintained, by arguments which are surely incontrovertible, that the rationalist conception of the powers of reason was seriously wrong. In doing so he took for granted an account of mathematical reasoning which we shall have to examine presently; nor did he attempt to explain why we have insight into relations of ideas in mathematics and not elsewhere. Nevertheless, it was clear from his time that rationalism can only be made to work if it recognizes some other type of necessity than the logical. But before we ask what that type is we must consider a further doctrine of Hume's.

2. Hume himself held that there is a further type of necessity besides the logical, namely, *psychological* necessity, and a leading point in his general case against rationalism is that all necessity outside that which depends on the principle of contradiction can be reduced to this form. Psychological necessity, in Hume's view, marks some of our knowledge of matters of fact. We have seen how he argued that, because the contrary of every matter of fact is always possible, we have no insight into the sphere of Nature. Our knowledge of the natural world (and the same is true of our knowledge of history) rests not on insight but on imaginative association. Experience teaches us to connect one idea with another, and this we do on the basis of various relations: resemblance, contiguity, cause and effect. We find, however, in considering the last and most important of these, that the connexion of ideas is apparently far closer than elsewhere. There seems to be a necessary connexion between any cause and its effect, just as there seems to be a peculiar necessity in the causal principle itself, a necessity which had led Leibniz to declare it to be a truth of reason. How are we to account for these facts?

(*a*) Hume had little difficulty in dealing with the first case. When we say that a cause is necessarily connected with its effect the necessity involved is purely subjective, brought about in our minds by the constant conjunction of the two. There is nothing in the cause which leads on inevitably to the effect, even in the case of human action. The causal relation is simply a regularity relation, not different in principle from any other piece of association.

(*b*) The case of the law of universal causation, however, proved more troublesome. That 'whatever begins to exist, must have a cause of existence' is 'a general maxim in philosophy', 'commonly taken for granted in all reasonings'.[1] ''Tis suppos'd to be founded

[1] *Treatise*, pp. 78–9, ed. Selby-Bigge.

on intuition, and to be one of those maxims, which tho' they may be deny'd with the lips, 'tis impossible for men in their hearts really to doubt of. But if we examine this maxim by the idea of knowledge above explain'd, we shall discover in it no mark of intuitive certainty, but on the contrary shall find, that 'tis of a nature quite foreign to that species of conviction.'[1] In other words, the general law of causality is not a logically necessary truth. So much is clear, but the question of the status of the law remains. Hume seems to have hesitated between two possible solutions: saying that the law is empirical, and saying that it is a principle appealed to by the imagination in the co-ordination of sense-data. The two views are not completely distinct, since on the second it is experience which suggests the law to the imagination: having met with many instances of causal connexions, we act as if such connexions were ubiquitous. But the imagination clearly goes beyond what experience warrants in making such an assumption.

Dismissing the purely empiricist account as impossible, let us concentrate on the alternative hypothesis. According to this view, Hume is saying that the necessity we attach to the general principle of causality is conferred on it by the imagination. Now it is of interest to note that this is not the only case in which Hume appealed to the imagination in this way. Another conspicuous instance is afforded by his remarks on 'Scepticism with regard to the Senses',[2] where he discusses our assumption that objects continue to exist when we are not sensing them. Our belief in continuing objects, he explains, is one we owe neither to pure sensation nor to reason but to the imagination. The latter has about it certain principles which are 'permanent, irresistible and universal',[3] in the light of which it supplements and interprets the actual data of sensation. We cannot hope to justify the appeal to these principles by any rational argument; but equally we cannot avoid the conclusion that they are used. It is a contingent fact about human nature that it appeals to these and no other principles: they have no internal necessity which compels their application. They are not truths of reason; though it must be said equally that they are not truths of fact in the ordinary sense of the term.

[1] Ibid.
[2] *Treatise*, Bk. I, part iv, section 2.
[3] *Treatise*, p. 225, ed. Selby-Bigge.

Hume thus complements his doctrine of logical necessity and completes the case for empiricism by arguing that so-called necessities of fact are really only subjective, and that our search for causes and our belief in continuing objects cannot be traced to any more elevated faculty than the imagination, which is on his view quite distinct from reason. How far his opinions are justified is a question I shall not ask at this point; it is sufficient to indicate his contribution to the problem, and to proceed to consider what, if anything, rationalists have to say in reply to it.[1]

It seems that rationalists can make two sorts of answer to the position we have outlined, each of which involves a further conception of necessity.

3. They may deny both the empiricist interpretation of truths of fact and their own doctrine of logical necessity by claiming that we can have a type of insight into real connexions which is essentially synthetic. The position is best approached from a consideration of the nature of inference. Formal inference, such as we meet with in mathematics, is commonly said not to lead to any new discoveries but merely to elicit knowledge already contained implicitly in the premisses from which it starts. As the reader will see without difficulty, thinking of this nature is an analytic activity in a sense closely bound up with Kant's. Now this account of the nature of inference was explicitly accepted by rationalists and empiricists alike in the seventeenth and eighteenth centuries, and is indeed very common to-day. But modern rationalists may hold that it is misconceived; and indeed they must do so if they are to give any plausibility to their case. They must maintain in its place that inference is not an analytic but a synthetic process, in which we make a genuine advance to new knowledge. This involves the assertion that when we investigate relations of ideas, to use Hume's phrase, we are not merely analysing our premisses in accordance with logical laws, but are going beyond them to discover real connexions which we had not previously suspected. Combining this conception of inference with a refusal to draw any sharp distinction between fact and idea, we reopen the way to a rationalist interpretation of natural science. Mathematics, thought of as consisting not of analytic but of synthetic judgements, will be reinstated in its place as the model of all scientific knowledge, and other branches of learning

[1] For a discussion of Hume's conception of the imagination, see Chapter VIII, § 3 below.

will be adjudged more or less reputable according to their distance from the mathematical ideal.

It is clear that this type of view, the most distinguished recent proponent of which is Mr. H. W. B. Joseph,[1] rests on a theory of intellectual intuition, and as such will have to be considered in the next chapter. What is of immediate importance here is to notice that it involves a conception of necessity separate from either of those we have hitherto considered, one which we may call *synthetic* or *intuitive*. A judgement possessed of this type of necessity will not be a necessary truth in the logical sense: there will be no contradiction in denying it. Nevertheless, it may claim a kind of evidence in itself in that it is established by an act of rational intuition. Many philosophers would account for what they take to be the certainty of ethical principles in such a way as this.

4. Alternatively, rationalists may accept the empiricist separation of idea and fact and even agree that rational insight in the latter sphere is impossible, but may yet hold that reason has a contribution of its own to make to knowledge. They can do that if they argue, like Kant, that those principles which Hume ascribed to imagination are in fact a product of the understanding. We have seen how Hume held that the imagination has about it certain settled principles of its own which it applies in the interpretation of experience. If pressed, Hume would have said that it was just a contingent fact about human nature that it applies these principles and no others. This was a proposition which Kant denied, arguing that it follows from the nature of our intelligence that we think on the lines that we do. Ours is a discursive and not an intuitive intelligence, deriving its raw material not from itself but the senses. Such a mind must combine the different parts of the given to attain knowledge, and if its knowledge is to be objective the combination must be carried out according to necessary principles. It was of these principles, Kant maintains, that Hume was thinking in his discussion of the problem of causality, though he did not see it, as he should, as the general problem of the synthetic *a priori*. Had he done so he must have anticipated Kant's own solution.

It is clear that to make out his case Kant must show more than that knowledge of objects presupposes thinking in accordance with

[1] Cf. *An Introduction to Logic, passim*. A similar view, though without the mathematical twist, is implied by many idealists.

principles of the understanding: he must show how particular principles of the understanding (e.g. the general law of causality) originate in the nature of intelligence as such. And this is a task which he thinks he can accomplish. We cannot, however, enter here into the details of his solution, nor discuss the plausibility of the general position, which will be considered in full at a later stage.[1] But we should notice that Kant is introducing in this doctrine a notion of necessity which is fundamentally new. He calls this type of necessity *transcendental*, employing that term in a purely arbitrary way to denote that which precedes experience as its *a priori* condition. A transcendentally necessary truth is a synthetic proposition, but it is neither logically necessary nor in any way self-guaranteeing. Its necessity is prescriptive rather than factual, and perhaps approximates to the necessity of the laws of logic itself.

§ 5. So much for the problem of necessity. Returning to the main subject of the present chapter, we must now examine briefly how the distinction of analytic from synthetic judgements clarifies the chief issues of epistemology. It was suggested above that an analytic judgement could be defined as one whose truth or falsehood can be determined by reference to logical laws alone, a synthetic judgement one for whose truth or falsehood a further criterion must be sought. In the light of these definitions I wish to maintain (1) that any fair-minded person must agree that there are both analytic and synthetic judgements in the senses specified, and (2) that the real problem for epistemologists concerns synthetic *a priori* judgements.

1. I say 'fair-minded person' here not in any invidious sense but because some philosophers, in the interest of a further theory,[2] are anxious either to deny the existence of a separate class of analytic judgements or to confine its membership to propositions of a wholly trivial and unimportant nature. These philosophers maintain that the only propositions which are indisputably analytic are tautologies of the old-fashioned kind like 'sheep are sheep'; and not unnaturally they refuse to attach great importance to these. But in fact the definition given is wide enough to cover judgements of far more obvious importance: for example, any syllogistic argument of the form 'If M is P and S is M, then S is P',

[1] Cf. Chapter VIII below, especially §§ 1–2.
[2] In this case the Coherence Theory of Truth. See below, pp. 82 ff.

as well as many of the judgements of everyday discourse, though the analytic character of the latter is often concealed behind an elliptical form of expression.[1] Quite apart from this is the suggestion, now strongly supported and widely though not universally accepted, that the whole of mathematics is made up of analytic judgements. It is argued that all mathematical propositions can be deduced by purely logical inference from a number of primary concepts and principles; and that in the process no particular experience, special insight, or knowledge of fact is presupposed. Clearly, if this contention, which we shall discuss shortly, can be made out, analytic judgements will be very important indeed.

2. Even so, it should be emphasized that there should be no dispute between rationalists and empiricists over analytic judgements. Acceptance of the possibility of judgements of this kind argues no special insight in the human intellect, and can hence be made by empiricists with the greatest equanimity. The situation here, in fact, is closely parallel to that examined in the early part of the chapter. In discussing there the two functions of the intellect, we argued that all philosophers should be prepared to accept the view that it has a 'logical' capacity; that empiricists should not jib at it as the first step to their undoing, nor rationalists seize on it as a stick with which to beat their opponents. Precisely the same can be said of analytic judgements. That the human intellect can form them is merely a consequence of its having a 'logical' capacity, and argues nothing either for or against its 'real' powers. And indeed the recognition of this fact in the present century has, as I have remarked already, made a considerable improvement possible in the modern presentation of the case for empiricism.

The real point at issue between empiricism and rationalism turns on the questions whether there are synthetic *a priori* judgements, what type of judgements they are, and on what basis they rest. This is the classical problem with which Kant confronted philosophers, and it remains to-day the main problem of theory of knowledge. Thus (*a*) there might be no valid synthetic *a priori* propositions: all synthetic judgements might be empirical. This is no doubt what all empiricists would like to believe, but it is a view

[1] We often express analytic judgements simply, stating their conclusions only, when in fact our thinking is much more complex. Thus we say that 'A must be *b*' when we mean that it must be if certain definitions are accepted and the laws of logic thought valid.

which the passage of time makes it increasingly hard to accept. Alternatively (*b*) there might be valid synthetic *a priori* propositions, but of a purely arbitrary kind, expressing the conventions within which the human mind, for no good reason, chose to work. Synthetic *a priori* judgements would in that case be a very special class, and would rest not on intellectual insight, but on the need to organize our experience in some way or other. Their justification, in a word, would be methodological or pragmatic. (*c*) Thirdly, we might argue, like Kant, that the class of synthetic *a priori* judgements is made up of those principles which the mind prescribes to experience, but that its doing so is by no means arbitrary or irrational. Or lastly (*d*), we could agree with rationalists of the more extreme school that some factual synthetic *a priori* judgements are possible, and ground our assertion on a belief in some form of intellectual intuition. In that case we should have to explain carefully just what that intuition amounts to and, if only to safeguard ourselves against misrepresentation, discuss its powers and limits.

I shall proceed to consider these four views and other questions suggested by this chapter almost immediately. Before doing so, however, I wish to make one further point about analytic and synthetic judgements. An analytic judgement was defined above as a judgement true or false in virtue of logical laws alone. Now it seems that if we accept this definition we already commit ourselves to synthetic *a priori* judgements of some sort. For what, we may ask, is the status of the laws of logic themselves? It is widely said to-day that the principles of logic are all analytic; but that could obviously not be true if analytic propositions are defined as we have defined them. The laws of logic cannot themselves be true in virtue of the laws of logic. Provisionally, at least, it looks as if we ought to describe them as synthetic, and, what is more, synthetic *a priori*, since we ascribe necessity and universality to them. Of course, to say this is not in itself to refute empiricism; for it may well be possible to show that the laws of logic form a class by themselves, and that our knowing them in no way justifies the hope that we might know synthetic *a priori* judgements of a different kind, such as the propositions of metaphysics or rational physics. I shall argue presently that this is in fact the case: that judgements can be divided into two classes, prescriptive and factual, and that while we can show that there are some genuine synthetic *a priori* judgements of the prescriptive type (including the principles of logic), we cannot point to any valid factual synthetic *a priori* propositions. On this account synthetic *a priori* judgements fall in a class of their own, and it may even be suggested that they are not judgements at all. Detailed discussion of these points must, however, await a later chapter, and in the meantime we must explore the possibilities of intellectual intuition.

IV

INTELLECTUAL INTUITION

§ 1. THE issue between rationalism and empiricism can now be put in the form of two questions:

(i) Has the human intellect a 'real' as well as a 'logical' function?

(ii) Are there genuine synthetic as well as analytic *a priori* judgements, and if so what are the conditions of their validity?

It seems reasonable to hold that the first of these questions, and the first half of the second, would be answered affirmatively, and the issue thus decided in favour of rationalism, if we could show that intellectual intuition is possible for human beings. Unfortunately, however, the term 'intellectual intuition' is generic rather than specific, and it will be necessary to begin by mentioning some of the main senses in which philosophers have thought it possible or at least worth considering.

I will begin with what might be called the full-blooded sense, expounded but, of course, not accepted by Kant.[1] Kant uses the idea of an intuitive intelligence to bring out his own notion of the human understanding. Arguing that sense and thought must co-operate in knowledge, and that each is ineffective without the other, he maintains that the parts they play are quite distinct. In sensation we are acquainted with particular presentations; thinking's business is to universalize these or, as Kant says, 'bring them to concepts'. Sensation thus provides the basic raw material of knowledge, which thought relates and interprets. This situation Kant describes by saying that sensation is, with human beings, an intuitive while thought is a discursive faculty; and this view of the relation of sense and thought is, of course, central in his philosophy. To underline and elucidate it he has recourse to the notion of a very different situation, one in which the same faculty at once intuits particulars and thinks them. Such would be the knowing of an intuitive understanding. It should be noticed from the first that Kant never says there actually *are* intelligences of this type:[2] he merely thinks it possible and profitable to inquire into the characteristics they would possess if

[1] See *Critique of Pure Reason*, especially the second edition version of the Transcendental Deduction, and *Critique of Judgment*, §§ 76–7.

[2] Though he clearly thought at one time that the divine intelligence was thus intuitive: compare *Dissertation*, § 10.

they were actual. And the burden of his answer is that in the knowing of an intuitive understanding there would be no separation, as there is with us, between the intuitive and the conceptual. Objects and their relations, if we can put the matter crudely, would present themselves to it in a single flash of insight, and it would know the universe not piecemeal but all at once. In consequence the thinking of an intuitive understanding would not be confined, as is human thinking, to general terms: its universals, if it could be said to possess any, would be concrete rather than abstract and would not so much contrast with particulars as afford particular knowledge themselves. But in truth the whole distinction of universal and particular would not exist for the type of intelligence here analysed, since there would be no question of its first originating raw material and then making judgements about it. The thinking of an intuitive intelligence would be in itself a knowing.

This description should suffice to give us an idea of intellectual intuition in its primary sense. Used in the meaning given to it by Kant it signifies a type of experience in which the normal antitheses of sense and thought, particular and universal, have been overcome and in which we know, in a single flash of insight, the particular in the universal or, in the Hegelian sense, know the individual. Although this form of intuiting is described as intellectual it clearly has no more to do with the discursive intellect than it has with the senses. It has transcended the antithesis of sense and understanding, which exists for a discursive intelligence alone.

A second sense of intellectual intuition is connected with our apprehension (or alleged apprehension) of self-evident truths. We have already discussed this matter briefly in Chapter III, and seen how rationalism in some of its forms can only be made to work if some rational insight into connexions of fact is allowed. The Cartesian notion of natural science clearly depends on a claim to such insight, as did, by a curious irony, the Aristotelian science Descartes was so anxious to overthrow. Aristotle has, indeed, a formal argument designed to show that there must be some self-evident truths of the type under consideration.[1] The proper form of every science, according to that philosopher—the form in which its results are presented in closest conformity with fact—is a deductive system. Now in such a system all propositions follow, by linear inference, from a number of basic principles or first

[1] *Posterior Analytics*, 72a 25 ff.

premisses. The justification for any particular proposition in the system is to point to these basic principles and trace the logical steps connecting them with the proposition under examination. But what justification can we produce for the basic principles themselves?

'Some hold that, owing to the necessity of knowing the primary premisses, there is no scientific knowledge. Others think there is, but that all truths are demonstrable. . . . The first school, assuming that there is no way of knowing other than by demonstration, maintain that an infinite regress is involved, on the ground that if behind the prior stands no primary, we could not know the posterior through the prior (wherein they are right, for one cannot traverse an infinite series): if on the other hand—they say—the series terminates and there are primary premisses, yet these are unknowable because incapable of demonstration, which according to them is the only form of knowledge. And since thus one cannot know the primary premisses, knowledge of the conclusions which follow from them is not pure scientific knowledge nor properly knowing at all, but rests on the mere supposition that the premisses are true. The other party agree with them as regards knowing, holding that it is only possible by demonstration, but they see no difficulty in holding that all truths are demonstrated, on the ground that demonstration may be circular and reciprocal.'[1]

'Our own doctrine', Aristotle continues, 'is that not all knowledge is demonstrative: on the contrary, knowledge of the immediate premisses is independent of demonstration.' And in a later passage[2] he proceeds to elaborate this theme, showing that we become familiar with the basic truths of science in the course of normal sense-perception, but owe our certainty of their truth not to sensation but to intuition (*νοῦς*). Intuition of the self-evident thus lies at the basis of all knowledge. We have only to supplement this with the theory of Descartes that inference itself reduces at its best to intuition to reach the rationalist doctrine of scientific knowledge in its strongest form.

A third theory of intellectual intuition concerns our apprehension of universals, and here again the stage for future discussion was set by Aristotle. As everybody knows, Aristotle believed that universals exist *in re*; and this view in itself involved him in a theory of intellectual intuition. We may take the question up by considering the well-worn Aristotelian antithesis of matter and form. Every concrete thing, according to Aristotle (and by the term he meant

[1] *Posterior Analytics*, 72^{b} 5 ff., translated by G. R. G. Mure.
[2] 99^{b} 15 ff.

something a good deal wider than we do by material object) is a συνόλον or composite of matter and form. The form of a thing is its intelligible structure, its matter that on which the form is imposed. Thus the form of a plant or a house is the way in which its different constituents are arranged; a plant, for instance, is not just a collection of cells but a collection of cells organized in a certain way and for a certain purpose; and it is just this element of structure which makes it what it is. Every concrete thing consists of a form embodied in a matter, but it is the form which is, as it were, the dominant partner in the combination. Indeed, if we ask what matter is apart from form we get into considerable difficulties. In the analysis of any given composite we can say what is form and what is matter; but if we turn to study the matter we see that it is susceptible of further analysis. That which stands as matter to form in one συνόλον is itself, when looked at from a different aspect, another συνόλον of matter and form, with a structure of its own;[1] and however far we push our analysis we always get the same result. Bare matter, πρώτη ὕλη, is thus nothing actual but merely the presupposition of the whole analysis.

Aristotle proceeds to elaborate his theory, in a way which has been historically important but which we need not consider in detail now, by developing his doctrine of essences, properties, and essential accidents. Every separate species of object has, he believes, an essential nature of its own, and the characteristics manifested by any individual of the species can be shown to depend more or less closely on this. It is the business of science to provide definitions: to point to the genus to which any given species belongs and indicate its differentia, and to show how its other qualities follow from its essential properties. The connexion of this view of the function of science with the notion that its proper form is a deductive system (p. 53 above) should be obvious.

I have described the form of a thing as its intelligible structure; and it is time to consider the theory of knowledge implied by the whole view. It is Aristotle's explicit doctrine[2] that in the process of knowing mind and its object (the form) are one; and this may suggest that he is pursuing a subjective theory. In actual fact nothing could be farther from the truth. Neither Plato nor

[1] To give a favourite Aristotelian example, the marble out of which a statue is cut is its matter; but from a different point of view it is a συνόλον itself, and the matter-form analysis can be applied to it in turn.

[2] *De Anima*, iii. 4.

Aristotle has any use for Conceptualism, the theory that universals exist not in fact but only in knowing minds: in terms of the famous medieval controversy they are both uncompromisingly Realists. They both set out from the view that the object of knowledge is independently real but is fully open to human knowledge; and while Plato suggests in a famous passage[1] that the mind or, as he says, soul (ψυχή) is 'akin' to the Forms, the most real of all things, there is no attempt by either philosopher to draw the implications of such a view in the way made familiar by later idealists. Thus in the present instance Aristotle would say that the form of an object is something which undoubtedly belongs to it, and that when known it passes over into the mind of the knower: the impetus here is entirely from the side of the object. All that can be ascribed to the mind is a capacity for grasping form as it exists *in re*, and this capacity is clearly a species of intellectual intuition. Knowing is thus for Aristotle primarily an intellectual act.[2]

It is perhaps unnecessary to point out that Plato's theory of universals, for all its differences from Aristotle's, has precisely the same epistemological implications. Indeed Plato starts with an explicit attack on the view that sensing can ever provide us with a stable object of knowledge. For that we must look to the Forms, which exist in a world of their own quite distinct from that we know in sensation. Our knowledge of the Forms is achieved by purely intellectual means. And indeed some such view is bound up with every Realist theory of universals.

There remains for consideration one further theory of intellectual intuition of some importance. This is the view to which reference has already been made in the last chapter, that all inference involves an element of intuition. Thus Mr. Mure writes in criticism of Kant's Transcendental Logic:

'Had Kant paid more attention to the nature of inference he might have found it less easy to deny to thought its native moment of intuition. The discursive factor in thought is not revealed only in the dispersion of an identical concept through a multiplicity of sensuous intuitions which instantiate it, but also in the movement of inference from

[1] *Republic*, 490^b 4; cf. *Phaedo*, 79^d 3.

[2] This statement needs qualification in the light of the facts that Aristotle 'maintains that in man sense-perception develops without a break into thought' (Mure: *Aristotle*, p. 113) and that his official account of sense-perception is that 'a sense is receptive of sensible forms without their matter' (*de Anima*, 424^a 17). But as he goes on to describe these forms as universal it is clear that he cannot be describing an act of pure sensation. For the whole subject see Mr. Mure's *Aristotle*, pp. 102 ff.

premisses to conclusion; and in the grasping of a conclusion a complementary factor of intellectual intuition is plainly manifest, not as an act separate from discursion but as the re-immediation of the discursive, mediatory movement.'[1]

The same sort of argument has been advanced in a rather different form in the writings of Dr. A. C. Ewing, more particularly in his British Academy lecture *Reason and Intuition*. Dr. Ewing holds that in whatever way the premisses of an argument are established, the insight that they necessitate the conclusion can be attained only by an act of intuition. The process of reasoning itself contains an intuitive factor, and to contrast reason with intuition is accordingly mistaken. Elsewhere[2] Dr. Ewing has laid great stress on the fact, or supposed fact, that in inference we advance from the known to the unknown; and indeed he identifies the problem of *a priori* synthesis with the problem of inference, i.e. with the question whether such an advance is possible. He holds that it is, saying that reasoning is essentially an attempt to apprehend necessary connexions between one fact and another, and arguing that inference is genuinely synthetic. But if it is, its synthetic character clearly depends on the factor of intuition which it contains. Dr. Ewing sees that his views are in agreement with the practice if not the theory of many of the classical rationalists,[3] though he would not necessarily endorse every synthetic inference those philosophers claimed to be able to make.

§ 2. So much by way of preliminary description of the various theories of intellectual intuition. In considering them in detail it will probably prove most convenient to begin with the last, which can be disposed of quite shortly.

It can scarcely be denied that reason does have insight into the following of a conclusion from its premisses, and that this insight approximates to intuition. We mark this fact in linguistic usage when we say that we *see* that the conclusion follows or that the premisses necessitate it: we do not of course mean that we visually apprehend the connexion or in any way sense it, but use 'see' as the precise and literal equivalent of 'intuit'. And this, so far as it goes, certainly suggests that the contrast between the intuitive

[1] *An Introduction to Hegel*, p. 96, n. 3.

[2] See especially *Idealism*, pp. 67 ff. and 251 ff.

[3] Something like Dr. Ewing's view is argued for by Descartes in the *Regulae* (III: Adam and Tannery, x. 369).

and the discursive in regard to human thinking is perhaps not so sharp as it has sometimes been said to be: if the human understanding is, in the main, a discursive instrument, it must also be credited with some intuitive functions. Intellectual intuition is a reality in inference at least, and this may seem decisive in favour of some form of rationalism.

Reference to the argument of Chapter III will, I hope, cast doubt on this conclusion. It will be remembered that a distinction was drawn there between two functions of the human intellect, which we called, in Kantian terminology, 'logical' and 'real'. The purpose of this distinction was to clear away certain misapprehensions of the issue between rationalism and empiricism and to prevent, if possible, the adducing as decisive of arguments which could be accepted with equanimity by both sides. We contended accordingly that both empiricists and rationalists should agree that the intellect has a part to play in knowing: its 'logical' functions, at any rate, are beyond question. Now it seems fairly clear that inferring is to be classed among these 'logical' functions. According to the traditional logic, the operations of the mind which the logician studies are conception, judgement, and inference; and this view would probably be accepted even by those who regard the content of the traditional logic as seriously wrong or at best quite inadequate. Of these operations it would no doubt be agreed without much ado that conception and judgement (along with its various attendant operations such as questioning and supposing) belong to the 'logical' activity of the intellect as we have defined it;[1] but a doubt might be expressed about inference. The reason for such a doubt would be found in the suggestion that inference is a process by which we reach new knowledge; to do this, we shall be told, is the function of the intellect in its 'real' capacity. And it is certainly true that if the mind has a 'real' function it must be a source of knowledge on its own account. But it may be questioned whether the knowledge we establish by formal inference at least is really new in the required sense. In formal inference we apply the rules of logic to what we know already and deduce our conclusions; our whole procedure is analytic, and we end by having explicitly before us what was at the beginning implicit only. No doubt this is often a considerable gain, and no doubt there is a

[1] Judgement certainly has another side to it as well, if we accept the mature Kantian view; but judgement as studied by formal logic conforms to the statement in the text.

sense in which our thinking results in new knowledge; but it is not new in the sense in which we establish new facts by sense-perception every minute of our conscious lives. Nor is the rationalist case established if we shift our attention from strict implication to probable reasoning. For though it is no doubt true, as Dr. Ewing says, that induction, too, involves an element of intuition, in so far as we must 'see' that our premisses enable us to conclude with just the right degree of probability, no one can maintain that it is the intuition which actually leads to the new knowledge in an inductive argument. On the contrary, induction is, as all philosophers know, a crying scandal, in that the advance to new knowledge which it produces cannot be justified on rational grounds.

We may conclude that the element of intuition which inference undoubtedly involves is not of major significance for theory of knowledge. Despite its presence formal thinking cannot lead to the discovery of genuinely new knowledge, though it can and does reveal implications of which we were formerly unaware. Formal thinking is, in fact, an analytic and not a synthetic activity. And while it is the case that we do discover new truths by inductive and causal reasoning, it can scarcely be said that our doing so is the result of acts of intuition. It is a philosophical commonplace that no causal argument can establish the existence of any particular cause; and, if only because of that, causal reasoning cannot give us that insight into the interconnexions of fact which is required to justify the rationalist view. The intuitional element in inference belongs to the 'logical' side of our nature and argues no special cognitive powers in the intellect. It should be acknowledged by rationalists and empiricists alike.

§ 3. The remaining theories of intellectual intuition require more protracted consideration. In the rest of the present chapter I shall be concerned with the first of the three views stated above (pp. 52–53), deferring the examination of the other two to Chapter V.

Perhaps it would be as well to indicate first why philosophers have inclined to a view so obviously difficult to sustain as the 'full-blooded' theory I have described. One of the primary metaphysical convictions which we all share is that everything in our experience is, in its own way, uniquely particular and individual. Experience presents us with a constant novelty of situation, which we strive to make intelligible by comparing with the past, but which we nevertheless believe to be no mere repetition or re-hash of the latter. Now many philosophers have argued that a discursive understanding, one whose whole capacity consisted, in Kant's words, in 'thinking' (conceptualizing) the data of the senses, could never do justice to the individuality of the real. The reason for this is to be found in the fact that the concepts of such an understanding are all general concepts, fitted to deal only with the common features of experience. And this, it is alleged, means that the real is inevitably distorted in discursive knowledge. Only an intelligence equipped with concepts of quite a different kind, which did not contrast with particulars but themselves determined them, could hope to grasp reality in its individual detail; and such an intelligence (if intelligence it should be called) is clearly intuitive. The contention is that we must admit intellectual intuition of the kind here described to be possible in principle unless we are to fall into complete scepticism about knowledge.

The argument has been put forward in different ways by different writers. It is to be found, for instance, in the *Ethics* of Spinoza, who makes but unfortunately does not elaborate a distinction between three ways of knowing—by *imaginatio*, by *ratio*, and by *scientia intuitiva*. The first of these is roughly equivalent to sense-perception (which Spinoza, like Leibniz, thought to be inevitably confused) and need not concern us now. *Ratio* is exemplified in the thinking of the scientist, who begins from 'common notions' (basic truths) and proceeds to draw general conclusions from these. The model for this type of thinking is to be found in (Euclidean) geometry, and Spinoza (like Descartes) might well have agreed that it progressed by a species of intuition. His main point about it, however, was that it terminated in universal truths, and so could give no knowledge of the individual. To do this was, apparently, the business of *scientia intuitiva*. To judge from Spinoza's few hints on the subject, he conceived it as a kind of knowledge in which the whole universe was seen in its relation to God's infinite essence; and it was, as he says himself in one passage,[1] a 'knowledge of individual things'. He seems to have been thinking of an intellectual intuition of the kind analysed by Kant, and he may have thought that his own philosophy, despite its geometrical expression, was based on such a concrete

[1] *Ethics*, v. 36, Scholium. For the whole subject see H. H. Joachim's *Study in the Ethics of Spinoza*, especially pp. 180–5, and the same author's commentary on Spinoza's *Tractatus de Intellectus Emendatione*, pp. 42–51.

intuition of reality as a whole. For the doctrine clearly has strong mystical tendencies, and the mysticism of the last book of the *Ethics* is notorious.

A second instance of the same point of view is to be found in the works of Bradley. The problem which exercised Bradley above all others was that of how we can know the individuality of the real. I have pointed out already how Bradley distinguished three stages in apprehension: feeling below the level of relations, relational thought, and feeling (if it can be so called) above the level of relations. The first of these is roughly equivalent to Kant's sensation and gives us immediate contact with reality. It is, however, quite inarticulate: by it we merely grasp a something which at this level we cannot characterize. To know the 'what' which complements the 'that' we must pass to the sphere of relational thought and bring the universals of (discursive) understanding to bear. But though this enables us to find experience meaningful, Bradley argues, it does not afford us true knowledge or abiding satisfaction. Relational thinking has two aspects: it is at once an attempt to break down and analyse what is given in feeling and an effort to reunite the parts in a more stable whole. But the task is one which can never be accomplished.

'Thought is relational and discursive, and, if it ceases to be this, it commits suicide; and yet, if it remains thus, how does it contain immediate presentation? Let us suppose the impossible accomplished; let us imagine a harmonious system of ideal contents united by relations, and reflecting itself in self-conscious harmony. This is to be reality, all reality; and there is nothing outside it. The delights and pains of the flesh, the agonies and raptures of the soul, these are fragmentary meteors falling from thought's harmonious system. But these burning experiences—how in any sense can they be mere pieces of thought's heaven? For, if the fall is real, there is a world outside thought's region, and, if the fall is apparent, then human error itself is not included there. Heaven, in brief, must either not be heaven, or else not all reality.'[1]

It is because of this failure by thought to incorporate the immediacy of feeling that its products remain, in the end, nothing more than a 'ghostly ballet of bloodless categories and spectral woof of impalpable abstractions'; because of it, too, that thinking must ultimately pass into something which is not thinking at all. This something,

[1] *Appearance and Reality*, pp. 150–1. Chap. XV of that work gives Bradley's main view on thought and reality; see also his index, *s.v.* 'feeling' and 'thought'.

of which we can gain an inadequate idea in immediate experience, is, on its cognitive side at least, strongly reminiscent of Kant's intellectual intuition, though Bradley would certainly have disputed the adjective. To what extent it can be reached in human apprehension is another question. Bradley was under no illusions as to the status of his own philosophy. 'Truth is one aspect of experience,' he says,[1] 'and is therefore made imperfect and limited by what it fails to include. So far as it is absolute it does however give the general type and character of all that possibly can be true or real. And the universe in this general character is known completely. It is not known, and it never can be known, in all its details. It is not known, and it never, as a whole, can be known, in such a sense that knowledge would be the same as experience or reality. For knowledge and truth—if we suppose them to possess that identity—would have been, therewith, absorbed and transmuted.' Philosophy cannot provide us with anything better than abstract general knowledge, though its truths are 'as true as truth can be'; but the question whether other forms of experience, not primarily cognitive, approximate to the concrete awareness we are seeking is perhaps left open in the qualifying clause 'as a whole'. We may suppose that Bradley would have said that awareness of this kind, just because it is not beyond our comprehension, is also not altogether beyond our grasp; and he might have pointed to artistic and religious experience[2] for partial examples of it. But in general he is content to say only that human knowledge points forward to absolute experience, and to leave the matter at that.

But if Bradley's views on the question of intellectual intuition are thus ambiguous, there seems to be no such difficulty with another philosopher whose initial thinking at least followed much the same lines. Henri Bergson agreed with Bradley that the intellect, condemned as it is to treat all experiences in general terms, cannot hope to grasp things in their individuality; but he went on to argue that it was never meant to do so. Biologically the function of the intellect is to facilitate action, not to produce knowledge for its own sake; and the distortion of reality which thinking involves, just because it proceeds in general terms, can hence be accepted with equanimity. Indeed, Bergson argues that distortion of this kind is indispensable for the purposes of action; for if we treated every case on its merits and allowed for its unique

[1] *Appearance and Reality*, p. 483.

[2] Bradley's philosophy clearly has a mystical basis, just as Spinoza's had.

character we should never act at all. Action requires the classification of things and situations as types, and the application of general rules; and in this process the individuality of the real is undoubtedly left out of account; but we need have no qualms about that so long as we remember that the 'knowledge' the discursive intellect produces is true for practical purposes only. This account holds, Bergson suggests, even of such refined products of the intellect as the physical sciences: indeed, the distinguishing mark of all of these is that they presuppose a special conception of spatialized or public time, which each of us can see on reflection to be different from the *durée* we personally experience. For real theoretical understanding of the universe we must accordingly have recourse not to the sciences but to intuition: it is intuition alone which gives us access to concrete reality and enables us to expose the erroneous character of accepted scientific concepts. Bergson does not say that he is here in effect reviving the view Kant rejected in the *Critique of Judgment,* but it is clear that he is. However, like Bradley, he would have firmly rejected the characterization of his intuition as 'intellectual', since he reserves that term to describe the processes of the discursive understanding. And just because of this terminology his doctrine can be viewed as anti-intellectual and anti-rationalist: Bergson has no more sympathy with rationalists of the pre-Kantian school than he has with advocates of the claims of science to produce metaphysical truth.[1]

To examine the doctrines of all these writers in detail would obviously be a lengthy and perhaps an ungrateful task; but it is fortunately unnecessary for us to undertake it. For we can consider the whole question of intellectual intuition in this primary sense by reference to the work of a single philosopher, Hegel. Hegel was influenced by Spinoza and himself influenced Bradley and (to some extent) Bergson; moreover, his philosophy was determined throughout by his attempt to avoid the difficulties to which he thought Kant had been brought by his view of the relation of sensing and thinking. I shall therefore devote the rest of this chapter to an attempt to elucidate and criticize Hegel's views on intellectual intuition—a task we shall find not altogether free from difficulty.

[1] Compare the attack in *L'Évolution créatrice* on mechanism and teleology alike. And for the general view compare Croce, in whose version of the theory the concepts of science are described as 'pseudo-concepts'. Croce is, however, more of a rationalist than Bergson.

§ 4. Hegel argued[1] that the discursive theory of human intellection, as represented by Kant, gave rise to two impossibilities: it made knowledge unintelligible, and it depended on the self-contradictory postulation of the thing in itself. Let us take up each of these points briefly. According to Kant (and indeed according to what may be called the common-sense view), knowledge is a compound of two elements, sense and thought. In a celebrated passage[2] in the *Critique of Pure Reason* Kant remarks that the two perhaps spring from a single, to us unknown, root; but in general he treats them as wholly separate. The functions of the two faculties are quite different, and while it is the business of sense to intuit sense-data or 'representations', the task of thought is to universalize or conceptualize these. To this account Hegel objects by asking how, if sense and thought are thus initially separate, we can expect them to co-operate. Why should the products of the senses be amenable to the processes of thought if the relation of sense and thought is what Kant says it is? Does not Kant make the whole of knowledge a standing miracle? Hegel maintains that he does, and holds moreover that Kant's view is bound up with the affirmation of the unintelligible thing in itself. I have referred to this matter before, and it will be necessary here only to summarize the Kantian position as Hegel saw it. We can put this in an antinomy: (*a*) Kant is committed to the thing in itself as the independent reality which is the source of the given element in knowledge, and (*b*) he cannot give any satisfactory account of our knowing even the existence of any such thing. If knowledge is (by definition) always a product of sense and thought in co-operation, how can we know something which in its very nature must lie outside the field of sensation? There is no doubt that, verbally at least, Kant had got himself into a muddle here, and Hegel had little difficulty in discomfiting Kant's supporters.

I shall not stop at this point to consider the propriety of these Hegelian objections, which in their author's eyes sufficed to discredit the Kantian attack on a metaphysics of the supersensible and to reopen the way to a rational science of Nature in the strong sense of that term,[3] but shall proceed at once to outline

[1] The reader may find it useful to compare the short summary of the following argument on pp. 27–9 above. For a fuller discussion of the subject see my article 'Hegel and Intellectual Intuition' in *Mind*, January 1946.

[2] B 29 = A 15.

[3] Kant himself believed in the possibility of rational science of Nature, but only in a weakened sense: reason could, in his mature view, establish the first principles

Hegel's positive theory. His first suggestion was that we must distinguish different levels of thought. Among these were (1) the confused picture thinking of common sense, with its constant recourse to images and sensible examples; (2) the clear thinking of the scientific understanding, with its abstract concepts; (3) the thinking of philosophy. Hegel maintained that these three forms were *dialectically* related members of a single developing series: that is to say, that they should be viewed as successive stages, related as thesis, antithesis, and synthesis, of a progression in which a single generic notion received increasingly adequate embodiment. The point he was making is that common-sense, scientific, and philosophical thinking are not, as might appear, alternative species of a single genus in the way horses and dogs, for instance, are alternative species of the genus animal, but are rather a series of attempts to do, with varying success, the *same* piece of work. Common-sense thinking, on this view, tends of its own nature to pass into scientific thinking, which in its turn gives way to the thinking of philosophy. Common-sense is thus to be regarded as inferior to scientific thinking, and the latter as inferior to philosophical thought. And in considering the relations of sense and thought we must not make the mistake of taking an inferior form of thinking as representative of the whole genus: we should rather judge the possibilities of thought by considering it at its best in the thinking of philosophy.

Hegel's second suggestion concerned the contrast between sense and thought. We have seen already how this was treated by Kant as virtually absolute: apart from the vague possibility of their having a common root, sensation and intellection were regarded as quite separate throughout the Kantian philosophy Hegel said that the true account of the matter was that sensation was thought's 'other'. In this rather mysterious language he was reviving the traditional rationalist doctrine (for which see Chapter II) that sensing and thinking are really parts of a single process. As with Aristotle and Leibniz, there was for Hegel an unbroken development from the lowest form of sensing to the highest form of thinking. However, Hegel did not leave the rationalist theory quite where he found it, for he went on to qualify the general view in the light of his doctrine of the dialectical relation of the forms of knowledge. Sensing and thinking were certainly con-

of natural science but had no insight into the working of particular laws in Nature. See *Metaphysical First Foundations of Natural Science*, published in 1785.

tinuous, but they were also opposites, at least so far as the lower ranges of thought were concerned. And it was because of this dual relationship that Hegel described sense as thought's 'other', marking by the term at once its affinity and its antipathy to thought.

If we now put these two suggestions together we can perhaps get some idea of what Hegel meant by the thinking of philosophy, which is clearly the key to the whole structure. We are to take it, I think, that sensation and the three forms of thinking distinguished above are all members of the same developing series, and that their relationship is dialectical. This means, first, that we must expect that they will somehow exhibit the familiar relationship of thesis, antithesis, and synthesis which Hegel regarded as of general application to all sides of experience; and, secondly, that just because of that the positive features of them all will be preserved in the series' highest member. We can find the thesis, antithesis, synthesis relation in the triad Sense—Thinking of Understanding—Thinking of Philosophy. As Kant and the empiricists had held, sense and discursive thought are sharply contrasted, and the one is everything the other is not. But the very existence of common-sense or imaginative thinking, according to Hegel, shows that the gulf between them is not absolute, and in fact the two are brought together in the thinking of philosophy. This 'thinking' must accordingly be quite different from the thinking described by empiricists and Kantians, since it must clearly contain something to match the intuitive or, as Hegel prefers to call it, immediate character of sensation; and in fact it is very difficult to see what it can be if it is not the concrete intellectual insight which Kant rejected in the third *Critique*.

The obvious way to test this conclusion is to examine Hegel's works and see what in fact he thought the function of philosophy to be, and in particular how it related to experience. It is here that we get into difficulties. Of course, it is beyond dispute that he thought there was a place for philosophy of Nature over and above the empirical natural sciences, and for philosophy of Spirit over and above history and the studies associated with it; but his view of the object of these philosophies is not so clear. I suggest that there are at least three possible views of the business of philosophy of Nature, if I may be allowed to concentrate on that for the sake of brevity. Philosophy of Nature might (*a*) merely consist in the analysis and clarification of the concepts used by natural scientists, more particularly those of them which cut across the frontiers of the various scientific disciplines. This would be the account given of it by empiricists, and in fact something like it is suggested by, for example, Mr. Ayer.[1] Alternatively (*b*) philosophy of Nature might be concerned with setting out the *a priori* presuppositions of natural science: its aim would be to discover the basic concepts and principles on which the scientist builds up his whole structure, and perhaps to offer some criticism or justification of these. It may be remarked that this is by no means a work of supererogation, though it would be idle to pretend that its value is appreciated by all scientists. It is the view of philosophy of Nature presented by Kant in his mature writings. Thirdly (*c*) philosophy of Nature might have a far more positive role, and claim not merely to forward but rather to supersede the empirical study of Nature by producing from its own resources necessary truths about the natural world. Such a claim would clearly have to rest on insight, or alleged insight, into the structure of the facts the empirical scientist investigates, and if it could be justified philosophy would without doubt be the most profitable and precious of all studies.[2]

Now which of these views did Hegel support? Let us examine his own statements on the subject. In § 12 of the *Encyclopaedia of the Philosophical Sciences*[3] we read that philosophy begins from experience, 'awakened' by which 'thought is vitally characterised by raising itself above the natural state of mind, above the senses and inferences from the senses, into its own unadulterated element'. This sounds uncompromising enough: philosophy needs experience only as a kind of ladder which can be dispensed with once it has been climbed. But it is not the impression Hegel wishes to give, for he goes on to say:

'The sciences, based upon experience, exert upon the mind a stimulus to overcome the form in which their varied contents are presented, and to elevate these contents to the rank of necessary truth. . . . In consequence of this stimulus thought is dragged out of its unrealised univer-

[1] *Language, Truth and Logic* (first edition), pp. 12–13 and 50 ff. Mr. Ayer does not mention philosophy of history, but presumably a parallel empiricist account of this would be possible.

[2] Is this classification exhaustive? It is not, because philosophy of Nature is treated by some as part of a wider metaphysical theory, in which a set of ideas derived from one branch of learning or experience is used as a key by which to interpret all aspects of reality. Whitehead's philosophy of organism would serve as an instance. For a discussion of this conception of metaphysics compare Chapter X, §§ 4–6 below.

[3] Quoted here in Wallace's translation (*The Logic of Hegel*).

sality and its fancied or merely possible satisfaction, and impelled onwards towards a development from itself. On the one hand this development only means that thought incorporates the contents of science, in all their speciality of detail as submitted. On the other it makes these contents imitate the action of the original creative thought and present the aspect of a free evolution determined by the logic of the fact alone.'[1]

Philosophy of Nature thus 'owes its development to the natural sciences' and is indeed entirely dependent for its material on them: all it can claim for its own part is a truer insight than the scientist possesses into the relations of the (empirically established) facts. It seems from this that though Hegel would like, if he could, to ascribe independent knowledge to the philosopher and thus subscribe to the third of the views of philosophy of Nature described on p. 67, his good sense holds him back at the last moment and he falls into a hybrid theory whose basis and justification are far from obvious.[2]

I suggest that the reason for this vacillation is recognition on Hegel's part of the impossibility of the view to which, according to the foregoing argument, he is logically committed. He should have pressed for the acceptance as valid of intellectual intuition in its full-blooded form, and, in fact, only that would enable him to surmount the barriers set by the conclusions of the Kantian philosophy. He comes near to doing so in much of his language: in his description of the concepts of reason (or, as he calls it, 'the Notion') as concrete universals, for instance, and in ascribing 'immediacy' to the highest form of thinking. But the quotations of the last paragraph show that this attitude is not consistently maintained, and the general procedure of his philosophies of Nature and Spirit is not, as we might expect, to give totally new accounts of their respective spheres, but rather to fit the facts as they are empirically discovered into the straight-jacket of the

[1] Compare the substantially similar account in *Encyclopaedia*, § 246 (introduction to the philosophy of Nature).

[2] Hegel's official reason for refusing to accept the possibility of philosophy of Nature in our third sense is the irrationality or, as he calls it, 'impotence' (*Ohnmacht*) of Nature itself. The very wealth of natural forms baffles the philosopher, with the result that knowledge of Nature is full of contingency. 'The impotence of Nature sets limits to philosophy, and it is most improper to demand of the Notion that it should conceive or (as the phrase is) construe and deduce contingencies of this kind' (ibid., § 250). As Mr. Stace says (*Philosophy of Hegel*, p. 307), this concept of the impotence of Nature is quite out of place in Hegel's system. It is, in fact, a relic of the much-denounced thing in itself.

Hegelian logic. This is the sort of thing any Kantian might have done, and, in fact, we find something like it in the pages of Kant's last work, the *Opus Postumum*.[1]

I have dealt with the case of Hegel at some length and, I fear, in too great detail for a work of this sort. My excuse must be not only the important place which Hegel holds in the rationalist tradition, but also the fact that in his case it is possible, thanks to the development of his philosophy from Kant's, to make the issue to be decided reasonably clear. I do not say that the refutation of Hegel entails the refutation of all philosophers who have inclined to intellectual intuition or something like it in the full-blooded sense; for it seems clear that some of them have referred to a non-rational intuition of the mystical type, and the case for this needs separate discussion.[2] But I do suggest that Kant produced decisive arguments against any non-mystical version of this form of intuition, and that Hegel's failure to justify his concept of concrete philosophical thinking underlines their effectiveness. These arguments are found in Kant's analysis, in the *Critique of Judgment*, of the idea of an intuitive understanding. For such an understanding (*a*) all universals would be concrete rather than abstract: in knowing a universal we should also know its instances; and (*b*) there would be no distinction between possible and actual, since whatever such an intelligence thought would *ipso facto* be real.[3] I do not see that anyone can claim that the human understanding is intuitive in this sense.

§ 5. It is impossible, however, not to recognize that the Hegelian type of criticism raises genuine questions, and to round off the discussion I propose to touch on some of these. The particular questions I shall consider (all, I fear, in a manner too summary for their deserts) are four: the problems of the thing in itself, of the co-operation of thought and sensibility, of the nature of philosophical thinking, and of knowledge of the individual.

1. The thing in itself is without doubt a sorry bugbear for Kantians. Like some disreputable relative who persists in dis-

[1] I must not be thought to applaud this attempt of Kant's, which I have discussed in a short paper on 'Kant's Conception of Scientific Knowledge', printed in *Mind* for October 1940.

[2] For some remarks on this subject see Chapter X, § 2 below.

[3] Translating the situation into discursive terms, we may say that for an intuitive understanding all propositions, including existence propositions, would be logically necessary.

gracing the family on whose charity he lives, it can neither be rendered respectable nor yet be got rid of altogether. For, as Kant's contemporaries already saw, the notion is both essential to Kant's whole theory and (to all appearances) impossible to maintain on that theory. The criticisms which Hegel brought against it merely repeated earlier complaints, and the chorus of disapproval has continued ever since.

Before we join in this chorus I think it is worth asking whether there is anything in the idea of the thing in itself which could make us *want* to preserve it: whether it answers to any special *need* in theory of knowledge. That Kant at any rate would have said it did is clear. For he would have said that it was a presupposition of our being able to make an analysis of human knowledge which stresses its *discursive* aspect that we should agree to the existence of a reality independent of human knowledge. A discursive intelligence is one which does not originate the materials of knowledge but accepts them as 'given'; and the metaphor of 'giving', Kant would say, implies a source. The source of the given is, in fact, the thing in itself, reality as it is out of relation to human thinking, in contrast to reality as it falls within experience, the world of appearances.

The thing in itself, then, was bound up for Kant with his theory of the discursivity of the human mind. Now that our consciousness is discursive is, so far as I can see, at least very likely; both positively (in so far as it fits in with what appear to be the obvious facts about human thinking) and negatively (in so far as alternative views, like Hegel's, appear to commit us to consequences which are quite impossible), it is as reasonably grounded as any philosophical theory can be. And if it is true that the discursive theory entails accepting the doctrine of the thing in itself, then we must make what attempt we can to preserve that doctrine, though we clearly cannot accept it as it stands.

But does the discursive theory entail accepting the reality of the thing in itself? There are many who would protest loudly against the assertion, including the bulk of the contemporary empiricist school. Kant, they would say, was deceived by a metaphor. Analysing the components of phenomenal reality into what the mind contributes and what is given to it, he failed to see that it was not sense to ask for the source of the given. Questions about sources (causal questions) were answerable only so far as applied to particular objects of experience; they could not be asked of the materials of experience itself. To talk about the cause or causes of sense-data was, in fact, meaningless, a piece of metaphysics of the kind whose pretensions Kant had himself exposed.

These empiricist critics offer a *phenomenalist* analysis of human experience: they say that all we need assume to explain it is the existence of sense-data and the minds that perceive them.[1] But there is a difficulty about this. To make the phenomenalist analysis work—to account for the beliefs to which we are committed in thinking a world of objects—we need to assume not merely the existence of the data we are actually sensing, but further that we might be sensing other data, if our point of view were different. For example, in the thought of the table I am now perceiving is included the thought that it has an underside; though in fact I do not see that. But I believe that if I were to get down and look, the appropriate data would be forthcoming. Now how is this to be explained on the phenomenalist theory? The stock answer is to say that we must talk in terms not just of sense-data, but also of sensibilia, possible sense-data. Sense-data are sensibilia actualized. And the suggestion seems to be that there is a vast realm of sensibilia, waiting to be sensed and conveniently appearing when needed. What exists, in fact, on the phenomenalist theory is not just minds and sense-data, but minds and sensibilia, sensed and unsensed.

That this is a possible hypothesis could not, I think, be denied: if anyone chooses to adopt it there is no means of finally refuting him. But that it is a very strange one must also be admitted; and it is legitimate to ask whether it is the most plausible theory that can be devised. To this I think the Kantian answer at least deserves careful consideration: that the thing in itself gives a better explanation. By accepting the notion of the thing in itself, of a reality of some sort of which different sense-data are to be thought as the appearances, and which persists whether or not it is being observed, we attain everything which the empiricist wants without falling into the improbabilities involved in his theory of unsensed sensibilia. Entities, particularly those which by definition lie beyond our knowledge, ought not to be multiplied unnecessarily. But then neither ought inherent improbabilities, such as the theory that the universe consists of sensibilia seems to contain.

If we do accept the thing in itself, are we to say that it exists

[1] Minds, in turn, are often by these critics resolved into collections of sense-data (perceptions, feelings, &c.), as by Hume.

and is the cause of appearances? Those would be odd statements to make of an entity which we must also admit to be beyond experience and knowledge. But perhaps the remedy here is to give up both sets of statements: to accept the thing in itself as a presupposition of knowledge, but to argue that nothing can be said about it. Anything we did say would be bound to make use of words and ideas appropriate only to the expression of what falls within experience. But our inability to express it would not take away from the necessity of thinking the thing in itself. We should have to think it to account for certain obvious features in knowledge; but in doing so we should not be determining an actual object (since determining an actual object means knowing something which falls within experience), but rather thinking what Kant himself called an Idea of Reason.[1] And if it is said that this is a difficult notion, the reply must be that it is still more difficult either to devise a more satisfactory theory of the thing in itself or to dispense with it altogether.

2. We have seen how Hegel held that on the discursive view no intelligible account could be given of knowledge, because there was nothing to guarantee that sensibility and thought, two wholly diverse faculties, would co-operate. Thought has to impose its forms on a matter provided by sensibility; but are we sure that it can do so? This is a problem which arises in some form for every type of philosophy, since it concerns our common assumption that all experience must be orderly. The point Hegel is making against Kant is that, despite his elaborate apparatus of forms of sensibility and categories of the understanding, he has no ultimate right to this assumption, because he thinks that the matter on which order is imposed is quite alien to the ordering intelligence. He would presumably have brought the same charge, *mutatis mutandis*, against most forms of empiricism.[2]

To attempt a solution of this problem we must first distinguish two questions: (*a*) How on the discursive view can we find *any* sort of order in the given? and (*b*) How on it can we find the *particular*

[1] See *Critique of Pure Reason*, Appendix to the Dialectic. The suggestion that the thing in itself is to be treated as a concept, not an existent, was originally made by the Marburg school in Germany. Though plausible in theory of knowledge, it raises serious difficulties in moral philosophy; but fortunately these need not be treated here.

[2] For a recent criticism of Kant stressing this Hegelian objection see Mr. H. W. B. Joseph's *Essays in Ancient and Modern Philosophy*, especially pp. 225–6 and 261 ff.

sort of order required for sense-data to be thought by an intelligence like ours? That these questions cannot be answered together is shown by the consideration that every part of experience might exhibit some sort of order, but that nevertheless experience as a whole might be so variegated that no system of general laws could be formulated which would describe it. This point will be elaborated in the sequel.

(A) Why do we assume that the given will always exhibit some kind of order? What right have we to think that the products of sense will be amenable to the forms of thought? The simple answer given to these questions by Kant was that we are justified because our knowledge is not of things in themselves but of appearances. This may strike many as a mere quibble, or again as valid only within a set of assumptions which no sensible man would make; but I think there is none the less a good deal of truth in it. For what, after all, is Kant saying if we strip his thought of the special terminology in which it is clothed? He is saying, in effect, that the sense-data in which we strive to find order are things which, in their very nature, fall within consciousness.[1] We may put this, if we like, by saying that the given, which forms the raw material of knowledge, is in fact given to a mind: and the problem we have to solve is how that mind can make sense of it. Now it seems perfectly clear that there is not the same difficulty in a mind's finding order in something which already falls within consciousness as in its doing so in something which falls wholly outside it; and indeed it is sometimes said that there is none at all. That which falls within consciousness must be in principle thinkable, we are told, just because of its having been experienced; if it were not we should reject it as unreal.[2] And it can be plausibly argued that epistemological analysis in terms of distinct faculties is here liable to be seriously misleading: sense and thought, on the discursive view, do not work separately but in co-operation, and sense-data and concepts are correlative terms. To suppose that there might be sense-data which could not be conceptualized would hence be absurd.

The form of this solution may not be fully satisfactory, but the

[1] This is, of course, not the same as saying that they are the creation of the mind that knows them.

[2] Cf. the remarks on this subject by Professor C. I. Lewis in *Mind and the World Order*, especially in chap. xi. Professor Lewis supposes, however, that there is *no* problem of getting order out of the given, ignoring in this the problems here discussed under (B).

argument seems at least to be on the right lines. I shall therefore pass on to the second question without further ado.

(B) It has often been pointed out that if we are to make sense and use of our experience it is not enough to assume that all sense-data will be thinkable in principle. We have to presuppose in the given not only order in general but also a particular type of order; and it is with this presupposition that we must now deal. Kant, who was perfectly well aware of this problem and discusses it both in the *Critique of Pure Reason* and in the *Critique of Judgment*, says that we must assume that Nature will display both homogeneity and specification: meaning that experience must not be either wholly diverse (consisting entirely of novelties of situation whose like has never before been experienced) or wholly lacking in diversity (consisting of the same situation repeated *ad infinitum*). To ensure ourselves of the fulfilment of these conditions, Kant says, we must think the idea of a God who adapts Nature to the requirements of our understandings, and this is an *a priori* demand. It is not a demand whose satisfaction we can guarantee, however, since there is no conceivable way in which we could know a supersensible being like God; and for this reason we must ultimately take it on trust that we shall find Nature orderly in the way science requires. A conclusion of fundamentally the same type is come to in Chapter XXII of Lord Keynes's *Treatise on Probability*, where it is pointed out that successful induction presupposes in Nature a law of limited independent variety. It is true that Lord Keynes speaks as if theory of knowledge might eventually establish the *a priori* probability of such a law; but he is compelled to admit that we cannot offer a justification of it now. He concludes (p. 264): 'The Inductive Hypothesis stands in a peculiar position in that it seems to be neither a self-evident axiom nor an object of direct acquaintance; and yet it is just as difficult, as though the inductive hypothesis were either of these, to remove from the organon of thought the inductive method which can only be based on it or something like it.' In a word, we must act as if Nature possessed the sort of order necessary for us to form generalizations about it, though we cannot justify the assumption.

These considerations suggest that while Hegel was wrong in regarding all co-operation between sense and thought as miraculous on the discursive view, he was nevertheless right in finding a difficulty over it. Unfortunately, his only way of dealing with the difficulty was the short one of declaring that it must be swept aside: that the discursive view must be given up and knowledge of the supersensible readmitted. As we have seen, this leads to more problems than it solves. It is true that the discursive theory as we have stated it does base knowledge, in an important sense, on faith, nor does it appear likely that it could be restated in a way which would eliminate this basing. It is true, too, that philosophers have always striven to avoid explanations which appeal to final inexplicabilities and unaccountable facts. But it may be questioned whether any philosophy (including here philosophies of the rationalist type) can attain this ideal completely. Unless we believe in the possibility of self-evident truths (which will be discussed in the next chapter) we are driven to say that every philosophy must take certain basic principles for granted. No doubt it is desirable that the number of these basic assumptions should be kept as small as possible, and true that not all assumptions are equally suitable as philosophical starting-points; no doubt, too, there is a sense in which interpretation of the detailed facts may be held to confirm or at least probabilify them, and unless there were it would be impossible to judge one system of philosophy against another. But the fact that a philosopher appeals, in a case such as we have been discussing, to a premiss he cannot immediately justify should not be taken as a fatal objection to his whole theory.

Perhaps we can sum up the question as follows. The discursive theory, which in other respects seems to accord pretty closely with the facts as we know them, certainly involves an assumption which we cannot justify in the shape of the principle of limited independent variety in Nature. And we may, if we like, find the theory wanting for that very reason. But if we do we have to consider whether there is an alternative which, as well as avoiding that particular defect, is in other respects free from difficulty. In the present case I can only say that I do not myself think there is.

3. I propose to deal with this point very briefly and dogmatically, since few are likely to dispute my opinion of it. Hegel is quite right in differentiating the thinking of philosophy from the thinking of understanding. But he is not right to ascribe any special intuition to the philosopher, who is, as he himself recognizes, dependent for his material on the various empirical disciplines. Nor could he claim that the philosopher has a clearer insight than the empirical inquirer into the structure of fact, though the proof

of this statement is still to come. A truer conception of the relationship is afforded if we recognize that while understanding is concerned with the direct pursuit of truth in history and the sciences, philosophy is indirect reflection on the conditions of the pursuit itself.

4. We are left with the question of knowledge of the individual, from which our whole discussion of this form of intellectual intuition started. Here again I must ask the reader to be content with a summary statement. It is, of course, quite correct to say that the terms in which we intellectually characterize what we know in sense-intuition are all general: if we say that this is round, or red, or a ball we are describing it in terms which are potentially applicable to any number of other objects. And the universal character of our predicates remains even when the subject of our thinking is highly complicated: when we are discussing the life of a large community, such as a university or a church, for instance, and using the complex intellectual ideas involved.[1] But I do not see that this prevents our having knowledge of the individual. According to the discursive theory knowledge is a compound of sense and thought, and if thought is necessarily universal, sense may equally be said to be necessarily particular. It is in sensation that we grasp the particularity of things, and this remains true even though we cannot find intellectual terms to do justice to that particularity. Perhaps we should lay stress here on the fact that, though all predicates are universal, existence is not a predicate.[2] This important truth, overlooked or misunderstood by many rationalists, enables us to account for our conviction that things are particular without abandoning the discursive theory of knowledge. That this or that exists, each in its unique particularity, we can say; what separates them from other things and constitutes their uniqueness we cannot explain, since every attempt at explanation makes use of general terms. No doubt this is an unfortunate situation, dissatisfaction with which is reflected in the preoccupation philosophers from Aristotle onwards have shown with the problem of the individual; but it is also one from which, so far at least, no satisfactory way of escape has been found.

[1] I mention this because it is sometimes said that the theory of concrete universals is misrepresented if we consider simple 'empirical' universals like redness only.

[2] As Kant, of course, was the first to point out: *Critique of Pure Reason*, B 626 = A 598.

V

INTELLECTUAL INTUITION: TWO FURTHER THEORIES

§ 1. THE arguments of the preceding chapter purport to show the folly of any attempt to ascribe to human beings a power of intellectual intuition in the primary or full-blooded sense, together with the neutral character, from the epistemological point of view, of the contention that all inference includes an element of intuition. But the case against intellectual intuition is by no means complete at this point. There remain for consideration two further theories, each of which has at various times and in various ways exercised an important influence on philosophical thought. The first of these theories holds that knowledge is reducible to, or at least depends on, intuition of the self-evident, the second that awareness of universals involves intellectual intuition. A preliminary exposition of the case for them was given on pages 53–6 above. In the present chapter §§ 2–5 will be devoted to the first theory, while the problem of universals will be more briefly considered in § 6.

§ 2. To do justice to the argument from self-evidence we must examine at length a doctrine touched on at several points in this book already, the classical rationalist theory of scientific knowledge. I use this term to cover a view of knowledge and scientific method which was commonly accepted, though, of course, with differences of detail and emphasis, by rationalist philosophers from Plato to Leibniz, and which, despite the great changes introduced into philosophy by the criticism of Hume and Kant and the new rationalism of Hegel, has continued to enjoy some support even in the present century.[1] The main theses of this theory can be set out as follows:

1. Knowledge consists entirely of necessary truths. There is an absolute difference between knowledge, which is certain and indubitable, and belief, which is uncertain and fallible.
2. Scientific results are properly expressed in a deductive system. In such a system basic premisses and conclusions alike are apprehended by a species of intellectual intuition.
3. Mathematics is the ideal science, and mathematical knowledge the ideal example of scientific knowledge.

[1] In this country, notably from the school of Cook Wilson, whose doctrines were developed on the basis of a close study of Aristotle.

4. Science consists not of hypothetical but of categorical propositions, which reveal and explain the structure of fact.

It will scarcely be necessary at this stage to elucidate or comment upon these points at any length. We may, however, note that Descartes, who in his *Regulae ad directionem ingenii* gave the most complete exposition of the theory in modern philosophy, thought that it offered both a universal account of scientific (systematic) knowledge and a clue to scientific advance. Progress in the sciences was to be ensured by a rigorous application of the method of doubt, leading to the rejection of all 'truths' which could not be clearly and distinctly conceived, i.e. which could not be seen by the light of reason to be self-evidently and therefore necessarily true. This doctrine led immediately to the expulsion of history from the body of knowledge, but that consequence was scarcely likely to worry so anti-historical an age as that of Descartes. What was important about the Cartesian theory was that it did justice to the main intellectual preoccupations of his time, mathematical physics and metaphysics. The rapid progress of physics, according to Descartes, was due primarily to the application to its problems of mathematical methods and mathematical insight. Similarly, metaphysics could hope to tread the sure path of science only if it emulated the clarity and logical order of mathematical thought. Descartes did not himself present the results of his metaphysical thinking in mathematical form, but the deficiency was supplied for him by Spinoza.

But though we must look to Descartes for the classical exposition of the theory, it is in Locke's *Essay* that we find its most interesting statement. Locke, as everybody knows, was the founder of English empiricism, concerned to show that all our ideas are derived from sensation and reflection. Despite this, his explicit theory of knowledge in the fourth book of the *Essay* is to a very important extent Cartesian. 'Knowledge', he says in § 2 of the opening chapter, 'seems to me to be nothing but the perception of the connexion and agreement, or disagreement and repugnancy, of any of our ideas. In this alone it consists. Where this perception is, there is knowledge; and where it is not, there, though we may fancy, guess or believe, yet we always come short of knowledge.' He goes on to explain in Chapter II that there are three degrees of knowledge. The first of these is intuitive, where 'the mind is at no pains of proving or examining, but perceives the truth, as the eye doth light, only by being directed towards it'. 'This part of knowledge is irresistible, and, like bright sunshine, forces itself immediately to be perceived as soon as ever the mind turns its view that way; and leaves no room for hesitation, doubt or examination, but the mind is presently filled with the clear light of it.'[1] The second degree of knowledge is demonstrative, where the agreement or disagreement of ideas is perceived as in intuitive knowledge, but only by means of intervening ideas. This form of knowledge is declared to be inferior because it involves memory and so is liable to error; but in its ideal form it reduces to a series of intuitions, since 'in every step reason makes in demonstrative knowledge, there is an intuitive knowledge of that agreement or disagreement it seeks with the next intermediate idea, which it uses as a proof'.[2] The last of the three, sensitive knowledge of particular existence, is a form about which Locke clearly has grave doubts. He sees that whatever comes short of intuition or demonstration cannot really claim to be knowledge; and committed as he is to the representative theory of perception, he cannot hold that we are immediately aware of external things. But he thinks that our conviction of the existence of such things exceeds probability even if it does not attain intuitive or demonstrative certainty, and so should pass under the name of knowledge.[3]

Now if we neglect sensitive knowledge for the present, as we quite legitimately may, we can see without difficulty that the analysis of knowledge Locke is offering is conceived on broadly rationalist lines. What is of more interest than this, however, is the view he puts forward of the extent of human knowledge. He explains in Chapter I that the agreement or disagreement of ideas in terms of which he defines knowledge can take four forms: identity or diversity; coexistence or necessary connexion; relation; real existence. And in Chapter III he goes on to state the extent of human knowledge under these four heads. So far as identity and diversity are concerned, our knowledge extends as far as our ideas; for of any idea we can say that it is what it is and not some other idea. In regard to coexistence our knowledge is 'very short, though in this consists the greatest and most material part of our knowledge concerning substances'.[4] The reason is to be found in the fact that 'the simple ideas whereof our complex ideas of substances are made up are, for the most part, such as carry with them, in their own nature, no visible necessary connexion or inconsistency

[1] Op. cit. IV. ii, § 1.
[2] Ibid., § 7.
[3] Ibid., § 14.
[4] Ibid. iii. 9.

with any other simple ideas, whose co-existence with them we would inform ourselves about'.[1] Knowledge of coexistence, in a word, is largely if not exclusively empirical: we have no insight into why our ideas coexist as they do, just as we have no insight into the real essences of species in the natural world. The extent of our potential knowledge of relations puzzles Locke: he thinks, nevertheless, that we have such knowledge in mathematics and might have it, if only we set about the matter in the right way, in morals. Lastly, we are said to have intuitive knowledge of our own existence, demonstrative knowledge of God's, and sensitive knowledge of the existence of 'some few' other things.

It will be seen from this that, while Locke is faithfully reproducing the Cartesian theory of knowledge in this part of his essay, he is also implicitly criticizing it. For the account he gives of the extent of human cognition shows that he must rule out the possibility of knowledge not only of history but also of Nature. For there to be knowledge of the natural world in the required sense we should need to formulate self-evidently true propositions about necessary connexions in Nature. But this, as Locke saw (and over this point his view has proved incontrovertible), is just what we cannot do. Ignorant alike of the real essences of substances and of the interconnexions of their properties, we have no insight into the sphere of fact. The Cartesian ideal of an *a priori* physics, every proposition of which was guaranteed by a separate act of intuition, thus broke down. And the breakdown was in fact final, though rationalists were slow to appreciate it, and needed both Hume's criticism of causality and Kant's discussion of analytic and synthetic judgements before they saw the point. Nor were they quite convinced even then, since they clung to the notion that mathematics at least conformed to their theory and provided an example which all other sciences should strive to imitate. The error of this way of thinking is a matter we shall discuss in § 4 below.

The Cartesian method was intended, as the title of the *Discourse* itself has it, to be a means of 'discovering truth in the sciences'. And the sciences Descartes had in mind were not only the different branches of mathematics, but various physical disciplines also, and above all medicine. When Descartes set out his conception of logic and scientific method in the *Regulae*, he supposed that science was one in the sense that every science could be advanced

[1] Op. cit. IV. iii. 10.

by the same means and must terminate in the same kind of result—intuition of the self-evident. But his own experience as a scientist and the analyses of the empiricists who followed him showed that the supposition was a false one, and that a quite different account of empirical knowledge was necessary. To have brought this out, even if he did not himself realize the point clearly, is perhaps Locke's greatest contribution to epistemology. The physical sciences at least do not consist of self-evident truths; yet it is hard to deny that they do contain genuine knowledge.

§ 3. It may be suggested at this point that, in turning our attention to the theory as it appears in Descartes and Locke, we have lost sight of the original argument for it produced by Aristotle (see pp. 53–4 above), which asserted not that every science *consists of* self-evident truths, but only that it *depends on* or *presupposes* such truths. This may well be thought to give rise to a more moderate and therefore more easily defensible form of the theory, for the notion that organized knowledge must rest on a basis of certainty is widely spread.

To try to decide the point we must go into the whole question of self-evidence and certainty.

We may note first that while philosophers of very different schools agree with Aristotle's formal argument that there cannot be an infinite regress in thinking if we are to avoid complete scepticism, there is a sharp difference of opinion between rationalists and empiricists about where to look for a certain basis for knowledge. Thus Aristotle, as we have seen, held that the propositions of every science were logically dependent on its primary premisses, and that these could not be proved but must be taken as evident in themselves. He included among the primary premisses of a science definitions of its subject-matter and of certain terms in it; he may also have included (their status in his theory is not quite certain) axioms, like the quantitative axioms in mathematics, taken to be common to the science in question and to others like it. These were all universal truths, and it was from the universal that Aristotle thought the ideal scientist at least would argue. But the empiricist view is very different. For though the empiricist agrees with Aristotle that science aims at being 'of the universal', he would say that it necessarily begins from inspection of the particular; and it is to particular judgements of sense, accordingly, that he looks for a basis of certainty.

If any statements are to be taken as beyond question, it is such judgements as that I am now sensing a coloured patch or aware of a loud noise. Unless these are accepted as self-evident, knowledge can have no firm basis, for it is upon them that the whole structure of science and learning rests.

We are thus presented with two theories of the self-evident, one of which presupposes, while the other does not, the reality of intellectual intuition. Before attempting to assess their merits, however, we must say something of an important doctrine which disputes them both—the Coherence Theory of Truth. This notion was first formulated by Hegel (there are traces of it in Kant), and rests on a denial of the whole Aristotelian argument for a certain basis for knowledge. Science, according to the theory, is built up neither by deduction from basic universal truths of the sort referred to by Aristotle nor by induction from unquestionable judgements of sense as the empiricists suppose. It is rather a system of mutually supporting judgements, none of them certain in themselves, but each deriving its claim on our credence from its place in the system as a whole. The suggestion is that every judgement is true only along with its conditions, and that these constitute the system to which it belongs. In the last resort, it is alleged, all judgements can be shown to fall within the same system: if taken sufficiently far back the conditions of all judgements are the same. That is why truth is said by those who support this theory to be 'the whole'. The idea is that no judgement short of the whole—no judgement except one, all of whose conditions were specified—could be absolutely true; whilst because even false judgements are made on a partially true basis no judgement can be said to be totally false. Thus the question whether any supposed system of knowledge is grounded in fact does not arise. Every coherent system of judgements has some truth in it; the only question is how much. And this analysis applies, if its supporters are to be believed, to all judgements and systems of judgement whatsoever—to simple judgements of sense, *a priori* propositions such as those of mathematics, principles like the general law of causality, and philosophical statements too.

It is obviously difficult to comment at all adequately on a theory of such scope within the limits of a context like the present. Nevertheless, some comment must be made in view of the theory's bearing on the question of intellectual intuition. In what follows I confine myself to two points: that the theory has a good deal of plausibility when applied to a very large number of propositions, including all ordinary empirical propositions, but that it fails to make proper allowance for different types of judgements and so involves itself in unnecessary paradoxes and difficulties.

1. The strength of the Coherence Theory lies in the very plausible account it gives of a great deal of our everyday thinking (including much of the thinking we do as scientists). No doubt it is natural for us to assume in the initial stages of philosophical analysis that the test of any statement of fact must be that it should be shown to be in accordance with independent reality; we take it for granted, that is to say, that any factual judgement will stand or fall on its own merits. But it is not difficult to show that in reality such judgements are only formulated in a context of other judgements; that they are not *bare* statements of fact, but statements indissolubly linked to other statements of the same kind. Now the contention of the Coherence Theory is that if we wish to determine the truth of any factual judgement we must look to its relationship to other judgements, i.e. to the context in which it is put forward. And that this view is much more convincing than may at first sight appear we can see by considering an example. Let us take one from the sphere of history. The judgement that Julius Caesar came to Britain in 55 B.C. would normally be said to be true because it was in accordance with the facts. But what are the facts in question? They are the facts that Caesar was Roman governor of Gaul, that he wrote an account of his doings that still survives, that he is in general a trustworthy writer, and so on. But these 'facts' are in reality *judgements* which we make on the strength of the evidence before us; and we take the judgement that Caesar came to Britain to be true because it coheres with these judgements. Nor is history the only sphere in which the theory works. If we consider the procedure of the natural scientist and ask questions about the truth of the laws he establishes, we can see that with him, too, the idea of truth as a system is highly important. The scientist does not assert the validity of any particular law on its own merits; he takes it as established because it coheres with the rest of his scientific beliefs. His judgements, in a word, are arrived at only within a certain context which they presuppose.

There are some philosophers who might admit the *prima facie* plausibility of the case I have put forward so far as it concerns the conclusions of the historian and the scientist, but would say that it was vitiated if offered as a general theory of truth because it failed to take account of their initial premisses. I have spoken of historical judgements as being based on evidence, and that scientific judgements rest in a more or less direct way on sense-experience is almost too obvious to mention. The contention we have to face at this point is that the propositions which state historical evidence in its primary form or express the simplest truths of sense-experience cannot be accounted for by the Coherence Theory. Simple judgements of sense, at least, it is argued, must be such that we can see them to be true on their own merits without reference to any other judgements. Thus, if I hear a loud noise I hear a loud noise; there is no sense in asking what other judgements I am prepared to assert at the time of hearing. But though this argument is a very strong one, I am not sure that it is really decisive. In the judgement 'I hear a loud noise' we can distinguish, as in other more complex assertions, two elements: a given element, supplied here by sensation, and an element of interpretation. And though the interpretative element is of minor importance in a case like this, it is none the less present. It is in virtue of it that I classify the experience as a noise and describe it as loud. But such a process of classification, in which appeal is made to general ideas (being a noise, loud, &c.), involves a reference beyond the context of the immediate experience, and so suggests that the judgement is not, after all, self-contained. It is not one experience, but a whole class of them, which I describe as being a noise. But if this is so it looks as if we must say of simple judgements of sense, as of other judgements, that their conditions lie partly outside themselves; that they are not to be accepted because they are evident in themselves, but only so far as they fit in with other judgements.[1]

It may be asked how, if this general argument is right, we can ever distinguish fact from fiction. Supporters of the Coherence Theory have sometimes been accused of confusing truth with consistency, and the point is certainly worth considering. The answer is that we have no difficulty in making the distinction because we place a deliberate limit on what we expect of the statements of fiction. We think, of course, that they must be

[1] The case for this point was argued most effectively by Bradley in the second chapter of his *Logic*. In reviving it I must not be thought to wish to deny the reality and importance of the given. But I hold (as I think Bradley did) that the given is a presupposition of experience rather than something we can express precisely in simple judgements. The given is known in feeling, not in judgement.

internally consistent, but we do not imagine that they will cohere with all our everyday factual judgements.[1] They are 'true' only within certain conventions which we create artificially and about which no adult person is likely to be deceived (though children often are). There is no such limit in the case of judgements of fact: we expect every supposed judgement of fact to cohere with every other, and regard it as indispensable that it should submit to this test. Any judgement which fails to satisfy it we dismiss as untrue. To the test of coherence that of comprehensiveness can thus be added, and when it is brought in many of the more obvious difficulties of the theory disappear.

2. But though the Coherence Theory thus has a good deal to be said for it, it cannot be claimed as beyond criticism of any sort. In particular, it would seem that its supporters have been far too forgetful of what may be called the departmental character of human thinking. Obsessed with the notion of a completed whole of human knowledge, they pass lightly over the weaknesses of the human mind, which is mostly content to deal with a single subject at a time and to make its examination on the basis of what may be alternatively taken as unjustified assumptions or self-evident principles. Thus every science or systematic study takes for granted notions which it does not itself examine: the idea of causal law in classical physics would be one example, that of purpose in history might be another. The classical physicist assumed in all his thinking the validity of the causal principle; the historian assumes (or at least it is arguable that he does) that the events he is treating can all be dealt with teleologically. What is the status of these assumptions, and how are we to justify them? The official way of dealing with them inside the Coherence Theory is to hold that they can be validated by precisely the same means as any other judgement, by showing that they cohere with the rest of our accepted beliefs. But this is to pass over a fundamental difference in types of judgement in far too cavalier a manner. The basic principles on which any given system of judgements is built up cannot be taken as on all fours with any particular judgement in the system.

Anticipating to some extent the results of future discussions, we may say that the Coherence Theory takes no adequate account

[1] We do think they must cohere with some: e.g., we demand that a novel should be 'true to life', in the sense that its characters should behave as real people would in the situation described.

of (*a*) the distinction of analytic from synthetic judgements, and (*b*) the special character of the synthetic *a priori*.

(*a*) Hegel and his English successors rejected the Kantian distinction of analytic and synthetic judgements for reasons which we have already stated (p. 39 above). They thought that all judgements were analytic and synthetic at once. But this sense of the terms, though perhaps justified in itself, is not that in which Kant and those who think with him use them. An analytic judgement is a judgement whose truth or falsity can be decided by reference to the laws of logic alone, a synthetic judgement one for whose truth a further criterion must be sought. And it seems clear, as we have argued, that there are analytic and synthetic judgements in the sense defined: Locke's knowledge of identity and diversity illustrates the former, while any empirical statement will exemplify the latter. But if the distinction is valid it is not allowed for in the Coherence Theory, according to which all judgements have to be brought to the same test—coherence with the rest of our accepted beliefs.

(*b*) In answer to this objection we may be told that even if the existence of a separate class of analytic judgements can be made out, the principle of the Coherence Theory is not affected, since the problem is thereby merely moved a stage farther back. Analytic judgements depend on the laws of logic; but how do we know that the laws of logic are valid themselves? The answer of the Coherence Theory was that they enjoy no special self-evidence or intuitive certainty, but must be justified in the same way as any other judgement. And here we come to another conspicuous weakness in the theory—its failure to allow for the special character of synthetic *a priori* truths. One of the main objects of those who formulated the Coherence Theory was to contest the notion of linear inference: in building up a body of knowledge, they said, the direction of our thought is not one way only, from premisses taken to be self-evident to conclusions which follow from them whether inductively or deductively. Rather there is a sense in which premisses and conclusions are established together, and serve to validate each other. And no doubt there are arguments for that point of view. But whatever its merits the fact remains that those who put it forward tended to overlook a further class of judgements which are neither premisses nor conclusions in an argument but nevertheless enter into it in a vital way: the principles in accordance with which that sort of thinking proceeds. All thinking proceeds in accordance with certain principles, some of which, such as the laws of logic, seem to be presupposed by thinking as such, whilst others are peculiar to special types of thinking (historical thinking, mathematical thinking, &c.). And these principles are (as we shall argue) not so much derived from experience as read into it: they represent the special contribution of the mind to knowledge. They are synthetic (since they include and do not depend on the laws of logic) and *a priori*, because they are taken as universally valid in their own province. Now there may be a sense in which *some* of these 'hypotheses', as Plato long ago called them,[1] can be 'destroyed' or confirmed as knowledge advances: what is assumed in one science may be proved in another. But it is most questionable whether there is possible, as he also suggested, a comprehensive discipline (whether universal science or philosophy) in the light of which they might *all* lose their 'hypothetical' character. Absolute presuppositions at least (to use Professor Collingwood's term) cannot be accounted for in this way if they deserve their name; and that there are such presuppositions follows from the nature of thinking as a questioning activity. But if there are, the Coherence Theory has nothing to say about them.[2]

We must return from this general discussion of Coherence to the problems of self-evidence and intellectual intuition. We may sum up the position about self-evidence as follows. (1) The empiricist account of self-evidence, which does not presuppose the reality of intellectual intuition, is almost certainly wrong. Every judgement of sense (and it is to such judgements that empiricists look for certainty) depends on conditions which fall outside the content judged, and so cannot be pronounced true or false in its own right. (2) But the opposing rationalist view, which finds self-evidence in the universal premisses from which the scientist argues, is also faulty. For the method of scientific advance is not, as Descartes at least supposed, by deduction from universal truths, but approximates far more to the mixture of deduction and induction for which the Coherence Theory argues. Outside mathematics, at least, the scientist does not begin from self-evident premisses, and so needs no appeal to intellectual intuition. The basis of

[1] See especially, *Republic* 510^{b}–511^{e}, 533^{b-d}.

[2] Clearly the best line for supporters of the Coherence Theory to take is to say that synthetic *a priori* presuppositions are not judgements, i.e. are not true or false, at all. On absolute presuppositions see below, pp. 126–9. The discussion in Chapter X below on the tests by which we may choose between conflicting metaphysical systems is also relevant: see pp. 243 ff.

certainty on which his work rests, and whose necessity Aristotle rightly saw, is to be found in two factors: in the given element which cannot be eliminated from knowledge, and in the synthetic *a priori* principles in accordance with which all thought proceeds. But, as we shall see in a later chapter, such principles are not factual truths about the real world, but rather represent the fundamental ways in which we order our experience. They are thus best described as prescriptive in character.

§ 4. So much for what we are calling the classical rationalist theory of scientific knowledge considered as an account of *all* human knowing. It remains to examine two fields in which its application has seemed especially plausible, the fields of mathematics and logic.

Of all the different branches of learning, mathematics is undoubtedly that which historically has had most fascination for philosophers. Here is a body of knowledge whose authority none can impugn, a science whose practical importance is as striking as are the clarity of its conclusions and the cogency of its proofs. And this science is, to all appearances, the product of pure thinking: reason here can not only establish truth, but can establish it beyond doubt or cavil. Is it surprising, in these circumstances, that Aristotle and Descartes alike took mathematics as the prime example of what a science should be, and proceeded, as we have seen, to judge all that claimed to be knowledge by comparison with it? Is it surprising that Spinoza and Leibniz thought that philosophy itself could only advance if it adopted mathematical methods and set out its results in mathematical form? No survey of the main problems of knowledge would be complete without some reference to the philosophy of mathematics, however ill equipped the writer might be to treat of that topic.

I shall begin by presenting very briefly the traditional rationalist view of the subject, and then discuss objections to it. It goes back to Aristotle, and runs more or less as follows. Mathematics is a purely deductive discipline, in which there is an unbroken chain of reasoning from a number of primary principles, taken to be true without question, to the conclusions which make up the body of the science. Its method is strictly logical: it appeals to no other source than the light of reason, which suffices to establish premisses and conclusions alike. And it is a science with a practical application because its premisses are not idle assumptions but general truths of fact. The different branches of mathematics are concerned, according to this theory, each with some very general department of reality, and logically they begin from intuitions of basic truths about these. Geometry, for example, is about space, and it begins from the apprehension of necessary truths about spatial relations. Arithmetic is about number, and its basis is a grasp of the fundamentals of the numerical system. We have only to reflect on space and number to see that anything they qualify must conform to the axioms of geometry and arithmetic; just as we have only to consider them to see the necessity of the axioms themselves.

Criticism of the rationalist philosophy of mathematics can be conveniently presented under three heads: that of old-fashioned empiricism, that of Kant, and that of modern empiricism.

Over the first of these it will not be necessary to linger for any length of time. Criticism of this sort is to be found in J. S. Mill's *Logic*,[1] and amounts to the claim that the primary principles of the mathematical sciences are not, as the rationalists said, self-evident truths apprehended by pure reason but rather empirical generalizations with which we are particularly familiar. So familiar with them are we, indeed, that we have come to believe them necessarily true, though in fact the necessity is in our minds only. The necessity of mathematical judgements, in Mill's view, is simply psychological, and to account for it we need no theory of intellectual intuition but a natural history of the human mind. As will be obvious, this old-fashioned empiricist view simply reverses the procedure of the rationalists, and instead of trying, as they did, to assimilate the empirical sciences to mathematics strives instead to reduce mathematics itself to the status of an empirical science. In neither case is the attempt successful, mainly because of an obstinate difference in the propositions of mathematics and those of even so well established a science as physics. The gap between them is shown if we attempt to deny propositions in the two sciences: to deny a true proposition in physics is to produce a falsehood, but to deny a valid mathematical proposition is to come near to talking nonsense. The implications of this will become clear in the sequel.

Kant's view of mathematics,[2] although now outmoded, is still

[1] Bk. II, chaps. v–vii.

[2] See *Critique of Pure Reason*, especially B 740 = A 712 ff., and *Prolegomena*, §§ 6 ff.

of some interest. Kant accepted the traditional view of the essential connexion of geometry with perceptual space, and even attempted to reinforce it by finding a parallel connexion between arithmetic and time.[1] But he went on to criticize the rationalist theory on the point whether mathematical inference proceeds by simple logical reasoning. To say that it did, he argued, was equivalent to maintaining that mathematical propositions were analytic; but in fact we could easily see that this was not the case. No amount of logical reflection on the concepts of five and seven, for instance, would enable us to say that their sum was twelve; just as we could think about the three interior angles of a triangle indefinitely without seeing that they were equivalent to two right angles. To prove a mathematical proposition we needed to construct a figure in intuition and so grasp the asserted connexion concretely. Mathematical reasoning thus involved an extra-logical element, and that indeed was the secret of its success. As for the nature of the intuition involved, it was, said Kant, an *a priori* intuition of space and time, which were not, as had been supposed in the traditional theory, concepts formed after acquaintance with particular spatial and temporal situations, but singular concrete wholes of which the human mind had a special quasi-sensible awareness. There is no doubt that Kant was influenced in formulating his view of space and time by the doctrines of Newton, who also thought space and time were singular concrete wholes; though in fact Kant modified these doctrines considerably by saying that space and time were, in an important sense, subjective rather than objective entities. Fortunately this complication can be neglected in discussing his view of pure mathematics, though it is important for his account of applied mathematics.

It is worth pointing out the ingenuity of the Kantian philosophy of mathematics in regard to Kant's general position over the issue between rationalism and empiricism. Mathematics, as we have already noticed, had long been the trump card in the hands of rationalists, the big stick which could always be brought out to chastise their opponents. Its propositions, as the rationalists said, were at once necessary and true of fact; they were, in Kant's own language, synthetic *a priori*. If judgements of this sort were

[1] In the inaugural *Dissertation* of 1770 Kant declares that the concept of number, the basis of arithmetic, is intellectual, but 'demands for its actualisation in the concrete the auxiliary notions of time and space (in the successive addition and simultaneous juxtaposition of a plurality)' (§ 12).

possible in mathematics why should they not be elsewhere? The Kantian account of mathematical truth completely turns the flank of this position by granting that mathematical truths are synthetic and necessary but denying that they are the unaided product of pure reason. The attainment of mathematical knowledge is only possible because of our special awareness of space and time. And because space and time are not concepts but singular entities, that awareness is not intellectual but a peculiar form of sense-intuition. The rationalist case thus falls to the ground entirely.

There are, nevertheless, serious difficulties in the Kantian theory. In the first place it is not worked out with any thoroughness. It owes its origin to a consideration of geometrical reasoning, and is strongest over its application to that. Kant is a good deal less satisfactory over arithmetic and even less clear over algebra, where the initial plausibility of his theory is at a minimum.[1] This is the less acceptable because the whole development of mathematics has been away from relatively concrete studies like Euclidean geometry to more and more abstract disciplines. But secondly, the centre of the Kantian position is challenged by the modern view that there is no special connexion between mathematics and space and time. Mathematics, on this account, is concerned with the examination and development of abstract types and systems of order, and is not primarily interested in whether or not these find concrete illustration in, for example, the spatial order as we know it in sense-perception. The development of systems of non-Euclidean geometry was a powerful factor in the formulation of this view, which would now be generally accepted by mathematicians. It may even be said that Kant's theory itself played a part in its genesis, since Kant's insistence on the necessity of sense-intuition for the geometer served to call attention to the imperfect character of geometrical reasoning in his time. But the general effect of the development of mathematics in the last fifty years has been to put any such philosophy of mathematics as Kant's out of court, and to make a thorough reconsideration of the whole problem necessary.

We have seen how, in the traditional rationalist account, mathematical knowledge depends on our possession of intellectual intuition, and we have examined two attempts to formulate an

[1] On Kant and arithmetic see Kemp Smith's *Commentary to Kant's* Critique of Pure Reason, pp. 128–34. On algebra see Paton: *Kant's Metaphysic of Experience*, vol. i, pp. 157–8.

alternative view, neither of them successful. It remains to ask what the situation is to-day. Here we come to what is probably the main achievement of modern empiricism, the working out for the first time of an adequate empiricist philosophy of mathematics. It is not too much to say that this development has changed the whole aspect of theory of knowledge.

The central contention of this empiricist doctrine is that all mathematical propositions are analytic or, as it is sometimes put, are 'tautologies'. This term is chosen to call attention to the fact, which is obviously crucial for the theory, that at no stage in his arguments does the mathematician have recourse to the intuition, sensible or intellectual, of any truth of fact. Mathematical reasoning is, as was argued in the rationalist doctrine, a matter of pure reason: its conclusions follow from its premisses by strictly logical rules. It is not the case, as Kant maintained, that mathematics has any special connexion with space and time, and depends for its progress on our ability to construct figures in intuition; if some of Euclid's conclusions cannot be reached from his premisses except by extra-logical aid that is not the fault of geometry as such but of Euclid's reasoning. But it is also not the case that the premisses from which the mathematician argues, the primary principles of his system, are self-evident truths established by intellectual insight. They are rather arbitrary assumptions, chosen by the mathematician without regard to their application to fact, and not fulfilling any other condition than that of being mutually consistent. It is because of the arbitrary character of the mathematician's starting-point that the development of, e.g., alternative systems of geometry presents no difficulty. If geometry were essentially connected, as earlier philosophers believed it was, with space, Euclidean and non-Euclidean geometries could scarcely subsist side by side; or if they did, one would have to be considered true and useful and the others arbitrary and useless. But if neither sort of geometry has any special relation to space the problem of their incompatibility does not arise.[1]

The main obvious difficulty for this theory, which makes pure mathematics out to be, in the words of its opponents, nothing but a

[1] It might, of course, be the case that Euclidean geometry applied to perceptual space and non-Euclidean geometries to other sorts of space (different parts of 'physical' space). But even if this were so the question whether the application were necessary or contingent would remain. Only if it follows from the nature of perceptual space that the axioms of Euclidean geometry must be true of it will their application be necessary.

game with symbols, is to explain the possibility of applied mathematics. But here no major obstruction should be encountered. The applicability of mathematical truths to the world we know in experience depends on the fact that both in mathematics and in the world of fact logical laws have absolute validity. In mathematics, as we have seen, conclusions follow from premisses by strictly logical rules. But logic is of equal importance in the world we know in experience, since it is a minimum requirement of anything we accept as fact that it should be consistent with all other facts. It follows that the truths of any mathematical system will have applicability to our experience provided that we can find in it situations which correspond to the system's primary premisses. Whether or not we are able to do so is a purely empirical question. Once we do establish a correlation between our system and fact the mathematics should apply because, to put it crudely, there is nothing in it but pure logic.

There can be no doubt that we have here the most effective counter to the rationalist theory yet devised. If Kant pointed the way to the position now reached, by insisting on the difference of the methods of mathematics and philosophy on the one hand, and mathematics and physics on the other, his formal philosophy of mathematics had the misfortune to be based on what mathematicians say was an accident of the Euclidean form of geometry. By contrast, the modern empiricist theory commends itself to philosophers and mathematicians alike. By ascribing to mathematical propositions the property of being logically necessary it does full justice to those features of mathematics on which rationalists had chiefly insisted and over which previous empiricist theories had conspicuously fallen down: in particular, to the clarity of the mathematician's insight into the relations of his ideas, and to the certain character of his results. But it effectively forbids any conclusion from these facts in favour of rationalism by its denial that the axioms of mathematics are self-evident truths of fact and its alternative account of them as arbitrary postulates taken as valid merely for purposes of argument. If it is accepted no appeal to intellectual intuition is needed to explain mathematical knowledge.

One of the advantages of this empiricist analysis, which I am proposing to take as substantially correct, is that it serves to explain our feeling, referred to already (see p. 89), that it is much more serious to deny a mathematical than an empirical proposition, however well established the latter may be. To deny that 2 and 2 = 4 is to make nonsense of the whole numerical system, since it follows from the principles of the system that the proposition must be true. No doubt we might have accepted different principles, yielding different conclusions; but granted our suppositions, the results we reach are logically certain. And the only reason why philosophers do not always admit this is that they insist on considering mathematical propositions in isolation and not as members of the system of judgements within which they fall.[1] But if we turn from mathematical to empirical truths and consider such a judgement as that Napoleon died in 1821, the certainty we ascribe to it is not and cannot be logical. It cannot be, because history, unlike mathematics, is not a deductive system; and what is true of history here is true of all empirical disciplines. Every statement the historian makes falls, as supporters of the Coherence Theory rightly point out, within a system; but it is not a deductive system. The system of historical judgements is one whose members mutually support one another rather than one where they depend one on another in a series which is essentially 'linear'. And because of that no empirical judgement can ever attain final certainty: as Hume says, the contrary of every matter of fact is always possible; though perhaps we should add that this does not imply that it is always likely, too.

A word should be said here on the supposed identity of mathematics and logic. I suggested above that, on the modern view, applied mathematics is possible because, to put the matter crudely, there is nothing in it but pure logic. This should not be misunderstood. For the purpose of showing the possibility of applied mathematics all that is necessary is to demonstrate the purely logical character of mathematical *inference*; the further question of the nature of mathematical *concepts* need not be considered. Now there is, of course, a famous theory of the concepts of mathematics, developed originally by Mr. Bertrand Russell and widely accepted to-day, which attempts to reduce them all to logical notions. The whole of mathematics, we are told by supporters of this view, can be deduced by purely logical reasoning from a set of ideas which are themselves purely logical. But we may perhaps be permitted to wonder whether, even so, mathematics is to be *identified* with logic. If there is any sense in saying of

[1] This is no doubt why Kant's argument that $7 + 5 = 12$ is synthetic is plausible.

logic that it is a second-order discipline, which takes its rise out of the attempt to formulate the rules of correct thinking (and however much we may want to emend that elementary definition, it is difficult to dispense with it altogether), must we not differentiate logic from mathematics, which is surely an example of first-order thinking? The difference between the two studies can perhaps be put in this way. In mathematics our business is to take certain ideas (whether they are purely logical or not does not enter the question) and develop their logical consequences; we are interested in the precise implications of that from which we start. But in logic it is not the system achieved but the principles on which it is constructed which occupy our attention; we are reflecting on the rules our thinking has assumed. That would give what at any rate seems to be an intelligible distinction between the two, and one that corresponds in some measure to the traditional view of their functions; but whether it is at all correct I could not presume to say.[1]

§ 5. This question of the relation of mathematics and logic is particularly important for our purposes now that it is clear that logic is, as it were, the key to mathematics. For it may be suggested that the propositions of logic at least give colour to the traditional theories of the rationalists. Logic thus becomes the last rationalist stronghold, the final refuge for the supporters of intellectual intuition. In a previous chapter (p. 50 above) it was argued that the very definition of analytic judgements suggests that the laws of logic are synthetic and *a priori*. The rationalist interpretation of this would be that they embody the results of human insight into the necessary nature of the world, and are thus factual truths of a very general kind.

The fashionable empiricist answer here is to treat logic as on an exact par with mathematics. We are assured[2] (*a*) that all logical judgements are purely analytic, and (*b*) that just as a plurality of mathematical systems, built up from different primary premisses, is possible, so is a plurality of logics. The idea of a single universal logic, whose propositions were based on intuitions of certain very general features of reality, would, if this were accepted, clearly be ruled out.

[1] I am not ignoring the theory that alternative logics are possible. I discuss this in the next section.

[2] Cf. C. I. Lewis, *Mind and the World Order*, chaps. vii–viii; A. J. Ayer, *Language, Truth and Logic* (first edition), pp. 107 ff.

But it is not clear that this empiricist view, despite its wide acceptance to-day, is capable of defence. To begin with the first point, the allegedly analytic character of the propositions of logic. If an analytic proposition is to be defined, as it was in Chapter III, as a proposition true in virtue of logical laws alone (and in fact most empiricists would probably accept this definition or something like it),[1] can we really describe the laws of logic as themselves analytic? Surely there is a difference in epistemological status between the principles in virtue of which a given set of propositions is to be adjudged valid or invalid, and those propositions themselves. The principles of logic cannot be necessary *in the same sense* as are those propositions which depend on them. This elementary point does not seem to be sufficiently appreciated in current discussions of the subject.

It will be replied that if the propositions of logic are not analytic, then they are not synthetic either; and this in fact takes us to the second point. The contention is that the fundamental principles of logic are to be viewed, not as propositions which might conceivably be false, but as expressing definitions. And definitions are taken, by those who support this theory, as essentially arbitrary. We can define a principle or understand by a concept whatever we please, and no one can say us nay. Now not all philosophers would subscribe to that view of definition, but their dissent from it as a general principle need not trouble empiricists in the case we are considering. For they can and do draw attention to the plurality of logical systems which ingenious logicians have succeeded in building up by varying the postulates and primitive propositions—i.e., the definitions—from which they set out. That such *alternative* logics can be built up is beyond dispute;[2] their significance for theory of knowledge we must now briefly consider.

The point which empiricists have to make here is a double one: first, that there is a plurality of possible logical systems, and second, that there is nothing to choose between such systems except in regard to convenience, elegance, and simplicity. Thus

[1] Mr. Ayer (op. cit., p. 103) says that 'a proposition is analytic when its validity depends solely on the definitions of the symbols it contains'. He would, however, presumably agree that in applying such definitions we need to have recourse to logical principles.

[2] The simplest kind of alternative logic would be one which disregarded the law of excluded middle and instead of saying that every proposition must be true or false, held that it might be true, false, or doubtful. This gives rise to what is known as a three-valued logic.

there is no reason why any particular logical law—say, the principle of the syllogism—should be included in any given system; and so long as we take care to frame our system in such a way that it really is excluded we can accordingly deny such a law with equanimity. Inside any logical system, of course, we must maintain consistency: as Professor Lewis puts it, 'for one who stands within a given system of logic, the denial of one of its principles will imply the principle itself'.[1] But he adds, 'this signifies nothing more profound than the fact that deductions in logic are inevitably circular'. There are no logical principles which must be regarded as absolutely valid, and consequently no final system of logic can be looked forward to.

Obviously if this view were to be sustained no rationalist interpretation of logic, either of the traditional sort or of any other, would be possible. But it may be questioned whether it can be sustained in entirety. Consider the following passage from Professor Lewis:

> 'Whoever denies a principle of logic, may either draw his own inferences according to the principle he denies, or he may *consistently* avoid that principle in deriving his conclusions. If one deny a principle of inference, but inadvertently reintroduce it in drawing conclusions from his statement, he will indeed find that he has *contradicted* himself and admitted what originally he denied. But if he denies a principle of inference and *consistently* reasons in accordance with his own statement, he will incur no *self-contradiction* whatever.'[1]

Here the words I have italicized illustrate the weakness of the empiricist view. It is a salient point of that theory that there is no difference between the status of the three Aristotelian laws of thought and that of other logical principles. But in the passage quoted these laws seem to be presupposed as something more fundamental than the other principles discussed; as a feature which must appear in every logical system. And the fact that we can talk about the compatibility of different logics and find a common basis on which to discuss and compare them may perhaps be taken as further evidence that there are certain ultimate principles which every logic must acknowledge.

But if there are such principles, what is their status? Mr. Joseph, who argues for the traditional rationalist view, says: 'There are certain very general principles exemplified in all thinking... known as the Law of Identity, the Law of Contradiction

[1] Op. cit., p. 207.

and the Law of Excluded Middle. . . . Now though these are called laws of thought, and in fact we cannot think except in accordance with them, yet they are really statements which we cannot but hold true about things. . . . The so-called necessity of thought is really the apprehension of a necessity in the being of things.'[1] Mr. Joseph is here influenced by the Aristotelian doctrine of the relations of thinking and fact: the view that thought must reproduce the articulations of the real world, and that successful thinking depends on our ability to grasp necessities of fact. We have seen how Aristotle's theory of demonstration, whose influence in the history of knowledge has certainly been enormous, was exploded successively in the empirical sciences and in mathematics; and in truth it seems to be no more successful in logic. A truer view of logic is that of Kant, who says that it abstracts from the matter of knowledge and concerns only its form. Logic is occupied not with thinking so far as it reflects fact but with thinking so far as it is formally valid: its laws prescribe the conditions under which such thinking must proceed. It is true that, because it is a minimum condition of any intelligible world that we can think about it in formal terms, the laws of logic do apply, and apply necessarily, to the world of fact. But we cannot infer from their so applying that they are based on insight into that world's necessary nature. The scope of logic is wider than the realm of actuality: as Leibniz saw, it covers the whole sphere of the possible, and indeed in a broad sense defines what the word 'possible' means.[2] Its principles can hence scarcely be of a factual nature: rather we should say that they prescribe the minimum conditions by which anything which is to be called fact must abide.

It thus appears that both the empiricist and traditional rationalist interpretations of logical principles are at fault. Empiricists err in trying to treat logic as precisely parallel to mathematics, making out that its propositions are all analytic and its nature essentially arbitrary. As we have seen, neither of these contentions can be defended. The principles of logic cannot themselves be described as analytic if an analytic proposition is one whose validity depends on logical laws. And again, it seems clear that however many alternative systems of logic we succeed in developing by varying the fundamental definitions from which we start, we do not all the same destroy the notion of a universal logic, whose

[1] *An Introduction to Logic*, p. 13 (2nd edition).

[2] Neglecting here the concept of 'real' as opposed to logical or formal possibility.

validity stands on a different level, in terms of which we compare such systems and whose principles they all presuppose. But such a universal logic cannot be held, as rationalists have thought it could, to be based on our insight into the necessary nature of the world of fact, since its sphere is not that of the actual but of the possible. Its propositions are in truth prescriptive rather than factual, and depend not on insight into the real world, but on the activity by which the mind constructs that world out of the given: an activity which we shall begin to explain in the next chapter.

With these considerations we must leave the subject of the intellectual intuition of principles. It is true that there is one aspect of it which has been passed over in silence: the question whether intellectual intuition of this kind is involved in moral thinking. There is a school of moral philosophers who would say that it certainly was. But to examine their arguments and the criticisms brought against them would demand a protracted inquiry, which I must ask to be excused in the present context. For the purposes of theory of knowledge I shall assume that the treatment of the issues raised by the classical rationalist theory is, if not complete, at least sufficiently comprehensive, and shall take it that the theory breaks down under criticism at every point. And this, if a negative success, would generally be agreed to be important.

§ 6. In the rest of this chapter I propose to consider briefly the problem of the status of universals, one of the most famous *cruces* in the history of philosophy. Such consideration is necessary because, as has been explained above, one of the standard theories of universals entails a theory of intellectual intuition. I hope to show, however, that there is no greater warrant for saying that we intuit universals intellectually than there is for saying that we intuit necessary truths of fact.

There are three stock views of the status of universals, which I will begin by stating summarily.

Nominalism maintains that universals are names only, corresponding to no reality. Everything which exists is particular; universals are simply a convenient dodge or fiction invented by a mind which cannot cope with unlimited variety and is content to take similarity for identity.

Conceptualism also begins with the view that whatever exists is, in an important sense, uniquely individual. It differs from

Nominalism in maintaining that universals are not names but thoughts or concepts formed by the knowing mind.

Realism is the view that universals have real existence. Historically it has taken two forms, one maintaining that universals exist in a realm of their own and that the things we know in sense-experience merely imitate or in some way participate in them, the other holding that the universal is in fact part and parcel of the real world and has no separate existence of its own. I shall refer to these alternatives as the Platonic and Aristotelian theories respectively.

Nominalism is the traditional empiricist theory of universals. We have had occasion in an earlier chapter, when discussing the 'logical' and 'real' functions of the intellect, to remark on the empiricist shyness of intellectual activities even of the most apparently innocuous kind. This shyness is well illustrated in the attitude empiricists take up to universals, which they strive to play down or write off to the maximum extent. Their hostility can be accounted for to a large degree by the behaviour of their opponents, who have tended to say that our awareness of universals is a decisive argument in their favour. It is an essential part of most rationalist philosophies of the traditional type to maintain both that universals are in an important sense real and that our knowledge of them argues the possession of intellectual insight.

Conceptualism stands in a somewhat uneasy position midway between Nominalism and Realism, beloved by neither and belaboured by both. Despite this it is, when properly stated, probably the most satisfactory theory of the three.

So much by way of general introduction: we must now consider some aspects of the three theories more closely. To begin with Nominalism. The impetus to accept this sort of view arises, I think, from a desire to follow the principle of Occam's razor and avoid postulating unnecessary entities. It is not denied that there is some sort of universal element in knowledge, only that universals exist in their own right. The function of the universal is discharged in different ways according to different versions of the theory. Thus in the account given by Berkeley[1] we read that 'an idea, which considered in itself is particular, becomes general, by being made to represent or stand for all other particular ideas of the same sort'. A universal is simply a particular regarded as standing for other particulars. In other versions emphasis is laid on the fact that such particular ideas are, as Hume puts it, 'annexed to

[1] *Principles*, Introduction, § 12. Cf. also pp. 31–2 above.

a certain term'.[1] Here it is the name which is thought to discharge the function of the universal, and this is of course the traditional form of the theory.[2]

The main objections to Nominalism are, however, decisive against the theory in all its forms. Thus if we take Berkeley's version of the argument we can ask what it is that makes one particular able to stand for another if it is not some feature they have in common. The fact that particulars are classified according to 'sorts' supports this criticism. Similarly, on the view that the universal function is discharged by names we can ask why we give the same name to different particulars. The official empiricist answer is that we give the same name to particulars which are similar to each other. But, as Bradley was never tired of asking, what is similarity but partial identity? To say that two things are similar is to say that they have some aspect in common. And in consequence a universal cannot be satisfactorily defined as a class of similar particulars, or in any such terms.[3]

Setting aside for the moment the difficulties of Conceptualism, which appears to be open to objections of much the same sort, let us consider next the merits of Realism. The most striking feature of this view is its oscillation between the two forms I have called Platonic and Aristotelian. In both versions universals are real—indeed, for Plato they have a reality far above that of mere particulars; but the account of their existence varies. Plato, whose primary interest is in mathematical and ethical universals, is impressed by the fact that these are never fully instantiated in everyday experience. No straight line we experience is ever absolutely straight, nor are any just acts just without qualification. Plato therefore looks on universals as prototypes existing in a world separate from the world of sense, and maintains that sensible things derive what reality they have from participating in or imitating such prototypes. It is in this sense that Plato, in Aristotle's words, 'separated the forms'. Aristotle himself denied

[1] *Treatise*, p. 17, ed. Selby-Bigge.

[2] It must not be supposed that Hume always thinks of the universal as a name. Professor Price (in his British Academy lecture *Thinking and Representation*) has argued that neither Berkeley nor Hume ought to be classed as a Nominalist. They should properly be described as 'Imagists', since in their view it is images which fulfil the function of the universal. This would put them half-way between Nominalism proper and Conceptualism of the old-fashioned (Lockian) sort. But even if this is right, it must be admitted that both thinkers have much of the Nominalist outlook, and, in my view, they make the main Nominalist mistakes.

[3] For a criticism of some recent forms of Nominalism cf. Price, op. cit., pp. 31 ff.

any such separation and argued for a doctrine of 'materiate forms'. The universal, for him, exists *in re*, as a constituent part of the world we know in everyday experience. It would seem that Aristotle was led to take this view not so much by tenderness for the senses as by his criticisms of Plato's attempts to relate universals and particulars. The difficulties of relating particular things to a separate world of universals appeared to Aristotle so great that he declared that to postulate the latter 'simply doubled the number of problems to be solved'; the universal must exist in particulars if it was to exist at all.

It will be seen that while Plato looks on the universal as a type to which things approximate, Aristotle regards it as a structure which they embody. Now in fact both these descriptions appear to be correct as far as they go. For, first, Plato is surely right in thinking that there are some universals which either have no instances or are only approximately instantiated. It may be the case, as Kant says, that a really just act has never been done; yet it is possible to form a perfectly clear notion of justice. We use this notion as a standard by which to judge particulars. But, secondly, if we take instances of a different kind, Aristotle's view grows in plausibility. Aristotle's primary interest was in Nature and the natural sciences, and he means by materiate form first and foremost the common structure exhibited by kinds and species. It seems absurd to regard this structure as something separate from particulars: if animals, e.g., do not embody animality, where shall we hope to find it?

What then is the solution to the Platonic-Aristotelian controversy? It can be found, I suggest, only if we abandon some of their common assumptions and so transform their theories that they can be amalgamated in an account which is not so much Realist as Conceptualist.

Both Plato and Aristotle assume that when we know there must be an object of knowledge which exists independently of the knowing act. Both presuppose that whatever the solution to the problem of universals, the universal must be somewhere. That is why Plato, for example, is not content to stop short at a Conceptualist solution of the puzzle. That the universal could be a concept and nothing more seems to him absurd; for every concept must have an object, and the controversy turns on the status of such objects.[1] Similarly, Aristotle's criticism of the Platonic theory

[1] *Parmenides*, 132^{b} 3 ff.

is built entirely round the problem how the two parallel worlds of universals and particulars could be related and yet retain their independence. Aristotle is clear enough that they cannot, but he never asks whether this whole way of putting the question is justified.

So long as we assume that universals, if they are to be objects of knowledge, must be things with an independent reality of their own, so long does a Realist theory of them seem the only possible one. It is true that our satisfaction with such a theory is marred by the Platonic-Aristotelian antinomy into which we fall and from which there is no obvious escape; we feel, nevertheless, that no other alternative is possible. But why do we make the initial assumption? What warrant is there for believing that universals exist apart from our knowledge? Can we not maintain conversely that universals have an essential connexion with a discursive intelligence, and should be thought of only in relation to such an intelligence? They are, as the Nominalists say, a device, but a device to which we must have recourse if we are to make sense of our experience. A different type of intelligence, one whose capacity for intuition was unlimited, would have no use for them.

It will perhaps be wise to emphasize and underline this point, even at the risk of some repetition, since the theory of Conceptualism stands or falls with it.[1] Thinking in terms of universals, we say, is the sort of thing a discursive intelligence does. What is a discursive intelligence? We use the phrase to describe a mind which, like our own, does not originate the raw material of knowledge but receives it from another source. In our own case the raw material of knowledge comes in the shape of the manifold of sensation, and the business of the intellect may be variously said to be to interpret or organize it. What is intended by both metaphors is finding features in it which relate to previous experience, whether by relations of similarity, by causal reasoning, or in some other way. In this process we conceptualize the given by bringing out its universal features—the aspects it shares with other parts of experience. But our mental activity here is not, as the wording of the last sentence might be taken to imply, so much a work of discovery as of interpretation and construction: we are not so much finding the universal in the given as interpreting the

[1] Some Conceptualists (e.g. Locke) would not accept any such arguments as these. But by avoiding them they expose themselves to the same sort of attack as is fatal to Nominalism.

given in universal terms. And the result of this process of interpretation is to transform the given into the world of experience, a world displaying both universal and particular features, a world which we can think about in intelligible terms. But it does not follow from the fact that minds like ours must go through some such process that the same would be true of all minds. For thinking in terms of universals is, after all, a *pis aller*, a device resorted to by an intelligence which cannot comprehend the real in its individuality. And that is, indeed, as we saw in the last chapter, the source of philosophical dissatisfaction with the theory of discursivity and of attempts to replace it by a doctrine of intellectual intuition of the full-blooded sort.

According to the view here put forward, universals are at once concepts in the mind and features of the world of experience. They are able to fill this dual role because the world of experience itself exists in essential relation to discursive consciousness. But we cannot draw the Realist conclusion that universals are part and parcel of ultimate reality, and that our apprehension of them is a primary source of knowledge. Such a conclusion is impossible because the world of experience, as we are calling it, is a world of appearance; it is to the thing in itself which lies behind the given that we must go if we are to know a reality which is truly independent. But whatever the truth about the thing in itself, we can certainly have no direct acquaintance with any such reality.

The reader will see that a whole theory of knowledge, or indeed, in one sense of that disputed term, a complete metaphysics, lies behind the view we have stated; and to expound it properly would involve a complex argument. Obviously no such exposition can be undertaken here. An elaboration, and some defence, of the main position will be found in succeeding chapters, and I must ask the reader to postpone judgement until he has read these. For the present I wish only to draw attention to the fact that Conceptualism in the form here expounded does justice to that dual aspect of the universal which makes us think of it as both type and structure. The universal can be regarded as a type because it is a concept in the mind, an ideal which no particular may actually embody but to which some particulars may approximate. But it is not necessary to think of all universals in this way, and indeed such an account seems in some cases highly unplausible. In these cases we can lay emphasis on the fact that, for the Conceptualist, universals exist in things just as much as in the mind, since things are, in an important sense, what they are because they are known by minds.

So much for the problem of universals. I hope that enough has been said to discount both Nominalism, which depends on the usual empiricist shyness of the intellect, and Realism, with its rationalist implications. Both these theories, if I am right, assume a naïve attitude to the problems of knowledge, and the difficulties of Realism in particular arise directly from that fact. The view suggested in their place has the merit of doing full justice to the universal and to its dual aspect as type and structure without entailing the epistemological consequences traditionally drawn by the rationalists. But to appreciate it more fully the reader must turn to the discussions of the next chapter.[1]

[1] Professor Price points out to me that the view of universals argued for in this section assumes that universals are *cum fundamento in re*, and says that this (Realist) feature must be found in all Conceptualist theories. With this I agree. On any theory, reality must be such that it can be thought in general terms. But I think it possible to bring this fact out without accepting Realism proper.

VI

REASON AND EXPERIENCE

§ 1. BEFORE beginning a new topic it will perhaps be useful to pause and consider the course of the argument so far. Our main aim is to decide, or at least to make progress towards deciding, between two rival theories of knowledge, rationalist and empiricist. In Chapter II we gave a preliminary exposition of these theories and pointed out the different forms they have historically taken. In Chapter III we attempted to make the issue between them more precise by the aid of two distinctions originally drawn by Kant. If the arguments of that chapter are accepted the problem which confronts us can be put in the questions: has the human intellect a 'real' as well as a 'logical' function, and can it know any valid synthetic *a priori* truths? And the purpose of our elaborate discussion of intellectual intuition has been to investigate a series of arguments put forward by rationalists to show that these questions must be answered affirmatively. If intellectual intuition either in its primary or in either of its main secondary senses could be shown to be possible, the mind would demonstrably have a 'real' function and would clearly know some synthetic *a priori* truths. But we have argued that the case for it breaks down at every point.

The question which must now be asked is whether the rejection of intellectual intuition entails the rejection of rationalism as such Before answering this we should notice that the arguments so far considered are all *direct* arguments for rationalism. They purport to show that the intellect is a primary source of knowledge, in much the same way as empiricists say that the senses are. In the most extreme of them, the full-blooded theory to which, as we saw, more than one philosopher has had leanings, the intellect tends not merely to supplement but actually to replace the senses as a means of knowing particulars. The remaining theories are more moderate, but in them too it is contended that the intellect is a source of significant knowledge in its own right. And it is this contention that we have in fact rejected: we have shown that all attempts to argue that we are intellectually acquainted with particulars, or have insight into necessities of fact, break down.

It follows from this that the case for rationalism, if there is a case, must from now on be based on *indirect* arguments. We must show, that is to say, not that the intellect is a source of knowledge on its own account, but that it necessarily co-operates with the senses in the production of knowledge. And to make the case out we shall need to demonstrate that this co-operation extends beyond the mere intellectualization of sense-data, since that is to be ascribed to the 'logical' side of the intellect's activities. In technical language, we must prove that the human understanding is not only a faculty of concepts, but a faculty of *a priori* concepts as well.

Can this be done? In the rest of this chapter and in the two following chapters I shall state and criticize a theory which holds that reason has just such powers. The human understanding, in this view, is not an intuitive faculty, but it is, for all that, the source of a number of *a priori* concepts or categories, which enter into the constitution of experience in a vital way. But before we investigate the details of this view it will perhaps be best to say something of the historical development of the notion of a category.

§ 2. The word 'category' is Aristotelian, but the idea that there are some features of the object of knowledge which are to be distinguished from all others is already found in Plato. In criticizing a sensationalist theory of knowledge in the *Theaetetus*[1] Plato points out that there are some characters which are not grasped by any of the special senses. He gives as instances of these common characters (*κοινά*): being and not-being, likeness and unlikeness, sameness and difference, 'unity and the rest of number', odd and even, beautiful and ugly, good and bad. Unfortunately no detailed discussion follows, and we merely learn that such characters, in contrast to things sensible, are apprehended by 'the soul acting by itself' (185 e). The subject is again treated in the *Sophist* (253 b ff.), where Plato, in defining sophistry, comes to consider the function of the philosopher. The philosopher's business is, apparently, to investigate forms (universals), and Plato suggests that, in view of the fact that some forms are of far wider application than others, and that they differ very largely in their compatibility with each other, it would be profitable to take some of the highest genera and consider their nature and interrelations. He selects rest, motion, being, sameness, and difference. As a result of the discussion we learn that the last three of these are all-pervasive characters, predicable of each other and of everything

[1] 184 b ff.

that is, while rest and motion apparently divide the world between them, one characterizing some things and the other all others. It is not clear what conclusions we are to draw for Plato's ultimate metaphysical view from either of these passages—in each case the whole subject is treated far too shortly for any interpretation to be certain—but their interest for our immediate purposes is not in doubt. Plato is recognizing, as he had not recognized in earlier dialogues like the *Phaedo* and the *Republic*, that to divide reality simply into intelligible forms and sense-particulars will not suffice.[1] We must realize that a new problem arises in the sphere of forms itself, since some forms are clearly of wider applicability than others. And the main preoccupation of the philosopher must be not with forms as such but with the highest and most general forms of all. These, if the indications of the *Theaetetus* are followed, are known not through the medium of any sense organ but by purely intellectual means; though Plato, of course, with his hostility to Conceptualism, would never have described them as *a priori* concepts. But despite that they correspond closely, in idea if not in content, to the concepts distinguished by later philosophers as categories.

Aristotle's conception of categories is of less interest. Aristotle was concerned, in the first place, simply to classify terms, as the treatise on *Categories* itself makes clear:

'Expressions which are in no way composite signify substance, quantity, quality, relation, place, time, position, state, action or affection. To sketch my meaning roughly, examples of substance are "man" or "the horse", of quantity, such terms as "two cubits long" or "three cubits long", of quality, such attributes as "white", "grammatical". "Double", "half", "greater", fall under the category of relation; "in the market place", "in the Lyceum", under that of place; "yesterday", "last year", under that of time. "Lying", "sitting", are terms indicating position; "shod", "armed", state; "to lance", "to cauterize", action; "to be lanced", "to be cauterized", affection.'[2]

What this amounts to is a statement of types of predicate,[3] which is the meaning of the word 'category' itself. Aristotle was constructing, by means of a purely empirical survey, a classification of the different ways in which things can be said to be; and his

[1] The criticism of the theory of forms in the *Parmenides* is no doubt to be connected with this recognition.

[2] *Categories*, 1^{b} 25 ff., translated by E. M. Edghill.

[3] Neglecting here the difficulties which arise about substance itself, with its division into primary and secondary substance (*Categories*, 2^{a} 11 ff.).

results are largely, though not exclusively, influenced by linguistic considerations. And the effect of his theory was to separate the ten categories from all other universals, but not to clarify, as Plato had at least proposed to do, their nature and interrelations. It is true that Aristotle has a clear idea of the relation of substantial and dependent being, and that he has much to say in his different writings about the category of substance itself; but he does not discuss the other categories in anything like the same detail, nor elaborate the general conception in the way we should have liked.

Passing from ancient to modern philosophy, we must now consider briefly a doctrine whose connexion with the present subject may not be immediately obvious—the theory of innate ideas. Everybody knows that Locke begins his *Essay* with a long and tedious attack on this theory, which appears from his pages to be such that no sensible man would hold it. Nevertheless, it was held by no less a philosopher than Descartes. What did Descartes intend by it? Initially at least he meant to draw a distinction, not in itself very different from that proposed by Plato, between the ideas we know when our sense organs are stimulated and those we form by pure intellection. The latter are innate to the mind, and apparently include extension, motion, number, duration, and God. Now it is easy enough to show, as Locke did, that the notion that we are literally born with such ideas is without foundation: ideas arise in our minds only on the occasion of experience. But it does not follow that experience (or, to put it less ambiguously, sensation) is the ground of all our ideas. And this suggests that the theory of innate ideas conceals, behind an objectionable and indeed childish terminology, a doctrine which can be restated in a far more defensible form. If we replace the notion of innate by that of *a priori* we produce a theory which is both more in accordance with philosophical tradition and very much less easy to refute.

The credit for doing this must go to Kant, with whose views we shall be principally concerned in the present chapter: they constitute what may be called the classical theory of the *a priori*, from which all subsequent discussion must start. It should be realized, however (and the purpose of the present section has been to point this out), that the Kantian theory is not an isolated phenomenon in philosophical history, but embodies ideas which were at any rate approached by earlier thinkers. Nor, for that matter, did Kant himself reach his final view in one leap: in 1766, when he wrote the *Träume eines Geistersehers*, he seems to have lacked the idea of *a priori* concepts altogether and to have believed that rationalism was ruled out because intellectual intuition could not be established, whilst four years later we find him arguing in his inaugural *Dissertation* that there are pure intellectual concepts, but that they refer not, like empirical ideas, to the phenomenal world we know in sense-perception, but to an intelligible sphere which is wholly transcendent of things sensible. It is only in 1781, with the publication of the *Critique of Pure Reason*, that the notion of the *a priori* as constitutive of objects, and the conception of the categories as defining the most general characteristics of the things we know in experience, were finally worked out.

§ 3. In presenting the Kantian type of theory in its mature form I shall first state the argument in quite general terms, and only proceed to elaborate it after considering one or two immediate objections which will occur to most readers. The general argument can be put as follows. Sensation, taken in a broad sense as including introspection, is the basis of knowledge, but it is not the whole of it: there is all the difference in the world, from the point of view of the epistemologist, between sensation and sense-perception. In sensation we become acquainted with (or, in Kantian language, we intuit) a multiplicity or manifold of sense-data; but we do not thereby know an objective and orderly world. The manifold of sensation is in itself lacking in determinate order; like Bradley's feeling (above, p. 61), it is below the level of relations. That does not mean, of course, as is sometimes suggested, that the given is, *qua* given, a mere undifferentiated mass; rather we should say that at this level its differences are implicit only. To become aware of the true character of what is given we must think it, bring it to the level of concepts, assert its nature in judgement; but in speaking of these processes we plainly pass beyond sensation as such. What we pass to is no longer sensation but sense-perception or sense-experience. It is in sense-experience that we are able to know a common world of objects, to transform private and subjective sensations into the objective reality we investigate in history and the sciences. The latter, in contrast to the former, is characterized by explicit order, and both the eliciting of order from the given and, in important respects, the ultimate forms which it takes are the work not of the senses but of the mind.

Sense-experience, in this view, is best regarded as a composite, embracing (*a*) a multiplicity of given impressions contributed by sensibility, and (*b*) an ordering element contributed by the mind. As we shall see in the sequel, this, if offered as a full analysis of sense-knowledge, is too crude, for knowledge of the objective involves processes of memory and imagination as well as elements of pure sensation and relational thought. But it remains true that sensation and thinking play a preponderant part in sense-knowledge, and that each is indispensable to the other.

There is one aspect of the present theory which must be clearly insisted on if our exposition of it is to be honest and complete. Earlier in this book, in dealing with the 'logical' activity of the intellect, we have already had occasion to point out the need for thinking to supplement sensation if we are to have genuine knowledge. We claimed that knowledge involves processes of conceptualization and judgement as well as sense-intuition, and urged that this could be asserted without prejudice to the ultimate issue between rationalism and empiricism. Now it must be made clear that the theory being put forward at present goes and must go beyond that position. It attempts to maintain that the intellect has a 'real' as well as a 'logical' function to perform in knowledge; and it does this by arguing that understanding not only elicits from the given an order which is implicit in it, but also imposes on it a very general order of its own. The mind, on this view, has as its business to make sense of the raw material of knowledge; but it approaches the task not as the *tabula rasa* of Locke's conception, but with certain preconceived principles of its own. And it is most important, if a conclusion in favour of any form of rationalism is to be drawn, both that the existence of such principles should be vindicated and that their origin should be traced to the understanding. For if it can be shown, as some writers have suggested, that, though we do delimit reality in accordance with *a priori* categorial principles, such principles are not the product of reason but of some other faculty (e.g. the imagination), the rationalist case will fall to the ground.

What we are arguing, then, in very general terms, is that knowledge of objects rests on experience, but that experience itself is composite, including both an intellectual (active) and a sensible (passive) factor. And while we hold that sensation has the primacy in knowledge in so far as our intellect is an instrument specifically fitted to deal with sense-data and unable to attain to any cognition on its own account, it does not follow that we should interpret these facts, as an intelligent empiricist would, by saying that the intellect's business is simply to bring sense-data to concepts. On the contrary, we claim that the mind brings certain principles of its own to bear in construing the given, and it is on this contention that our whole case turns.

§ 4. At this point we shall do well to consider certain obvious objections. We shall be told that the view expressed (*a*) depends on an arbitrary and unwarranted conception of experience, and (*b*) would if true take away the independence of the object of knowledge and so destroy the possibility of knowledge itself. I shall refer to these as the empiricist and realist objections respectively.[1]

(*a*) The empiricist line of attack is to claim that our theory reads more into the conception of experience than it has any right to do. For what, after all, do we mean by experience? The essence of the view we are examining is that experience cannot be identified with bare sensation. Sensation is subjective and fragmentary, and cannot in itself give rise to objective knowledge of an orderly world. But, say the empiricist critics of our theory, all this was recognized by Hume before Kant; yet the conclusions the two philosophers drew from the facts are strikingly different. Kant argues that because sensation is insufficient to give us knowledge of objects we must go beyond it and postulate an experience which will give just such knowledge; Hume infers that objective knowledge is impossible, and that our reasoning about matters of fact depends on subjective principles whose application to the given can never be rationally justified. Of these solutions the critics prefer that of Hume. Despite his enormous efforts, they say, Kant was never able to produce a satisfactory proof of the necessity of his principles of the understanding as principles of experience, since the experience to which he attempted to relate them was itself nothing more than a rationalist fiction. The notion

[1] What I am calling the empiricist objection was first formulated by those contemporary German critics of Kant who were under the influence of British empiricism, e.g. Platner, Maimon, G. E. Schulze. An account of their views is given in H. J. de Vleeschauwer, *La déduction transcendentale dans l'œuvre de Kant*, t. iii, pp. 380–5. M. Vleeschauwer himself sympathizes with this type of criticism: see t. ii, pp. 394–7 of the same work. What I call the realist objection was developed by Cook Wilson and forms the basis of Professor Prichard's criticism of Kant in his book *Kant's Theory of Knowledge*.

that it is the prime duty of a philosopher to explain how we can know an orderly world itself depends on showing that our world *is* orderly; but palpable experience, what we know of reality in immediate sensation and introspection, will not show any such thing. Kant's demand that we invoke an elaborate theory of *a priori* concepts and principles conditioning whatever we know in order to account for the orderliness and necessities of Nature is thus yet another instance of the truth of Berkeley's dictum, that philosophers first raise a dust and then complain that they cannot see.

The same point is sometimes put (e.g. by M. Vleeschauwer) by saying that the Kantian type of view depends on an illegitimate conception of *possible* experience. All readers of the *Critique of Pure Reason* will remember the great play Kant makes with this idea. Thus, at a vital stage in the argument of the first edition version of the Transcendental Deduction (A 111), he claims that 'the *a priori* conditions of a possible experience in general are at the same time conditions of the possibility of objects of the experience', and goes on to maintain that the categories are 'nothing else than the conditions of thinking in a possible experience, just as space and time are conditions of [sense-]intuition for it'. He concludes that the categories are objectively valid. In the *Prolegomena* (§ 36) there is a passage in which Kant says that Nature understood in the formal sense and possible experience are to be taken as absolutely identical (*ganz und gar einerlei*). Now Nature understood in the formal sense is always contrasted by Kant with Nature understood as the totality of appearances, i.e. with the sort of Nature whose existence would be admitted by empiricists. And the empiricist criticism of Kant in the passages I have quoted (and indeed throughout his theory of knowledge) would be that in assuming that there is any other aspect of Nature he is fundamentally mistaken. Kant supposes that it is possible to unite all our impressions, however diverse and fragmentary, in a single experience, the different parts of which will be connected together according to necessary rules. But the hope is chimerical, if not absurd. Possible experience is a conception whose reality cannot be made out.

So much for the objection. To deal with it fully and satisfactorily at this stage is clearly impossible, since it calls in question many points in the Kantian theory which so far we have not even mentioned. A complete answer would presuppose a complete exposition of the theory, and could be given only along with that. But in the meantime the following discussion may be of preliminary use.

Kant is in effect recognizing two levels or stages of experience, which we may call immediate and developed;[1] his opponents recognize the former only. In trying to decide between them we must ask whether immediate experience is in fact adequate to provide knowledge. And here we must insist that if immediate experience is to be equated with sensation (and if it is not, with what is it to be equated?), it is quite inadequate for the production of knowledge. We have seen in earlier chapters how sensing needs to be complemented by intellectual processes: at the least we must recognize and classify what we sense. It is this act of *judgement* (as it in fact is) which transforms sensation into the kind of sense-experience of which we have spoken in § 3. But sense-experience, we claim, cannot differ from sensation only in so far as in it sense-data are intellectualized. In knowing objects, as we shall argue in detail later, far more is involved than the having and classifying of sense-impressions: we need to supplement what we have before us by acts both of memory and of pure imagination, and our procedure throughout is governed by the thought of objects as things whose different appearances are necessarily bound up together. And we may fairly argue that the onus of proving that no such thought is involved must be borne by those who deny it; for it seems plain that organized knowledge, most effectively exemplified in the sciences, does presuppose just such a conception. The sciences, history, and common sense alike proceed on the assumption that whatever we sense will be so far orderly that it can be connected with past and future sense-data. Unless we could make such an assumption intelligent thinking about immediate experience would be impossible. But if it is made we are saying that immediate experience must be regarded as a fragment of or

[1] In a celebrated passage in the *Prolegomena* (§ 18) Kant drew a distinction between two types of judgement: judgements of perception (*Wahrnehmungsurteile*), whose validity is subjective only, and judgements of experience (*Erfahrungsurteile*) which are objectively valid because based on the categories. This is perhaps the clearest expression in his writings of the contrast to which we are drawing attention. But the terminology of the passage, as commentators have pointed out, is unduly favourable to the empiricists; for to say that there can be *judgements* of perception which are only subjectively valid is to make the possibility of any other sort of judgement precarious in the extreme. Kant did not use this antithesis elsewhere in his writings, and his considered doctrine was that the categories are involved in judgement as such: see below, Chapter VIII.

extract from a wider *possible* experience—in fact, the possible experience of which Kant wrote.

It should be noted that the claim just made is quite consistent with recognizing that immediate experience is subjective and incomplete. And indeed empiricists might do well to reflect on just these qualities of it. It is too often assumed by writers of this school that immediate experience will provide knowledge in itself, though, as we have seen, this is far from being the case. The battle-cry of the empiricists, that all genuine knowledge is derived from experience, owes much of its plausibility to the essential ambiguity of the term 'experience' itself. The ambiguity is acknowledged by sophisticated writers like Hume, who have their own means of dealing with the problems it raises; but less subtle thinkers are apt to gloss over it altogether. Hence the denunciations of the nineteenth-century 'school of experience' made by Bradley and Green.

(*b*) We can now pass to the realist objection. According to the view we have stated, the mind not only elicits the order implicit in the given, but also imposes on it a very general order of its own (how it does it, of course, remains to be examined). Now it is objected to this sort of theory that it commits us to the impossible position that reality is *created* in the act of knowing. But this, it is said, contradicts the notion of knowledge itself; for it is axiomatic that the object of knowledge should be independent of the knowing mind if knowledge is to be possible. As Professor Prichard puts it:

> 'Knowledge unconditionally presupposes that the reality known exists independently of the knowledge of it, and that we know it as it exists in this independence. It is simply *impossible* to think that any reality depends upon our knowledge of it, or upon any knowledge of it. If there is to be knowledge, there must first *be* something to be known. In other words, knowledge is essentially discovery, or the finding of what already is. If a reality could only be or come to be in virtue of some activity or process on the part of the mind, that activity or process would not be "knowing", but "making" or "creating", and to make and to know must in the end be admitted to be mutually exclusive.'[1]

It must be confessed that the idea that the mind in any sense makes reality in the act of knowing it is a paradoxical one; but whether it is as absurd as Professor Prichard supposes is another matter. We may begin by noting two points about his view. First, that it is arbitrary to hold, as he does, that we *cannot* think

[1] *Kant's Theory of Knowledge*, p. 118.

that any reality depends on our knowledge of it, or on any knowledge of it. Surely there is nothing *self-contradictory* in such a supposition; if there were, it would scarcely have been made by competent, if misguided, philosophers like Gentile. And secondly, that he is assuming that the term 'reality' itself is completely free from ambiguity. According to the realist analysis, knowing is the progressive discovery of more and more facts about a pre-existing real. Particular truths about real things are known to us in perception; universal truths are grasped by acts of intellectual insight. In either case the real is directly present to us, and is emphatically not known through any mental intermediary. The mind perceives, but what it perceives is not in the mind but in the object; the mind thinks, but its universals are not mere concepts or ideas: they are rather independently existing features of fact.

This analysis has its merits as an attack both on the representative theory of perception as it appeared in Locke and on the vaguer forms of 'constructivism' favoured by some nineteenth-century idealists; but it is for all that seriously misleading. For surely we must draw at least a *prima facie* distinction between three types or levels of reality: the given, the common world which we construct from the given, and the independent reality which lies behind it. The given is the form in which reality first presents itself to consciousness: it is the real as known in immediate experience. But immediate experience is private to the individual percipient, and so we must differentiate its content from the common world we know in sense-perception. And because in the investigation of that world we take for granted certain principles which, though they are *a priori*, nevertheless belong essentially to a particular type of consciousness, we must recognize a further reality beyond it in the shape of the source of the given, the independent thing in itself. We can only ignore or slur over these distinctions by supposing an awareness by which we directly apprehend facts, whether particular truths such as are known in sense-perception, or universal truths of the kind established by scientists. But the case for such a veridical awareness—a pure intuition as it would in fact have to be—can easily be shown to be doubtful. It depends on (1) precisely the confusion between sensation and sense-perception against which we have continuously protested, and (2) a belief, already seen to be false, that intellectual insight into the necessary relations of fact is the only foundation for science and learning.

1. The point here is the old one that we do not apprehend any *facts* in sensation. Sensation is a passive state in which the given presents itself to us; but once we pronounce on its nature we have passed beyond sensation itself. Strictly speaking, facts are not independently existent realities but the product of judgement.[1] And judgement, though it enters into perception, is no part of pure sensation. Moreover, once we begin to judge we open the way not only to truth but also to error. Sensation cannot be mistaken, but sense-perception emphatically can.

2. Similarly we cannot hold, in the way old-fashioned rationalists did, that the business of thought is simply to reflect the necessities of things. It may be that science, and organized knowledge generally, do presuppose necessary truths; but if they do, they are neither premisses from which the scientist argues nor conclusions to which he comes. We have insisted on this point at length in Chapter V.

It may be asked here how, on the supposition of different levels of reality, we can hope to pass from one to another. How can we start from the given, supposed to be private to the individual percipient, and pass to a world which is common to all percipients of the same type? And what assurance have we that the processes by which I construct the 'common' world are the same as those you follow? These are all pertinent questions, deserving a careful answer. They cannot, however, be answered fully until the theory we are defending has been set out in detail; and for the present we must content ourselves with certain preliminary observations. We must point out that, while it is true that the contents of my sense-awareness are private to me in the sense that only I can be aware of them, it is nevertheless possible for you to have similar or comparable sensations, since one presupposition of the sort of analysis we are offering is that behind the data of sensation there exists a reality independent of both of us; and that we can construct a common world from our diverse experiences because the structure of our minds is fundamentally the same. The processes of understanding—conception, judgement, and inference—and the *a priori* principles which, if our argument is right, we use as criteria in our construction, are not private in the way sensations are.[2] And that is why, though we cannot

[1] The word 'fact' is itself ambiguous, like 'experience' and 'reality'.

[2] My acts of thinking are private to me; but *what* I think is (or ought to be) universal.

impart our particular experiences to other people, we can nevertheless describe them in terms they can understand, so that the correlation of one person's experiences with another's becomes possible.

Our reply to the realist argument will accordingly run as follows. First, we hold that it is not self-evident that knowing excludes making in the way the criticism supposes. But secondly we must emphasize that to say, even on our theory, that the world of experience is created in the act of knowing it is highly misleading. For though it is true that the common world is constructed out of the given, the construction is not an act of creation so much as of interpretation; and its results are determined in their details entirely by the nature of the material itself. The element contributed by the mind is confined to (*a*) what we call the conceptualization of the given, and (*b*) the provision of certain very general criteria of objectivity as such. These criteria, as we shall see, are purely formal in the sense that they apply to any and every object, and do not determine in any way what objects we are to know. And they are not employed by this thinker or that, considered as individuals; rather they belong to thinking as such. They constitute the content of what Kant called *Bewusstsein überhaupt*.

§ 5. The time has now come to attempt a more detailed account of the theory of *a priori* concepts as conditioning objective experience than has so far been possible. We may approach the subject through a consideration of the question how we can have knowledge of objects. Common sense, of course, assumes that there is no problem here: that there exists a world of objects fully formed, which merely awaits our apprehension. We have seen some of the difficulties of that view in discussing its presentation by modern realists, and it will scarcely be necessary to go into them again. Instead, we must ask what we have to put in the place of the common-sense theory once we abandon it. For if we deny that objects exist without regard to our knowledge of them, have we any right to belief in the objective at all?

I propose to tackle the problem by considering it as it appears in the works of the classical writers on theory of knowledge. Between the time of Descartes and Hume rationalists and empiricists were agreed that we can have no direct acquaintance in sense-perception with external things: we know them only through the medium of ideas, which are private to individual percipients.

How then could we talk of objective reality?[1] Descartes's answer to the question was that among our ideas are some which are clear and distinct, and that the goodness of God guarantees that these at least are objectively valid. There was, in fact, more in this solution than meets the eye, since Descartes was at least feeling his way towards the conception of the objective as depending on certain universal features of our thinking;[2] but it broke down on formal grounds, because its author assumed the principle of clear and distinct ideas in proving the existence of God, and nevertheless thought the principle itself dependent on God's goodness. In the speculations of the empiricists who followed comparatively little account was taken of the Cartesian solution. Locke held that the problem of objectivity could be solved because our ideas of primary, as opposed to those of secondary, qualities were undoubtedly veridical: there was an objective world independent of human consciousness, but we could know its primary qualities only. But Berkeley had little difficulty in showing that there was no real ground for this suggestion. Not only was it a psychological impossibility, he argued, to think of the ideas of primary qualities without endowing them with secondary qualities too (we could not, e.g., imagine anything extended without also thinking of it as coloured); but even if we could form abstract ideas of primary qualities we should have no means of knowing that they corresponded to objective things in the way Locke said they did. For the first premiss of Locke's theory was that ideas are the only objects of our immediate acquaintance.

Berkeley's own theory of objects, sketchy and imperfect as it is, is of some importance as the first example of what is now called a phenomenalist analysis. Convinced that we have no means of penetrating beyond ideas to their originals, he proceeded to define an object as a collection of ideas. In § 1 of *The Principles of Human Knowledge* we read that 'a certain colour, taste, smell, figure and consistence having been observed to go together, are accounted one distinct thing, signified by the name *apple*. Other collections of ideas constitute a stone, a tree, a book and the like sensible things.' In § 38 Berkeley speaks of 'the several combinations of

[1] The problem of objective knowledge is not identical with that of our knowledge of the external world, but discussion of the two necessarily proceeds together, since to say that there is an external world is one way of accounting for our ability to make (some) objective judgements.

[2] A clear and distinct idea was not a percept but a concept, and Descartes had a tendency to regard all such ideas as innate: see above, § 2.

sensible qualities, which are called *things*'. In § 99 he says: 'The objects of sense are nothing but . . . sensations combined, blended or (if one may so speak) concreted together.' In the third *Dialogue* (pp. 282–3 of the Everyman edition) there is a passage giving a more detailed account.

> 'Strictly speaking, Hylas, we do not see the same object that we feel; neither is the same object perceived by the microscope, which was by the naked eye. But in case every variation was thought sufficient to constitute a new kind or individual, the endless number or confusion of names would render language impracticable. Therefore to avoid this as well as other inconveniences which are obvious upon a little thought, men combine together several ideas, apprehended by divers senses, or by the same sense at different times, or in different circumstances, but observed however to have some connexion in nature, either with respect to co-existence or succession; all which they refer to one name, and consider as one thing.'

Now what is conspicuously lacking in all this is an adequate account of the process of collecting, combining, or 'concreting' of ideas.[1] Berkeley tells us that the different aspects of an object are held together by being perceived by a spirit (*Principles*, § 91); and he gives some indication (though he does not discuss the subject as he should) of what ideas go together, viz. those that 'are observed to attend each other' (third *Dialogue*, p. 287). But he seems to be quite unaware of the general problem which exists for a theory of his type—to give an account of objective knowledge on a radically subjective basis.

Hume's theory of objects, although a great deal more subtle and suggestive than Berkeley's, is nevertheless in the end not much more satisfactory. Hume begins the *Treatise* by thinking of objects in a way substantially like Berkeley's, as collections of impressions or ideas;[2] and he retains this point of view, as if it gave rise to no problems, throughout his famous discussion of causality. But in the section on 'Scepticism with regard to the Senses' (Book I, Part IV, § 2) he suddenly reveals the difficulties to which a simple phenomenalism is exposed by the fragmentary nature of immediate experience, and subjects the common assumption of a world of continuing and independent

[1] It should be remembered that Berkeley is offering this analysis as valid of sensible objects only. The being of spirits is not *percipi* but *percipere*. It is much to be wished that Berkeley had written Part II of the *Principles* and developed his conception of spirits.

[2] See, e.g., p. 2 in Selby-Bigge's edition (on complex ideas).

objects to a most searching criticism. Hume argues that it is only by means of an illegitimate process of the imagination that we are led to assume such objects, and that philosophical reflection shows that such a process is contrary to reason. In our philosophical moments, accordingly, we must give up the belief in objects as an irrational fiction. But this is surely a despairing conclusion, one, moreover, which appears to be contrary to the dictum with which Hume opens his discussion, that 'we may well ask, what causes induce us to believe in the existence of body? but 'tis in vain to ask, whether there be body or not?'[1] For on any theory (even on one like Hume's) we have to distinguish the subjective from the objective, that which exists for my mind only from that which exists for all minds. It is true that Hume might have held that the very existence of other minds than his own was a postulate incapable of rational justification; but the problem breaks out again in a different form inside a single mind, and Hume does not solve it.[2]

How are we to speak of a common world if the sense-data which are the immediate objects of our acquaintance are private to the consciousness which perceives them? How can there be a tolerable account of objectivity on a phenomenalist basis? It is the merit of Kant to have realized the force of these questions, and to have offered a theory designed to answer them. We must accordingly proceed to examine the main lines of his solution.

We may take up first the Kantian doctrine of the threefold synthesis necessary for knowledge of objects.[3] Kant points out that knowledge begins when we are acquainted with a manifold of sense-representations, but cannot be confined to such acquaintance. It demands (i) that the given manifold be apprehended as one manifold; (ii) that we supplement present sense-data by past sense-data, thus making it possible to consider simultaneously different aspects of a single object, and (iii) that we recognize that these different aspects belong together by forming the concept of

[1] *Treatise*, p. 187, ed. Selby-Bigge.

[2] Hume's failure to solve the problem of objective knowledge is partly due to his loose use of the term 'imagination'. The imagination is, in his view, the faculty responsible for the uniting of one idea with another, or for the transition from an impression to its associated idea. But it is not until comparatively late in Bk. I of the *Treatise* that Hume makes clear that not all principles of imagination are of equal validity. He sets out to reduce thinking about matters of fact to association, but ends by recognizing that much of what he calls association is uncommonly like thinking as normally understood. See below, Chapter VIII, § 3.

[3] *Critique of Pure Reason*, A 98 ff.

the object to which they relate. In other words, the first requisite of objective knowledge is that we should synthetize the given, supplementing sensation by processes of memory, imagination, and understanding. We may add that the part imagination plays is greater than Kant himself brings out, since it is needed not only to parade past sense-data alongside present ones, but to fill gaps in present sensations themselves. Every blink breaks the continuity of sensation, yet we continue to act as if no breaks occurred, and are indeed unaware that they do.[1]

To say, however, that objective knowledge demands synthesis is only to begin the solution of the problem. For, after all, both Berkeley and Hume had in effect held this view, though they had failed to work out its details in the way they should. What marks Kant's view off from theirs is that he propounds a theory not merely of empirical but also of *a priori* synthesis. He holds that an object is not just a collection of sense-data, but a collection of sense-data necessarily united together. And it is in the necessity, supplied by mind yet independent of any particular mind, that he finds the essence of objectivity.

We must now attempt to throw light on this difficult and (let it be admitted) paradoxical idea. We may begin by taking up a point which Kant makes more than once,[2] a point which explains why he cannot accept a solution like Hume's. According to the threefold synthesis argument, all knowledge includes a process of imaginative association, whereby we supplement present by past sense-data (this is the process which Bradley was to call 'redintegration'). Now why cannot we explain all objective knowledge by recourse to such a principle? According to Kant we are unable to do so because carrying out the process of redintegration involves an assumption, that the course of Nature is governed by rules. If Nature were disorderly, if, as Kant puts it, 'cinnabar [red lead] were now red, now black, now light, now heavy, if men appeared in the shape now of this, now of that animal, or if on the longest day the country were covered one year with fruits, another with snow and ice', all the normal processes of association, whereby we proceed (in Kant's example) from the redness of red lead to its heavy quality, would be quite untrust-

[1] The important part played by imagination in sense-perception was one of the major discoveries of Hume. Among contemporary philosophers it has been most stressed by Mr. Russell and Professor Price.

[2] Especially in the first edition version of the Transcendental Deduction: see *Critique of Pure Reason*, A 100 ff., A 112 ff.

worthy. Association itself, in other words, presupposes a certain regularity in phenomena. But how can any such regularity be guaranteed?

Kant's answer[1] is that our world is orderly because in the end we make it so. In knowledge, as we have seen, we start from the given, which, however, because of the serial nature of our apprehension, we are compelled to synthetize or hold together. And a synthesis of this sort is only complete when we are in a position to be conscious of the rule in accordance with which it has proceeded: when we can attain explicit awareness of the concept or thought which has dominated it. Now though it is true that most of the concepts which operate in our knowing processes are suggested by the nature of the given, it does not follow that they are all of this nature. Kant's case is that objective knowledge requires not merely empirical concepts, which depend on the sort of material dealt with, but *a priori* concepts as well, operative in all processes of objective synthesis. Such concepts may be described, in contradistinction to those which refer to this type of object or that, as 'concepts of an object in general'; they are of universal application, being predicable of whatever is to be considered a part of the objective world. They are, in a word, categorial concepts, defining the criteria by which we delimit the objective as such.

It would be a gross misunderstanding of the Kantian position to suppose that his assertion of the need for *a priori* concepts or categories is in any way arbitrary. In particular, he is anxious to show that it is not just a contingent fact about human nature that it thinks in this way. He holds rather that we must have recourse to the categories if we are to solve a problem which confronts every type of discursive consciousness: the problem of distinguishing the objective from the subjective, the real from the illusory. Sensation presents us with a mass of data of all sorts, and our task is to reduce those data to order. *What* order we find obviously depends in a fundamental way on what is given; but our search for order cannot even start unless we have some preconceived notion of the ultimate sorts of order for which we are looking. We must have some idea of the sort of thing an orderly or objective world would be if we are to establish the details of

[1] The problem of the orderliness of Nature for Kant comes up at two stages, and what follows concerns the first stage only. See Chapter IV, § 5, for some discussion of the more ultimate difficulties involved.

such a world empirically. And such an idea would properly be called *a priori*, both because it was one to which we held without regard to the nature of the given and applied to whatever was given, and because it could not conceivably be derived from immediate experience.

All this can be summarized by saying that experience in the developed sense involves not only empirical thinking but *a priori* thinking too. It involves empirical thinking because, as we have seen many times already, the given must be conceptualized and judged if it is to be known; and it involves *a priori* thinking because only if we start with the thought of what it is to be an object can we hope to determine what is in fact objective. But it should be stressed that though in this account we have set *a priori* and empirical thinking over against one another, they are not to be thought of as really separate. There is no such thing as pure *a priori* thinking (though we may consider the *a priori* component in thought separately when we philosophize): the *a priori* synthesis is only real in so far as it operates in and controls particular empirical syntheses. And conversely, all empirical thinking is accompanied by *a priori* thinking, and every empirical concept will fall under the categories.

Kant's theory of objects and the objective world can accordingly be put if we say that the objective is, in a phrase of Bosanquet's, 'what we necessarily think'. But the phrase should not be misunderstood. For in the first place it should be emphasized that though on the view we have expounded there is a sense in which it can be said that the mind makes Nature, yet this is not to be interpreted as meaning that *particular* minds make it. The categories are not the peculiar invention of my mind or yours; and, indeed, if they were their use would be self-defeating. For the whole point of saying that knowledge must contain categorial thinking is to account for our belief in an objective or common world. The categories belong, as Kant say, to 'consciousness in general': they are applied by the understanding, and there is good reason to suppose this to be identical in each one of us.[1] And secondly, to find the essence of objectivity in necessity, and hold that the objective world is a world governed by necessary rules, is not to subscribe to any absurd doctrine about the logical relations of facts. The necessity which Kant postulates in Nature,

[1] For discussion of the suggestion that the categories have a history and vary in content from age to age, see Chapter VIII, § 5 below.

and which is the basis of all scientific law, is not *logical* necessity: there is no suggestion with him, any more than with Hume, that one fact or law entails another in the way in which propositions are related in a deductive system. Kant is not saying, as his rationalist predecessors had, that the truth about Nature must be expressible in analytic judgements: on the contrary, he holds that both particular laws of Nature and those universal principles which derive from the categories are unquestionably synthetic. The necessity of the objective, for Kant, depends on the fact that we impose on the raw material of knowledge a very general form. Whatever falls within experience, we hold, must conform to certain rules if it is to be accounted objective at all; but it does not follow from this that we can determine in advance of experience what objects we shall meet with. In other words, no inference is possible from concepts of an object in general to empirical concepts. From knowledge of the categories we can infer nothing about the detailed relations which hold in the actual world.

The above must suffice as a general description of the Kantian theory,[1] which we may summarize as follows. Kant is claiming that the possibility of objective knowledge, such as is presupposed by organized learning and common sense alike, depends on our bringing *a priori* as well as empirical concepts to bear on the interpretation of immediate experience. Such concepts, distinguished by the name of 'category', have a special part to play in knowledge, and they represent the contribution of the pure understanding to it. Because of their presence we may say that the human intellect has a 'real' as well as a 'logical' function, and is the source of certain synthetic *a priori* principles. And if these positions can be made out rationalism of a sort, though not of the sort favoured by Descartes or Hegel, will be established. Rationalism in Kant has a firm empiricist basis, since he holds that no truth of fact can be validated except by reference to the details of experience; but

[1] In explaining Kant's theory I have deliberately abstracted from two factors which could only cause confusion in the present context: the argument that *a priori* synthesis is necessary if we are to have self-consciousness, and the distinction, made in § 24 of the second edition version of the Transcendental Deduction, between the intellectual and the figurative synthesis, the former involving the pure, the latter the schematized, categories. Much of Kant's detailed argument depends on his conceiving his problem as that of explaining our knowledge of a single world of objects unified in one space and time; but the reference to space and time is not essential to consideration of the general position, though it cannot be avoided, as we shall see in the next chapter, when we come to consider individual categories.

it deserves its name for all that, since he also holds that over and above truths of fact there are some truths of reason, and indeed that without the latter there could be no facts. But we must postpone further discussion of the nature and relations of these two types of truth to a later section.[1]

§ 6. It may be helpful for the understanding of the Kantian position if we restate the argument for an *a priori* factor in developed experience from a different point of view. It is a point of view taken, but not pressed, by Kant himself (it appears most clearly in the *Prolegomena*), and in recent years it has been argued with singular vigour and clarity by Professor Collingwood in his *Essay on Metaphysics*. In this new approach we begin not from objects but from our study of the objective, and the question we must attempt to answer is how, and on what presuppositions, such study is possible. That there are forms of systematic inquiry, in the shape of the sciences and history, each with a technique and a subject-matter of its own, is a fact which no one disputes. What is of interest to us is to know what sort of a thing a science (if we can use that word generically) is, and what, if anything, it involves in the way of *a priori* thinking.

We may take it that the classical rationalist conception of science, which equated scientific with *a priori* knowledge, has been sufficiently disposed of in the last chapter. What of its empiricist rival? The official empiricist account is that the only inquiries worth the name of positive science proceed by purely empirical methods. They attempt to discover the truth about some portion or aspect of reality without making any presuppositions. A scientist is a man who subordinates himself, wholly and without reservations, to 'the facts': who strives to avoid all preconceived ideas, or any confusion of his own suppositions with the truth he uncovers. His thinking is strictly empirical, and the introduction into it of an *a priori* element would serve only to mar and confuse it.

Now although this empiricist theory contains an important element of truth, it is not difficult to show its shortcomings. (A) It proceeds on the assumption that every science is separate from every other. Each science is supposed to deal with a single part of reality, and to pursue its inquiries without regard to those of other sciences. But this is obviously false. Sciences overlap, and the results of some are clearly taken for granted by others.

[1] See § 8 below.

Thus the results of physics are accepted without question in chemistry, and those of both in biology. Neither the chemist nor the biologist approaches purely physical questions with an open mind: he assumes that the laws formulated by the physicist will answer them. Nor is the phenomenon confined to the physical sciences. The labours of the historian result in the establishment not of laws but of individual facts; but these results are taken for granted by the economist or the sociologist in much the same way in which those of the physicist are assumed by chemists or physiologists. And (B) it is not true that empirical sciences are free from presuppositions. All systematic inquiries involve some assumptions which they do not themselves justify. Thus the physical sciences assume that anything they investigate will be measurable, and that whatever is not capable of precise measurement may be ignored for their purposes. History assumes certain criteria for the assessing of historical evidence (a possible example is the principle, suggested by Bradley, that whatever we accept as historical fact must bear some analogy to our own present experience),[1] but does not itself make these criteria matters of question. To lay bare such assumptions, indeed, is the business not of the sciences themselves but of philosophy.

What justification do we have for saying that all sciences involve presuppositions which they do not justify? There is a celebrated passage in Kant which supplies an answer to this question. 'Reason', we read in the preface to the *Critique of Pure Reason*, 'must approach Nature with a view, indeed, of receiving information from it, not, however, in the character of a pupil, who listens to all that his master chooses to tell him, but in that of a judge, who compels the witnesses to reply to those questions which he himself thinks fit to propose.'[2] In this sentence Kant brought out a feature of scientific thinking of very considerable importance: that it proceeds by means of question and answer. The process of establishing scientific (or historical) facts is not one of passive apprehension: before we can learn anything we must have some idea of what we hope to find out. And this explains why all organized inquiries make presuppositions: what is presupposed is the terms in which their questions are to be answered. Nor is this procedure in any way inconsistent with the fundamentally empirical character of such inquiries. For even if we do approach

[1] Cf. *The Presuppositions of Critical History* (reprinted in *Collected Essays*, vol. i).
[2] B xiii (translated by J. M. D. Meiklejohn).

Nature (or history for that matter) in the character of a (continental) judge, prepared with certain questions to put, it does not follow that we know in advance of experience the answers we shall get, any more than the judge knows in advance what witnesses will say under cross-examination. In either case experience has the last word, though it cannot be said to have the first one, too.

Now it may be suggested here that though it is true that the sciences (or some of them) proceed on principles which they do not themselves justify, nothing significant can be inferred from the fact. For what is assumed in one branch of learning may be justified in another. To meet this point we must follow Professor Collingwood in drawing a distinction between 'absolute' and 'relative' presuppositions.[1] Presuppositions are relative when they are assumptions made for the sake of some particular inquiry, but are nevertheless answers to questions which fall outside the inquiry. It is in this sense that, for example, the laws of physics are presupposed in biology or the results of the historian in economics. By contrast absolute presuppositions, if there were any, would be principles which could not be shown to be the answers to *any* questions whatsoever, but were the fundamental assumptions upon which our whole questioning activity proceeded.

Are there any absolute presuppositions in this sense? Collingwood thought he could show by a formal logical argument that there must be. If we take any statement, he argued, we must regard it as either the answer to a question or the presupposition of one. But this in itself shows that there must be absolute presuppositions, since questions clearly precede answers (are logically prior to them). And this conclusion is confirmed if we turn to concrete examples of organized learning. There seems to be a good case for holding that there are absolute presuppositions of particular *kinds* of thinking (e.g. thinking in physics, in biology, in history, &c.), and some case for adding that certain principles (the general law of causality might be an example) are presupposed in *all* thinking. Principles like the law that we must always look for a cause are not peculiar to any department of human knowledge, however broad our conception of such departments, but appear to be involved in objective thinking of any sort. Such principles might be taken as expressing the ultimate criteria by means of which we define the objective or delimit the real.

[1] Compare *An Essay on Metaphysics*, pp. 21 ff., and, on the logic of question and answer, *Autobiography*, chap. v.

It seems clear that if there are absolute presuppositions, whether of specialized thinking or of thought as such, we may say that knowledge involves an *a priori* element. But this should not give rise to premature conclusions. For we have still to ask for the *source* of our presuppositions, and to decide whether they can really be connected, as rationalists have supposed, with reason or understanding. The possibility remains, after all, that they spring from the non-rational side of our nature: from that mysterious faculty, half intelligent and half instinctive, which Hume called the imagination. I mention this possibility here not because I am proposing to discuss it—I shall do that later in the book[1]—but simply as a warning to anyone who thinks rationalists can set up their trophy at this point and withdraw from the field. There is a good deal more fighting to be done before either side can be pronounced victorious in this struggle.

§ 7. We have now stated the case for an *a priori* element in thinking from two points of view. Objective knowledge, we have argued, requires that we bring to the interpretation of the given not merely empirical but *a priori* concepts also, these being best regarded as 'concepts of an object in general'. And again, all systematic inquiries proceed upon presuppositions which are unquestioned, and these, whatever the solution of the difficulties raised in the last paragraph, can be set down as, in a general sense, the product of the mind. The two points of view can be brought together if we recognize that it is upon the categories that our absolute presuppositions are based. The former are in the sphere of concepts what the latter are in the sphere of judgements.

It remains to determine more precisely what can be known by means of the categories: what limits, if any, we must set to the powers of *a priori* thinking. The problem is important because it might be thought from what has been said that the categories, as concepts of an object in general, were capable of *metaphysical* use, i.e. that they could reveal to us, or help us to infer, the essential structure of reality. But this, as I hope to show, is a statement which at least needs serious qualification.

We have seen already that the notion of categories, the idea that among our universals are some which are (*a*) all-pervasive in character, and (*b*) knowable by the pure intellect alone, was familiar to Plato. But we owe to the Greeks not only the conception

[1] In Chapter VIII.

of a category but that of metaphysics too. Book Γ of Aristotle's *Metaphysics* begins with the words: 'There is a science which investigates what is real simply as real (τὸ ὂν ᾗ ὄν), together with the attributes which inhere in it in virtue of its own nature. It is not identical with any of the departmental sciences. No other inquiry considers reality as such universally; they each cut off a part of being and study its necessary attribute.' The purport of this passage is clear enough: Aristotle is suggesting that over and above the special sciences, each of them concerned with a part or, as he puts it elsewhere,[1] a 'kind' of reality, there is room for a further discipline, first philosophy or metaphysics, which investigates being as such. Such a science would be universal in a way no special science could be, since its business would be to consider not this thing or that but the basic structure which underlies all particular appearances; and for the same reason it could be regarded as raising the most fundamental of all questions. Elsewhere (especially in book Λ of the *Metaphysics*) Aristotle puts forward a different conception of metaphysics, as concerned not with being as such but with the most real of all things. Metaphysics is here the science of pure form, manifested in God and the intelligences which move the heavenly spheres, and for that reason Aristotle sometimes calls it θεολογική. It is not clear whether the two conceptions can, as Aristotle himself supposed,[2] be reconciled, or whether the second should not be regarded, as Jaeger suggested, as a relic of a Platonic view which Aristotle later outgrew. Fortunately, however, the issue is of no importance for our purposes, since both views of the nature of metaphysics were influential in determining subsequent speculation. Metaphysics as traditionally conceived (e.g. in the works of the successors of Leibniz) included both an ontology (a doctrine of being as such) and a treatment of the problems of God, Freedom, and Immortality (an attempt to understand the most real of all things). And in both its aspects it was viewed as a strictly intellectual discipline leading to knowledge of a reality lying beyond sensible appearances; for the fundamental structure which ontology was to reveal was just as remote from the things of sense as were the more obviously intelligible entities with which rational cosmology, rational psychology, and natural theology concerned themselves.

Now it is natural to think that pure intellectual concepts of the type for which Kant argued would be available for the construc-

[1] Cf. *Post. An.*, 87^{a} 38, *Metaphysics*, 1025^{b} 8.

[2] Cf. ibid. 1026^{a} 23 ff.

tion of just such a metaphysics of the supersensible; and indeed Kant himself at one point in his career supposed that they were. In the dissertation 'On the Form and Principles of the Sensible and Intelligible Worlds', written to inaugurate Kant's tenure of the professorship of logic and metaphysics at Koenigsberg in 1770, it was argued that though all our knowledge of things sensible was knowledge of appearances only, because it was all bound up with space and time, subjective forms of human perception, metaphysics in the traditional sense was none the less possible. We could have some knowledge of the essential nature of reality because there were in the intellect certain pure concepts of 'things or relations' (§ 5), which it could discover by reflection on its own operations on the occasion of experience (§ 8). Kant gives as instances of such concepts (ibid.) 'possibility, existence, necessity, substance, cause, &c., with their opposites or correlatives', and these all belong to the later list of categories. He explains his view of the function of pure intellectual concepts in the passage immediately following:

'The concepts of understanding have, in especial, two functions: (*a*) In their *critical* use, they perform the negative service of keeping sensitive concepts from being applied to noumena. Though they advance knowledge not at all, they yet keep it free from the contagion of errors. (*b*) In their *dogmatic* use, the general principles of pure understanding, such as are dealt with in ontology or rational psychology, issue in some exemplar, which is conceivable only by pure intellect, and is the common measure of all other things as far as real. This exemplar—*Perfectio noumenon*—is perfection either in a theoretical or in a practical sense. In the former, it is the supreme being, God; in the latter, moral perfection.'[1]

It is not easy to see how much is meant by this (to us) unfamiliar language; but it must mean at least that our intellect gives us some sort of idea of what later philosophy was to call the Absolute. Kant is careful to emphasize (§ 10) that he is not claiming any intuition of things intellectual: our knowledge of them is symbolic (by description?) only. But he does think we can know reality up to a point, and it is because we possess pure intellectual concepts that this is possible.[2]

[1] *Dissertation*, § 9, translated by J. Handyside (Open Court Publishing Company, 1929.)

[2] Kant's view in the *Dissertation* contrasts most sharply with the theory he had stated four years earlier in the *Träume*, where he argued from the absence of intellectual intuition to the impossibility of metaphysics without even considering *a priori* concepts.

Despite the confident tone of the *Dissertation*, Kant was very soon dissatisfied with its positive doctrines. And the question which exercised him above all others was this: how, if we grant unrestricted validity to the pure concepts of the understanding and hold that they apply to an intelligible world, can we guarantee this application? How can we know that such concepts are valid of objects? For, after all, we have no acquaintance with any reality other than that we know in sense-experience; and that being so the possibility remains that pure concepts determine no object whatever—that they are empty thoughts without objective reference. Indeed, some empiricists would say that this was, in fact, the case.

Kant's answer was to reformulate his whole theory of the relations of empirical and *a priori* thinking. In the *Dissertation* he had held that the two were sharply separate: that the first was exercised in sciences like physics and referred to the phenomenal world of sense-perception, whilst the second was exercised in metaphysics and referred to the real world of things in themselves. In the *Critique of Pure Reason* all this is changed: pure and empirical thinking now go together, and neither exists without the other. The suggestion that we might use the *a priori* concepts of the understanding to determine the sphere of things in themselves is discarded, along with the belief in the possibility of a metaphysics of the supersensible. *A priori* concepts or categories are held to play an essential part in knowledge, but it is knowledge of the sensible world. And without this reference to things sensible they are thought to have no content or objective validity.

To understand Kant's mature theory we must grasp one point about it above all others: that the categories are no longer conceived as denoting independently existing 'things or relations', but rather as concepts of the ultimate ways in which we give unity to our sense-experience. All concepts, in Kant's view, stand in relation to those processes of synthesis which, as we have seen, are indispensable for human knowledge: they express the rules in accordance with which such processes of synthesis proceed. Every such synthesis involves both an empirical and an *a priori* element, the former in so far as we unite our sense-data under the concept of this object rather than that, the latter in so far as we think of the resulting object, whatever its empirical nature, as forming part of a single objective world, the same for all percipients. And this belief in the essential connexion of concepts with processes of synthesis explains both Kant's insistence on and his answer to Hume's question 'from what impression was that idea derived?' He is always asking what intuitions give reality to a concept because he holds that concepts in their nature relate to intuitions; and he thinks he can show that pure concepts have objective validity because, though they have no direct relation to intuitions, they have nevertheless an indirect relation. But the intuitions to which they relate are *sense* intuitions; and in consequence it is only in reference to the sensible world that they can be said to have significance. Their use for the purposes of metaphysical cognition is entirely precluded.

The sections of the *Critique* in which this argument is worked out, the Transcendental Deduction and the Schematism of the Categories, are undoubtedly among the most difficult in philosophical literature; but the fault is not wholly due to the obscurities of Kant's style and manner of argument. In particular there is one complication which in the nature of the case seems unavoidable, and yet renders both the exposition and the understanding of Kant's thought far more difficult than it would otherwise be. This is the fact that Kant thinks of the categories as coming up at two stages, more and less abstract, the former belonging to discursive consciousness as such, the latter to discursive consciousness in its human form.

To explain this complication we must say something of the knowing of a discursive intelligence. A discursive intelligence, as we have seen in earlier chapters, is one which cannot itself originate the matter of knowledge, but only operate upon data given to it from without. In its knowing there are in consequence two elements, called by Kant 'receptivity of impressions' and 'spontaneity of concepts'. The material of knowledge is contributed by sensibility, its form by the understanding. And Kant would say that this account was true of all possible intelligences of the discursive type. But he also holds that though understanding does not vary from one type of discursive intelligence to another, sensibility very well may. Our human intelligence stands in relation to a sensibility whose *a priori* forms are time and space; but it would be rash to assume that ours is the only possible sort of discursive intelligence. There is no contradiction in assuming intelligences related to sensibilities whose *a priori* forms are quite different from space and time. Such intelligences would not perceive things as spatial and temporal as we do, though the principles in accordance with which they ordered their experience would be fundamentally the same as ours.

Nevertheless, they would not be *quite* the same; and here we come to the crucial point. Concepts, as we have seen, stand in Kant's view in essential relation to intuitions; it is from intuitions that they derive what has sometimes been called their cash-value. Now though it is true that *a priori* concepts spring from the nature of the understanding, i.e. belong to discursive intelligence as such, they cannot remain unaffected by their relationship to intuitions of a specific type. In the case of human thinking they stand in special connexion with the pure intuitions of space and time, supposed by Kant to accompany all empirical intuition. And in virtue of this connexion they lose their abstract character and acquire a concrete significance. In their pure form—considered as the basic concepts underlying the processes of synthesis carried out by discursive consciousness as such—they are so vague as to be useless for knowledge of objects. It is only if they are schematized and considered in relation to space and time (particularly the latter) that we can show that they do determine an object and have a genuine part to play in knowledge.

Whatever the difficulty of the details of this argument (which can scarcely be considered here), its consequences should be tolerably clear. We began by thinking that the categories, because of their non-empirical origin and because they relate to objects in general, might enable us to describe the essential structure of the world, i.e. to discover the real which lies beyond sensible appearances. The categories would here be used in a metaphysical way, being supposed, in Kantian terminology, to be valid of 'things in general'. But further consideration shows the suggestion to be doubly unjustified. In the first place the categories are not concepts of 'things or relations' but of processes of synthesis; and a synthesis is not intelligible save so far as we consider what is combined in it. Except when something is given, synthesis just does not take place. But a discursive intelligence is such that it can only synthetize a manifold given from without, i.e. by sensibility. And secondly, when we scrutinize the content of the categories closely we see that they derive it not just from standing in relation to the given but from standing in relation to the particular sort of data available for human cognition, viz. spatio-temporal data. The categories, in other words, only acquire a determinate content when considered as they operate in human experience, as expressing the principles in accordance with which we think a common world of objects *in one space and one time*. In their pure (unschematized) form they cannot be characterized with any precision.[1]

It follows from all this that any rationalist hope that the categories might be used for metaphysical purposes, in the Aristotelian sense of that term, must be vain. Pure concepts of the understanding cannot, as was argued in the *Dissertation*, take us beyond sensible experience altogether: they should rather be regarded as giving us insight into the necessary form of things sensible. Of course, if anyone chooses to call that insight metaphysical Kant has no quarrel with him; indeed he actively supports the suggestion. But it should be quite clear that this 'metaphysic of experience', as it has been called by Professor Paton, is very different from the old metaphysics of the supersensible. Again, we should recognize plainly that it is one thing to know the categories and another to know the empirical concepts which fall under them. As we have seen in earlier sections, there can be no inference from one to the other; if the categories prescribe the general form of experience, it is to sensation and empirical thinking that we must go for its particular nature. The position of the categories in the structure of human knowledge is, in fact, a quite special one; they are concepts, but concepts of a very peculiar kind. And indeed it would seem to be over this point that their whole difficulty for philosophers has consisted.

§ 8. To bring this statement of the Kantian theory to a close it will be useful to express Kant's conclusions in terms not of concepts but of judgements. This should enable us to elucidate a distinction to which we have appealed more than once in earlier chapters—that between prescriptive and factual truths.

We may begin by taking up a point made in Chapter II. It was argued there that one way of putting the issue between rationalism and empiricism was to use Leibniz's terms and ask whether there are truths of fact *and* truths of reason, and whether either type is reducible to the other. Empiricists, as we saw, tended to deny the existence of truths of reason altogether; rationalists to

[1] Despite this Kant holds that the unschematized categories can be used to *think* non-sensible objects, though not to know them: cf. *Critique of Pure Reason*, B 166 n. This is a puzzling doctrine connected with his moral theology, but, like the latter, never sufficiently worked out.

hold that they were the model of all knowledge, and that truths of fact could be shown in principle to follow from them. It is over the arguments with which these diverse views have been supported that the main controversies of theory of knowledge have turned.

What is Kant's answer to these crucial questions? It is clear enough that he agrees with neither the empiricist nor the rationalist contentions. For first, he holds, with Leibniz, that over and above truths of fact we can distinguish truths of reason; but he refuses to follow the Leibnizians in seeing in these the type of all knowledge. Truths of fact are determined by truths of reason, but by no stretch of the imagination or extension of the normal powers of the understanding could they be elevated to the rank of the latter.[1] But, on the other hand, it is equally impossible to maintain, as many empiricists have done, that all truths of reason can be reduced to truths of fact (e.g. by showing that they are empirical generalizations). For developed experience, as we have seen, involves principles which cannot conceivably be derived from sensation in the strict sense of that term.

Kant's real contribution to the problem was a new conception of the nature of truths of reason, which in turn revolutionized his view of truths of fact.

Truths of fact, as conceived by empiricists and rationalists alike, contained factual knowledge about the world based on sense-experience; truths of reason were simply bigger and better truths of fact. The whole controversy between the two schools turned on whether there were such truths. What is perhaps most remarkable about the whole thing is the vagueness of the dividing line between the two. Thus, if we turn to Baumgarten's *Metaphysica* (1739) we learn that psychology, for instance, has both a rational and an empirical part, the former consisting of truths of reason, the latter of truths of fact. Reason, it appears, has insight into the nature of the soul, but only of a limited kind; after enunciating certain propositions it must fall back on experience. Similarly with cosmology: the general nature of the world can be stated in the necessary truths of metaphysics, but for the rest we must turn to empirical sciences like physics. Theology is a little different, since there it is not reason and experience which contend for the spoils, but reason and revelation. But the principle involved is the same: there are some truths which reason can establish, others that we must accept on other than rational grounds.

[1] This is why Kant could never have agreed with Hegel: see above, Chapter IV, § 4.

To clear up this muddle it was necessary for Kant (*a*) to distinguish analytic from synthetic judgements, and (*b*) to recognize that there is a fundamental difference in kind between synthetic *a priori* and synthetic *a posteriori* judgements. We can put this difference most conveniently (though it is language which Kant himself does not use) by saying that the former are expressible in prescriptive, the latter in factual judgements.

We may explain this distinction somewhat crudely as follows. A factual judgement states a fact known in some kind of experience, and all empirical judgements are factual. Thus many of the propositions of everyday discourse and all the propositions which make up the raw material of the empirical sciences and history, together with the scientific laws established by induction and the considered judgements of the historian, are factual. In contrast, prescriptive judgements say nothing about particular matters of fact, but express certain general laws with which all matters of fact must comply. To adopt Kant's distinction, they concern themselves not with the matter of knowledge but with its form. Because prescriptive judgements (*a*) have nothing to do with particular facts, and (*b*) express conditions which all matters of fact *must* fulfil, they are all *a priori*. Among prescriptive judgements seem to be (1) the absolute presuppositions of knowledge of which we have already spoken, and (2) the laws of logic. We may add that Kant himself would have regarded mathematical judgements as at least quasi-prescriptive,[1] though it is by no means certain that we can follow him in this course.[2]

Two general remarks must be made on this distinction before we go on to show its bearing on our present problems. First, though all empirical judgements are factual, there is no reason in principle why all factual judgements should be empirical, in the sense of based on *sense*-experience. For it might be the case that we had some other primary source of information than the senses (e.g. intellectual or mystical intuition), and if we thus had insight into a non-sensible world we could discover factual truths about it. But in fact all our information seems to come from the senses, and thus the proposition 'all empirical judgements are factual' can

[1] In Kant mathematical knowledge depends on our awareness of the necessary nature of space and time, which we know by pure (sensible) intuition, and thus appears to be a queer sort of factual knowledge. But since he holds that whatever is true of space and time as such must apply to whatever falls within space and time (i.e. must be true of the world of experience), it turns out to be prescriptive after all.

[2] See above, Chapter V, § 4.

be converted *simpliciter*. Secondly, there clearly is a division within the class of prescriptive judgements, some applying to all types of object, others only to objects of a particular kind. Thus the laws of logic apply to all objects of discursive consciousness whatever, while those of Euclidean geometry (if we accept Kant's view of that science) apply only to things in perceptual space. We can distinguish the two classes by calling them generally and specially prescriptive.

Now how does all this illuminate the controversy about truths of fact and truths of reason? The answer is that it brings out the real distinction between the two types of truth. There are genuine truths of reason over and above truths of fact; but they are not just bigger and better versions of the latter. They are not propositions like 'there is a God' which are supposed to rest not on normal experience but on supersensible insight. They consist rather of the principles which determine the basic structure of fact. These principles are of varying kinds, some being generally, others specially, prescriptive; but in every case it is clear that to understand their meaning we must consider that to which they prescribe. Thus truths of reason cannot in themselves afford a separate source of knowledge or form the basis of a metaphysics of the supersensible. Nor again can there be any question of a transition from truths of reason to truths of fact, or *vice versa*. All factual judgements imply prescriptive judgements (and here the traditional account of them must be revised); but it is obviously absurd to suppose that they could either be deduced from the latter or be elevated to their status. For there is all the difference in the world between a fact and its presuppositions; and no amount of philosophical argument can break that distinction down.

Perhaps the most puzzling problem about the whole distinction is that of the sense in which prescriptive judgements are true (or, for that matter, are judgements). All judgements are, by definition, true or false, and there is no difficulty in seeing how this applies to factual judgements. But prescriptive judgements are another matter. Quite obviously, no fact of experience can validate them, since they themselves determine the structure of fact; and equally they cannot, as synthetic, claim any intuitive validity or evidence in themselves. Yet there must be some sense in which they are valid, since alternative sets of them appear to be possible. Can we show that one among these possible sets has the primacy, as Kant thought he could, by connecting it with the inner nature of reason? Or must we hold, as others have suggested, that convenience alone dictates what presuppositions we choose, and that philosophy can only discover what prescriptive judgements have been made, not what should have been? For some discussion of these questions I must refer the reader to Chapter VIII.

VII

SUBSTANCE, CAUSE, AND THINGHOOD

§ 1. THE case for the functioning in experience of *a priori* concepts or categories is now complete in outline; but before we proceed it will be as well to indicate explicitly the limitations within which it has been presented. In the first place we must disclaim any intention of having been primarily concerned to expound the doctrines of Kant. Kant's theory of *a priori* thinking as constitutive of objects occurs in a context of particular assumptions and distinctions; and no honest summary of it, however brief, could fail to lay due stress on the most important of these. Yet in the previous chapter our procedure has been, to say the least, highly selective. Thus, to take an example which will occur to anyone familiar with the *Critique of Pure Reason*, we have said little or nothing of the unity of apperception, though that is central in Kant's own exposition. Kant argues that a process of synthesis must be presupposed in experience if the empirical fact of self-consciousness is to be explained; for a discursive intelligence can be aware of its own unity only in so far as it is active. This argument we have passed over in silence, partly because the whole subject of the unity of apperception is to be discussed later,[1] partly because it seemed important in the present context to stress not so much the fact of self-consciousness as the identity of the function by which different minds constitute a common world. Again, though we were compelled, in explaining the details of Kant's doctrine, to say something of his peculiar conception of space and time as *a priori* intuitions, we made no attempt to analyse and criticize this conception. And, once more, we did not so much as mention the important distinction Kant drew within the sphere of *a priori* concepts between categories of the understanding and ideas of reason. Over and above the categories, which are properly described as concepts of an object in general, there are, Kant thinks, other *a priori* notions which function, though in an indirect fashion, in experience; and these he calls ideas. But this refinement we have passed over altogether.

What justification, if any, can we offer for these glaring omissions? The only tolerable answer is to claim that our purpose was to expound not so much *the* Kantian as *a* Kantian theory. We

[1] See Chapter IX, § 3 below.

have aimed, in other words, at stating what seem to be the essentials of Kant's doctrines rather than at presenting them in the precise way and with the precise emphases that their author laid on them. For that, after all, we can go to the *Critique of Pure Reason*. And while it cannot be denied that selection of the kind followed here involves some distortion of an author's meaning, the procedure should not be regarded as philosophically objectionable. For it is surely possible to take a view and consider it on its own merits, without regard to the special context in which it was originally put forward. To deny that would seem equivalent to denying that we can ever separate the important from the unimportant in a piece of philosophical thinking. But if we could not make such a separation, with what purpose should we study the history of philosophy?

I can see no reason in principle why the main argument of the last chapter, that *a priori* must accompany empirical thinking if it is to lead to knowledge of objects, should not be thought true and valuable, even if we disagree with Kant's view of the nature of space and time, or again with his conception of the unity of apperception. Though closely bound up with those doctrines, it neither entails nor is entailed by them. It is based on independent arguments and, as such, entitled to independent consideration. Nor again are we justified in rejecting it because we cannot accept the special application Kant himself makes of it. We may look on Kant's attempted derivation of his list of categories from a table of judgement forms supposed to be established by formal logic as nothing more than a bad conjuring trick; we may regard the results of that operation as either hopelessly incomplete (as Hegel did) or demonstrably erroneous (e.g. in its inclusion of modal categories): but none of this affects the main principle of the Kantian position. Everything Kant says about particular categories may be wrong, and yet his general argument for categorial thinking may be completely acceptable.

Nevertheless, it must be confessed that to confine ourselves, as we have done so far, to stating the theory in purely general terms is scarcely satisfactory. At the very least we want to test it by examples: to see what sort of a thing is meant by a category and how it could relate to empirical concepts. Only if we do that shall we be able to bring the theory into relation to the speculations of other philosophers and so realize its full implications. I therefore propose in this chapter to take one or two of the most widely accepted Kantian categories and explore their general nature. But I must warn the reader that once again my main aim is not to expound Kant in detail so much as to discover, if I can, the independent value of his contribution to the problem. I shall therefore have as much to say about other philosophers as about Kant himself.

Perhaps I should mention first that, over and above the 'pure' intuitions of space and time, Kant recognized twelve categories and three ideas of reason. With the ideas of reason we are not concerned at present: they raise special problems of their own. The twelve categories fall into four groups, called by Kant Quantity, Quality, Relation, and Modality. The categories of Quantity, broadly speaking, explain the possibility of applied mathematics by assuring us that whatever falls within experience will have extensive quantity. The categories of Quality are, in Kant's opinion, the basis of our belief that whatever qualities we meet with in experience will be determinate in the sense that they can be arranged on a scale varying from 0 to 1. This, if justified, would explain why we think qualitative differences can be treated in quantitative terms. The categories of Modality are said by Kant himself not to determine the object of knowledge but 'merely to express its relation to the faculty of cognition'.[1] Their presence in a list of concepts of an object in general is hence somewhat surprising. But it is to the categories of Relation, Substance, Cause, and Reciprocity that we must turn for what is obviously the most important part of the Kantian theory. Not only did Kant himself pay very great attention to these particular concepts; he was treating, under the head of Relation, of ideas which had played a leading role in European speculation from the Greeks onwards. I therefore propose to devote the next section to substance, and the one after that to causation.

§ 2. The conception of substance is both one of the oldest and one of the most puzzling in European philosophy. Perhaps the chief source of its difficulty is that it appears to be affected by a radical ambiguity. At different times in the history of philosophy it has been used to cover what appear to be the quite separate notions of (1) that which is the true subject of predicates, whatever it is that has qualities and relations and is not reducible to them, and (2) that which persists through change, the hard core

[1] *Critique of Pure Reason*, B 266 = A 219.

of things as opposed to their surface show. In the first of these meanings substance is thought of as the independently real (that which has reality in its own right), in the second as the ultimate stuff out of which what we know in everyday experience is formed.

The two meanings can be illustrated in a sufficiently striking manner from the history of Greek philosophy. We all know that philosophy began in Ionia when Thales said that everything was water. His successors, who replied that on the contrary it was air, or fire, or 'the boundless', differed from him in the answers to their questions, but not in their presuppositions. All these early Greek thinkers were assuming that the different objects to be met with in experience could be shown to be in some way made up of a single stuff, a permanent which underlay change. They were agreed in thinking that there must be a primary substance, and differed only in what they took that substance to be. They conceived their inquiry, in the main, as physical not metaphysical: in asking 'what is substance?' they were asking what was the stuff of things in the natural world. And indeed they thought that the answer would be found in some element with which we were familiar in everyday life, such as air or fire or water.

We find a very different state of affairs if we turn from the pre-Socratics to the writings of Aristotle. Substance as a technical term in philosophy was invented by Aristotle, though the idea, as he recognized, was far from new.[1] But the meaning he attached to the term was very different from that of the early Ionians. Substance, for Aristotle, was the independently real, and substantial contrasted with accidental being. Thus Socrates was a substance because he was a subject of predicates and not himself a predicate, while whiteness was an attribute predicable of substances and having no independent being in itself. The whole universe could be described as a collection of interrelated substances. But Aristotle thought that more could be said of substance than that it was the subject of predicates. Socrates, as an individual subject, was primary substance (*πρώτη οὐσία*); but substance had also a secondary meaning. For we could distinguish among the characteristics of any given subject some which were substantial and belonged to its essence, and others which were clearly accidental and non-essential (e.g. we could distinguish Socrates's

[1] He speaks in one place of 'the ancient problem of being, now and always with us' (*Met.* 1028b 2). The problem of being (τὸ ὄν) was in fact identical with that of substance (*οὐσία*), as Aristotle himself pointed out.

humanity from his being the husband of Xanthippe). The essential or substantial characters of a thing constituted its nature or form, and it was in the light of them that the thing as a whole was to be understood. In view of the importance of the antithesis of matter and form in Aristotelian metaphysics the significance of this doctrine is not likely to be underrated.

Now though we have described these two conceptions of substance as separate, they do nevertheless have a tendency to coalesce. We can see this if we turn to the philosophy of Leibniz. At the beginning of the *Monadology*, in which he sets out the main heads of his mature views, Leibniz makes it quite clear that he regards his monads as the ultimate stuff of the universe. The monad, we read in the opening paragraph, 'is nothing but a simple substance which enters into compounds; *simple*, that is to say, without parts'. He goes on: 'And there must be simple substances, because there are compounds; for the compound is nothing but a collection or *aggregatum* of simples. Now where there are no parts, there neither extension, nor shape, nor divisibility is possible. And these monads are the true atoms of nature and, in a word, the elements of things.'[1] Here we find Leibniz using the notion of substance as ultimate stuff. But it is also obvious that in describing the monad as a simple substance containing the source of its changes in itself,[2] Leibniz is making use of the other conception of substance as the ultimate subject of predicates. And, indeed, one of the most striking suggestions of modern Leibnizian scholarship has been that there is a close connexion between Leibniz's conception of the monad and his logical view that in every true proposition the predicate is contained in the subject.[3]

What justified Leibniz in thus combining the two senses of substance we have distinguished? The answer is to be found in the fact that he regarded the problem of substance as in all its aspects a *metaphysical* problem. There was no question of his looking, like the pre-Socratics, for some *physical* substance out of which all familiar things came to be, for he regarded the physical world itself as metaphysically unreal. The physical world, in his view, had no reality in itself but was merely a confused representation of something whose true nature could be apprehended by pure

[1] Translated by Mary Morris (*The Philosophical Writings of Leibniz*, Everyman's Library, p. 3).

[2] *Monadology*, §§ 11 ff.

[3] See B. Russell, *Philosophy of Leibniz*; L. Couturat, *La Logique de Leibniz*.

intellect alone. Hence the monad was not a sensible but an intelligible entity: not a microscopic bit of matter, like the atoms of classical physics, but a being of the nature of spirit. Thus conceived, the monad could clearly also be viewed as the ultimate subject of predicates and endowed with all the peculiar characteristics which Leibniz assigned to it.

It is against the background of this tendency to think of substance in a purely metaphysical way (which Leibniz shared with the Cartesians and Spinoza) that we must approach empiricist discussions of the concept. Locke, who wrote before Leibniz himself but was familiar with the Scholastic tradition which Leibniz continued, did not reject substance altogether. He pointed out, however, that our idea of substance in general was 'obscure and relative', containing in fact nothing more than the notion of an unknown support of accidents. 'If anyone will examine himself concerning his notion of pure substance in general, he will find he has no other idea of it at all, but only a supposition of he knows not what support of such qualities which are capable of producing simple ideas in us; which qualities are commonly called "accidents".'[1] Substance was the substratum in which simple ideas subsisted; but we could hope for no direct knowledge of it. And ideas of particular substances were collections of simple ideas 'by experience and observation of men's senses taken notice of to exist together', taken along with this 'confused' notion of a substratum in which they subsisted.[2] All this was in accord with Locke's general rejection of Aristotelianism and with his view that human beings must rest content with knowledge of the nominal essences of things: with the real essence (i.e., with the substantial nature) of mind and body alike they could not hope to be acquainted.[3]

Locke thus hoped to save the conception of substance by playing down its metaphysical features and emphasizing its connexion with the familiar things of everyday experience. But Hume would have none of this compromise. Substance for him was an 'unintelligible chimaera', and he was prepared to apply the description to all accounts of the concept. It is true, he argued, that we do, as Locke suggested, very easily fall into thinking that the different qualities which go together to constitute a thing inhere in something which lies beyond them, which something is then supposed

[1] *Essay*, Bk. II, chap. xxiii, § 2. [2] Ibid. 3.
[3] See ibid. 5, with ibid. Bk. III, chap. iii, §§ 15–18.

to persist independently of our perceptions; but our action in so doing cannot be justified by any rational argument. The supposition that our perceptions are united by belonging to a substance is a fiction of the imagination, and the whole distinction of substance and accident belongs not to science but to superstition. For the idea of substance, whether conceived as ultimate stuff or as ultimate subject, is one to which we can find no corresponding impressions; and in default of such impressions we must pronounce it wholly without meaning.[1]

Philosophy here seemed to have reached a complete *impasse*, with the rationalist school, following Leibniz, thinking of substance as a key concept in the study of the universe, whilst Hume rejected it unhesitatingly on empiricist grounds. It remained for Kant, here as elsewhere, to find a way out. Kant agreed with Hume in his criticism of substance as a metaphysical idea: if by substance we understood something which lay altogether beyond the bounds of possible sense-experience, then our use of the concept could not be justified. But he refused to accept Hume's inference that substance is therefore an idea belonging not to science but to superstition. On the contrary, he thought it could be shown to play an important, if rather a strange, part in experience itself: we must, in his view, think of the objects of experience as determinations or states of an underlying permanent substance. We could not say in advance of experience *what* permanent we should find; but look for *some* permanent we must, for the principle of substance was one of those principles by which we built up the objective world.

In all this, as the reader will observe, Kant was returning to the point of view of the pre-Socratics.[2] Retaining the traditional notion of substance as an *a priori* idea, he nevertheless strove to find a use for it not in the metaphysical but in the physical sphere: to invoke it in the explanation of (empirical) change. Substance applied in this way (what Kant called *substantia phaenomenon*) became identical with the conception of the *permanent*, i.e. of the ultimate stuff of the physical universe which persists through change. And Kant thought he could show not only that we do

[1] For Hume's views on substance see *Treatise*, Bk. I, part iv, sections 3 and 5.

[2] Nevertheless Kant held to the alternative conception of substance as the ultimate subject of predicates, and maintained that this was the content of the pure category which lay behind the schematized category of substance as the permanent persisting through change. But it is not clear how he would have justified this belief if seriously challenged.

commonly suppose that behind the changing phenomena of perceptual experience there is something permanent, but further that we must make that supposition. For only if we presuppose something permanent in the physical world, he argued, can we find anything to represent an all-important characteristic of time: its abiding quality. Time itself cannot be perceived, yet all human experience is temporal. If we are to have awareness of objective time-relations we must measure temporal changes against a permanent background; and to be sure that this is possible we must read the concept of substance into experience.[1]

The argument is not wholly convincing, for it is not clear how the notion that there is something permanent in the physical world helps us to measure the flow of time if the permanent cannot be itself observed.[2] Nor again is the transition from the abiding quality of time to the permanent which 'represents' it altogether lucid: one feels here that more than one metaphor needs to be explained. Yet even if the formal argument fails, the theory can claim strong empirical confirmation from the history of science. The concept of substance, understood in the way Kant suggests, does appear to have played a most important part in scientific thinking from the Greeks onwards. It is true, of course, that Kant's own views were coloured to an important extent by the physics of his own day: he thought the category of substance exemplified in the matter of which scientists then talked. But it is wrong to suppose that the whole theory is refuted if we give up the matter of classical physics. For Kant was not arguing that we must find any particular sort of permanent in experience, only that we must look for some permanent. And he would not have been unduly distressed if told that the ultimate stuff of the universe was not to be thought of as solid matter at all, but rather as electrical charges (or in whatever way contemporary physics regards it). For so long as the notion of an ultimate stuff is appealed to the essentials of the Kantian category remain.[3]

It is true, of course, that some philosophers say that science is

[1] For the argument of this paragraph compare *Critique of Pure Reason*, First Analogy of Experience.

[2] According to Kant, what we observe are changing states of the underlying substance. In assessing his argument we must remember that he denied any reality to time except as a form of experience.

[3] Kant's own conception of matter, which is perhaps not altogether orthodox by the standards of classical physics, is set out in his *Metaphysical First Foundations of Natural Science*. It is summarized in Professor Paton's *Kant's Metaphysic of Experience*, ii. 209 ff.

now abandoning (or has abandoned) not only the matter of classical physics but the notion of the permanent itself. Professor Collingwood, for instance, informs us on the authority of Whitehead that physics no longer draws a distinction between the body to which events happen and the events themselves. 'Nature is not body as distinct from event; it is body, no doubt, but body itself is only a complex of events; and, since events take time, it takes time for nature to exist.'[1] But it is not clear to me how far this involves, as Collingwood says it does, a 'flat contradiction' of Kant's principle of substance. For even if Nature is reduced to a stream of events (a proposition which Kant himself might in a certain sense have accepted),[2] it may still be necessary to regard those events *as if* they were connected as the states of something itself not an event; for, as Kant pointed out, change itself presupposes the notion of the permanent. But if this is the case the category of substance will have its place in scientific thinking after all.

The upshot of Kant's discussion of substance is, then, a vindication of the objective validity of the concept, but only if we interpret it in reference to sense-experience. This involves a return to the original notion of substance as ultimate stuff maintained by the early Greek philosophers, and an abandonment (or virtual abandonment) of all attempts to use the concept in a more metaphysical way. It is true that Kant himself believed that to grant the existence of substance was to grant that of substances, and thought of such substances as possessing a certain unity in themselves, entitling them to be regarded as true subjects of predicates. But here he seems, like Locke, to have been confusing the concept of substance with that of thinghood, and we must postpone further consideration of his views on the matter to § 4.

§ 3. I propose now to say something on the well-worn topic of causality. Every tyro in philosophy knows that Kant made an important contribution to the elucidation of this problem, and most of them believe that it consisted of producing a refutation of Hume. But this, to say the least, is a highly misleading judgement. The agreement of Kant and Hume over causality is at least

[1] *An Essay on Metaphysics*, p. 267.

[2] *Natura materialiter spectata* is, for Kant, a complex of representations; it is to *natura formaliter spectata* that the principle of substance applies. On the general principles of his theory of knowledge, Kant can scarcely assert the existence of any permanent other than a permanent possibility of sensation.

as striking as their differences. For Hume, despite his radically empiricist approach, does not deny that the causal principle is valid throughout the sphere of sense-experience;[1] while Kant, for all his rationalist upbringing, is just as anxious as Hume to argue that the necessity of the causal relation cannot be logical. Kant, it is true, bases causality on the understanding, while Hume grounds it in the imagination; but, as we shall see in the next chapter, the distinction between these two faculties is perhaps not so sharp as has sometimes been thought.

The true importance of the Kantian view can be brought out if we contrast it (*a*) with that of rationalist writers like Leibniz, and (*b*) with that of simple empiricists like John Stuart Mill. But we should remember that in each case what is primarily in question is the validity of the general law of causality itself rather than that of a particular analysis of the causal relationship. Indeed the nature of the causal relation is a subject which Kant nowhere discusses at length; for though he tells us that cause and effect are connected as what necessarily precedes with what necessarily follows, he does not say whether this is the sole tie between them. He is concerned to vindicate causality in its minimum meaning, and accordingly many of the problems connected with causation are not relevant to our present discussion.

Leibniz, if Mr. Russell is right,[2] held that the general law of causality is itself a truth of reason. On this view the causal principle applies, and applies necessarily, to all possible worlds; for if a truth is analytic, as truths of reason are, everything we conceive must be in accordance with it. The concept of cause is thus an *a priori* concept, valid, in Kantian language, of things in general, and capable therefore of a metaphysical as well as an empirical use. Although this notion of causation was not explicitly affirmed by other rationalists, it seems to have been widely accepted by them. Indeed, the principle that whatever exists must have a cause seems to have been generally assumed by philosophers before the time of Hume as valid without restriction of object.[3] Empiricists like Locke and materialists like Hobbes

[1] This comes out very strongly in his essay on miracles (in the *Enquiry*).

[2] See *The Philosophy of Leibniz*, chap. iii. Mr. Russell points out that Leibniz thought that particular causal connexions were synthetic, not analytic.

[3] Strictly the principle commonly accepted was that whatever *begins to* exist must have a cause: compare the quotation from Hume in the next paragraph. The point of the qualification was to preserve the notion of God as an uncaused First Cause.

made no more bones about it than rationalists like Spinoza. The principle was widely used in the argument for God's existence *a contingentia mundi* (an argument which goes back to Aristotle), as well as in discussions of the reality of the external world.

Yet, as Hume showed in one of his most devastating chapters,[1] we really have no warrant for so using it. The maxim that 'whatever begins to exist, must have a cause of existence', though general in philosophy, is by no means intuitively certain. If it were, the relation between cause and effect would have to fall under one of the four relations of resemblance, proportion in quantity and number, degrees in quality and contrariety which alone, in Hume's view, give rise to knowledge strictly so called; and it plainly does not. Nor can we be impressed by the various attempts made to demonstrate the validity of the causal principle, such as Locke's argument that anything produced without a cause must be produced by nothing, or Clarke's contention that in default of causes things must produce themselves. All such attempts, as Hume says, are 'founded on the same fallacy, and are derived from the same turn of thought. 'Tis sufficient only to observe, that when we exclude all causes we really do exclude them, and neither suppose nothing nor the object itself to be the causes of the existence; and consequently can draw no argument from the absurdity of these suppositions to prove the absurdity of that exclusion.'[1]

In other words, the causal principle is neither itself a self-evident truth of reason nor derived from any such truth. It is synthetic, not analytic, and the questions of its validity and of the field of its application require careful investigation. And here we may note that the tendency to think there are no such problems arises from the all too easy confusion between the relation of cause and effect and that of ground and consequent. Ground and consequent is a logical relation, universally valid within the sphere of judgements. It is sense to ask of any judgement what reason we have for making it, i.e. what our ground for asserting it is, though the answer may not always be another judgement. But it does not follow that we can give unrestricted validity to the concept of cause, which applies not to judgements but to matters of fact. For though the relation of cause and effect bears some analogy to that of ground and consequent, it is plainly not identical

[1] *Treatise*, Bk. I, part iii, § 3.
[2] *Treatise*, p. 81, edited by Selby-Bigge.

with it, or we should be able to infer effect from cause without any reference to experience.

So much for the rationalist account of causation: what of the empiricist alternative? If the causal principle is synthetic, it is at least worth seeing whether it is not also empirical. That it is was maintained by, among others, J. S. Mill. To understand Mill's view we must say something first of his notion of the causal relation. He begins his discussion by remarking that 'when in the course of this inquiry I speak of the cause of any phenomenon, I do not mean a cause which is not itself a phenomenon; I make no research into the ultimate or ontological cause of anything.'[1] In other words, Mill is proposing to investigate causality only as it falls within experience. And he thinks there are no difficulties in finding an empirical meaning for the concept. Our experience exhibits certain uniformities of succession, in which one kind of event (or, as Mill says, phenomenon) is always followed by another; and these are causal successions. A cause just is the invariable and unconditional antecedent of a phenomenon; there is no further intrinsic connexion between them. Mill holds not only that this is obvious, but further that because we have experience of a great many causal successions we can infer that every event must have a cause. The causal principle is itself a generalization from experience, i.e. a synthetic *a posteriori* truth.

Now it is easy enough to show that this conclusion cannot possibly be justified. However much experience we have had of causal successions in the past, we have no right to expect similar successions in the future. For (to repeat a very familiar philosophical truth) no amount of empirical generalization can give rise to a truly universal proposition. Yet our attitude—or at least Mill's attitude—to the general law of causality is that it applies to all phenomena whatsoever, past, present, and future. To say that such a law is a generalization like any other is to misrepresent its logical status; it cannot be derived from experience since it is one of the principles which determine developed experience itself. Mill's argument, in fact, here and elsewhere, suffers from his undue simplicity of mind: from his desire to explain all knowledge in terms of a single principle. We see the same simplicity of mind in Mill when he is dealing with the closely connected problem of the analysis of the causal relation, where he undoubtedly exaggerates the extent to which we can *observe* uniform sequences, and

[1] *Logic*, Bk. III, chap. v, § 2.

fails to bring out the fact that discovery of causes is often a complicated operation, involving the piecing together of information, much of which is fragmentary, and from which a consistent picture by no means always emerges at first sight. Yet Mill is surely right in his approach to the problem: in saying that we must investigate causality as it falls within experience. And once we do that, we cannot avoid seeing that causality is a relation involving sequence, or at least order,[1] in time, and therefore applicable only to such objects as themselves fall within time. To apply it to the timeless objects of traditional metaphysics, and thus give it an unrestricted use, is accordingly impossible.

If we turn now to Kant's discussion of causality in the Second Analogy and elsewhere in the *Critique of Pure Reason* we should have no difficulty in understanding his position. Kant has two main points to make: that cause and effect is, despite the empiricists, an *a priori* concept, a category prescribed to experience rather than derived from it, and yet that it cannot, as the rationalists supposed, be used to determine things in general. And he supports the first of these contentions by an argument which, if admitted, leads straight to the second. Cause and effect is a category presupposed in developed experience, he says, because without it we should be unable to distinguish objective from subjective time sequences. We find in immediate experience that the order in which we experience things is not necessarily the order in which they really happen. If I am looking at a large object—the view from a mountain top, for instance—I cannot apprehend it all at once but am compelled to look first at one part and then at another. But the order in which I apprehend the different parts is quite arbitrary so far as the object is concerned, for they all, I believe, exist simultaneously. In other cases, however, the order of my apprehending is fixed. Suppose that I am watching a football match and see the centre-forward shoot the ball into the goal: I cannot first see the ball in the net and then watch the centre-forward shoot. How then are we to distinguish subjective from objective successions? Kant answers that we can only do it if we hold that the objectively successive is that which follows necessarily according to a rule. We must think that there are necessary precedences and successions in the object, and experience of the

[1] It was pointed out by Kant that though it is not true that all causal sequences involve a lapse of time between cause and effect, the temporal order of the two is nevertheless fixed: *Critique of Pure Reason*, B 248 = A 203.

objective is built up when we establish such sequences. But this, in Kant's view, is equivalent to saying that we must interpret our immediate experience in accordance with the general law of causality, for the relation of cause and effect in human experience, whatever else it is, at least includes a relation of necessary precedence and succession.

Kant's argument for the objectivity of causality here follows the general lines of his theory of objects, and should therefore be intelligible in the light of the preceding chapter. The objective, according to him, is what we necessarily think, and objective causal successions are distinguished from other successions by following according to a necessary rule. But this should not be misunderstood. Kant is emphatically not saying that some kind of inner necessity binds cause to effect, still less that we can know in advance of experience what causes what. All we can know in advance of experience is that every event has some cause; what that cause is we must discover by the recognized empirical methods. The necessity which marks the causal relation is accordingly derived wholly from the necessity of the general principle of causality itself. Granted the cause, we believe that the effect will, *ceteris paribus*, follow. But the ground of our belief is not insight into the causal relation; it is a general conviction that all developed experience is governed by causal law.

The all-important conclusion that the relation of causation holds only within the sphere of the sensible (a conclusion in which Kant had been anticipated by Hume)[1] follows simply from this conception of causation. We apply the category of cause and effect to distinguish objective from subjective time sequences; and except in relation to time we cannot give it a determinate content. But time, in Kant's view, has no independent existence: it is only a form of human sensibility, a way in which we look at things. And even those who disagree with this account of the ontological status of time can scarcely deny Kant's main conclusion. For it is surely impossible, on any theory, to separate time from sensible experience, and to assert that temporal relations characterize intelligible entities such as the traditional metaphysicians postulated. Metaphysicians themselves assure us that they make no such assertion, and mystics too tell us that the objects (or Object) they claim to experience are out of and beyond time altogether. But if this is so, there can be no transition by means of the causal principle

[1] *Treatise*, p. 212, edited Selby-Bigge.

from the sphere of the sensible to that of the supersensible. To make such a transition legitimate we should have to find an interpretation of the causal principle which made no reference to time whatsoever; but how we are to do that is a question which has yet to be answered.[1]

In this connexion it is perhaps worth making a rather obvious point. We may be told that Kant's difficulties with causation arise from his acceptance of Hume's view that causation is simply regular sequence. Such an account, we are assured, does less than justice to the theory we all entertain that a cause in some way produces its effect, and so must be abandoned in favour of an analysis in terms of activity. Now it might be replied to this criticism that, as we have said before, Kant is characterizing causality in its minimum meaning only, and that some of his statements lead one to suppose that he himself held the activity view. But quite apart from the truth of this contention, we must insist that merely to accept an account of the causal relation in terms of activity will not affect Kant's conclusions about the scope of the general principle of causality, unless we can dissociate causality from temporal sequence altogether. But whether we can do that without reviving the deservedly obsolete theory that the relation of cause and effect is just that of ground and consequent seems to me highly doubtful.

Kant's theory of causality has indeed been subjected to a violent attack by a distinguished modern philosopher on the very ground that it does rely on this reference to time. Professor Collingwood in his *Essay on Metaphysics* (especially pp. 285 ff.) offers an enterprising discussion of the whole subject of causation in contemporary scientific thought, in the course of which he argues (i) that the Kantian view of causality is self-contradictory, since it makes use of two quite different and incompatible notions of causation, and (ii) that physics to-day has dispensed with the notion of cause altogether, replacing it by that of law. He points out that Newton himself recognized two classes of events, caused and uncaused, instances of the latter being afforded by the 'free' and (in some cases) the 'relative' motion of a body. 'If it were possible to show either that all motion is "free", that is to say, takes place according to laws having the same logical character as the

[1] Causality through the will presents features which do not hold in the sphere of mechanical causation, and it is arguable that it offers a closer relation between cause and effect than is evident in Nature. But cause precedes effect there too.

Newtonian laws of motion; or that all motion is "relative"; then on Newton's own principles it would follow that no motion is caused. . . . This is what modern physics has done' (p. 327).

It is not clear to me just how seriously all this is to be taken, and how far physicists would subscribe to point (ii). Granted that the primary laws of physics do not state one-way connexions of cause and effect, but, as Eddington says, symmetrical relations, we have still to ask what the logical status of these laws is. Again, we can inquire where the reference to time comes in in physics. If there is no such reference, how does it explain our actual experience? If there is, can we dispense with the Kantian type of view altogether? For, as regards point (i), it is to be noted that Collingwood ignores entirely Kant's remark, referred to above (p. 152 n.), that the causal relation involves not so much a lapse as an order in time. Yet surely this is of decisive importance when the whole problem takes its rise out of the difficulty of distinguishing objective from subjective successions.

Professor Collingwood makes it quite clear (pp. 316–18) that he is not arguing for a reinstatement of the rationalist conception of the causal relation: his point is rather that cause and effect is an out-of-date category. In his own terminology, the causal principle used to be an absolute presupposition of experience, but no longer is. We shall have to discuss the problems raised by this type of view in the next chapter. In the meantime, I shall close this section with a very brief reference to another development which has cast doubt on the Kantian conception of causality, a development in modern physics. Kant held that the general law of causality has universal application throughout the physical world: that every event has a cause on which it necessarily follows. But physicists tell us that even if this is true of the world of macroscopic objects, it does not hold among sub-atomic phenomena. There we cannot describe the facts without invoking the notion of what Sir Arthur Eddington called 'objective probability',[1] a real indeterminacy in events. The laws governing sub-atomic phenomena are not causal but statistical; they state probabilities only, not necessary connexions. And as it seems possible to extend this account, with due alterations, to the sphere of macroscopic phenomena also, it has been suggested that the category of cause should now give way to that of probability. But it is surely a little premature to take this step. The notion of objective probability is an

[1] *New Pathways in Science*, chap. vi.

excessively odd one, and it may be that physicists themselves have not said the last word about it. Nor is it clear that probability itself can be understood if all reference to causation is suppressed. Causality as a category may indeed be doomed to destruction, but we had better be quite sure of its death before we appoint a successor.

§ 4. Besides substance and cause Kant thinks there is a third category falling under the general head of Relation, namely, Reciprocity (*Wechselwirkung*). We need the idea of reciprocity if we are to think of the physical world as not merely governed throughout by causal law, but as consisting of things in causal interaction. As with causality, Kant begins from a question arising out of ordinary perception. We find that we are able to view certain things in an order which is completely indifferent: e.g., we can look first at the fire and then at the street outside, or first at the street and then at the fire (I am assuming a situation in which we cannot see them both at once). Where such arbitrariness in the order of our perceiving is met with, we say that the objects perceived coexist. But if we are to be sure that we can always pass from the perception of one object to that of another coexistent with it (provided that the conditions remain unchanged), we must, says Kant, hold that each is in some way responsible for the present state of the other, i.e. we must hold that the objects themselves are in causal interaction. But this means, on a theory like Kant's, that we must combine or, if we like, interpret the given in accordance with a special principle, that based on the category of reciprocity. The category of reciprocity is needed to explain objective coexistence, just as that of causality is to explain objective succession.[1]

Here again Kant has taken a traditional metaphysical idea, though this time not a particularly obvious one, and interpreted it as valid in reference to experience. The notion of a community (*Gemeinschaft*) of substances, each of which determines the states of the rest and is in turn determined by them, might well be applied metaphysically, though in fact the traditional metaphysicians mostly defined substance in a way which excluded the interaction of one substance with another. Thus the Cartesians and Leibniz, who thought that substance was that which is independently real, argued that no substance could directly affect another,

[1] See *Critique of Pure Reason*, Third Analogy.

and so were compelled to have recourse to Occasionalism and the Pre-established Harmony respectively to explain the obvious facts of psycho-physical interaction. But there were other metaphysicians (Spinoza is the most obvious instance) who were prepared to use the principle of reciprocity as an argument against both the two-substance theory of Descartes and pluralistic theories like that of Leibniz, and who held instead that we must accept the existence of only one substance, 'God or Nature', the different parts or modes of which reciprocally determined each other. And this form of monism, though robbed by its theological implications of any immediate influence on philosophical thought, was to be reproduced in some important respects in the Absolute Idealism of Hegel and his successors.

Now Kant has no more use for this kind of speculation than Hume. Whether substances in the metaphysical sense interact or are solely responsible for their own changes, whether the universe is ultimately one or many: these are questions which the human mind has no means of answering. Interaction, like substance and cause, can only be a useful idea if we can give it an empirical meaning. This does not, of course, imply that we must show it to be an empirical concept: it may still remain, as the rationalists had said, *a priori*. But it must no longer be thought valid of 'things in general' but only of 'objects in general', i.e. of objects of experience: it must be exhibited as one of the concepts defining the objective as such. And this, as we have seen, is what the argument of the Third Analogy professes to do.

Of more interest, perhaps, than the category of reciprocity itself is the idea of thinghood which it seems to imply. We saw earlier how Kant thought that to prove that a permanent substance underlies change is in itself to grant the existence of substances in the plural. His reason for this is simple. Matter, which he identifies with phenomenal substance, fills space, and space is infinitely divisible. Matter itself is divisible *ad indefinitum*, and every part of it is as well entitled to be called substance as the whole. But when we speak of the reciprocal causality of substances, as in the principle of interaction, we are surely thinking of substances in a different sense from this. If I am not mistaken, we are thinking of something like the things of common sense, which are held to be in some sense unitary and persistent through time (to be, in Mr. W. E. Johnson's word,[1] 'continuants'), though

[1] Compare his *Logic*, Vol. III, chap. vii.

not to be permanent in the sense of everlasting. And this notion of thinghood, as Hume in effect showed in his discussion of it in the *Treatise*,[1] is itself categorial, since it most certainly cannot be derived from immediate experience. We cannot know by experience that things persist when we are not observing them, nor can we see the way in which their different properties are united, either at any one time, or at many different times. Yet we make constant use of the idea of thinghood in empirical thinking; and unless we are to declare it, as Hume does, a 'fiction', we have no choice but to think it a category.

It seems clear that it was of thinghood rather than substance as Kant was to understand it that Locke was thinking when he discussed substance in the *Essay*. He was interested in what it was that gave unity to the different ideas we group together as one thing. It is true that he could not find anything to account for that unity, save the 'confused' notion of a substratum in which the qualities responsible for the different ideas were supposed to inhere; and this was, in fact, as Berkeley and Hume showed, to explain *obscurum per obscurius*. But if Locke's analysis of what is involved in thinghood is unacceptable, it does not follow that the concept itself should be given up.

We may be asked why Kant himself does not discuss the category, though he seems to take it for granted in his account of reciprocity. One answer to this question would run as follows. Though Kant set out to show that the categories were involved in all experience, and based his proofs of individual categories on difficulties which arise in normal perception, he seems to have thought that the true test of any categorial idea was whether it was used by the physical sciences. He tended to equate experience as such with the experience of the scientist. Whether he was justified in this—whether in so doing he did not restrict the range of his categories unduly—are important questions which we shall have to take up later.[2] For the present, we must be content simply to record the fact, and to note that he said nothing of thinghood because physics has nothing to say of thinghood. Neither classical nor modern physics recognizes the existence of separate things corresponding to the things of common-sense thinking: chairs and tables, for the physicist, are analysable into sets of spatio-temporal events. It is true that classical physics

[1] Of Scepticism with regard to the Senses, *Treatise*, Bk. I, part iv, § 2.
[2] See Chapter X below.

assumed that these events happened in an underlying substance, namely, in particles of matter; but this makes no difference to the present issue. For even if we are compelled, as Kant held, to think of the physical world as substantial, it does not follow that we must think of it as made up of separate things.

There is, however, a second and altogether different answer to our question. It is that Kant after all *did* discuss the subject, and indeed that it is one of the things in which he was most interested. For the whole Transcendental Deduction, whose argument we have set out in general terms in Chapter VI, is an attempt to explain how we know objects; and by objects we mean the things of common sense. Nor is Kant without an account of the unity of an object. That which gives unity to the different appearances of a thing is not to be looked for in the thing itself but in the formal unity of consciousness which combines the appearances and thinks them as belonging together. Thus the guiding thread which Locke could find only in a mysterious something behind what was given to sense, and which Hume roundly declared to be fictitious, was found by Kant in the mind of the observer for whom the world of appearances itself existed.

Which of these answers is right? In a sense, they both are. For of course it is idle to deny that Kant was concerned with our consciousness of such things as chairs and tables. He most certainly was. But it is also true that while he discusses the concept of an object in general at length, he has little to say of the notion of thinghood as used in ordinary human experience. He seems to have thought that the problem of how we know objects is identical with that of how we know an objective world. But the two problems are after all separate, for it is possible, as the procedure of the scientist shows, to believe in an objective world which contains no separate *things* at all.[1]

§ 5. The intention of the above discussion of Kant's three categories of Relation has been to enable the reader to grasp more clearly the sort of thing the Kantian theory of *a priori* thinking

[1] Kant's apparent slurring over the problem of our consciousness of material objects has its parallel in Hume. In discussing causality, Hume assumes that it is between objects that the causal relation holds (e.g. one billiard ball and another). But later in the *Treatise* he rejects the whole notion of continuing objects as fictitious. He should plainly have considered the two problems together.

It is perhaps worth remarking here that only if we separate the category of substance from that of thinghood can we clear up the ambiguity in substance itself referred to on pp. 142–3 above.

is. We undertook to examine this view, after rejecting intellectual intuition in its various forms, because it appeared to offer ground for a further defence of rationalism. The intellect, it claims, though not in itself the source of any factual truths, may yet be held to produce certain concepts of its own, and on the basis of these to prescribe to experience its general form. And if this is accepted, it will be shown to have a 'real' as well as a 'logical' use.

Whether the Kantian theory can be taken as established, and in particular whether we can accept its crucial claim that the categories proceed from the intellect in the strict sense of that term, are questions which remain to be decided. All we have done so far is to expound and illustrate the doctrine of categories, not to offer a final justification of it. But we can perhaps argue that certain obstacles to the unprejudiced appraisal of any such doctrine have been cleared away. In particular, we have sought to show, both in general terms and by individual examples, that the categories as Kant understands them are not metaphysical concepts in the old-fashioned sense of the word metaphysics: they apply not to all possible objects of thought, but only to what can fall within our sort of experience. And again, while they cannot themselves be derived from experience, since it is in terms of them that developed experience must itself be understood, that does not mean that they compromise the fundamentally empirical character of all knowledge of matters of fact. For by knowing that whatever falls within experience must conform to the categories we know nothing of what will fall within experience: it is to sensation (or some other form of immediate intuition) that we must go to discover the detailed nature of reality. Of *a priori* more than of any other concepts is it true that without intuitions they are empty forms of thought.

In short, this form of rationalism, if it descends from what some would regard as a primeval monster, must be confessed to be itself a very tame beast. It need hold no terrors for any empiricist, so long at least as he prefers truth to dogma. And indeed it may turn out, on further inspection, to be something of an empiricist itself.

Before ending this chapter, I should like to say a word about a matter so far passed over in almost complete silence—Kant's technical distinction between reason and understanding. Kant uses 'reason' in two senses: to denote both the intellect generally and a particular part of it. In its narrower sense reason is primarily the faculty of drawing conclusions, as opposed to understanding whose business it is to make judgements.[1] Now this sounds artificial to a degree, and it may be thought that the distinction Kant proceeds to draw in the sphere of *a priori* concepts between categories of the understanding and ideas of reason is worthless. But it does look as if Kant is pointing out something of real importance, though the way in which he expounds it is far from lucid. We can put his view very roughly by saying that the presuppositions of our thinking are not exhausted when we have specified those principles which define the objective as such. There are certain peculiar assumptions we make over and above these. I have already given an instance of the sort of thing of which Kant is thinking in an earlier chapter (pp. 72 ff.), when discussing the question of the co-operation of thought and sensibility. If we are to find order in our experience—if we are to be able to reduce it to a system of laws—we need to make assumptions not only about its general form, but, in a broad sense, about its matter too. Thus in all scientific thinking we must take for granted not only the applicability of the general law of causality to the manifold of sensation, but further that the manifold itself will, *in its particular detail*, be such as to make the discovery of scientific laws possible. It is not enough to know that every event will fall under some causal law or other; we must show further that actual causal laws can be discovered. In the language Kant uses in the *Critique of Pure Reason*, we must believe that the manifold will show both homogeneity and specification: that it will be neither too uniform nor too diverse for an intellect like ours to understand. But this, in Kant's view, is equivalent to saying that we must believe that a supersensible intelligence has adapted Nature to the needs of our understanding. The concept of such an intelligence is an idea of reason, which guides the empirical procedure of understanding, but cannot itself be verified in any possible experience.[2]

There can be no doubt that Kant was dealing with a genuine problem in all this, and that his case for the assumption of something like an idea of reason is a strong one. It should, however,

[1] This is the doctrine of the first *Critique*. Modifications introduced later are discussed below.

[2] See *Critique of Pure Reason*, Appendix to Transcendental Dialectic (B 670 = A 642 ff.). Kant thinks we use the idea of the soul as well as that of God in a regulative fashion.

be mentioned that when he came to write the *Critique of Judgment* (published in 1790, nine years after the first edition of the *Critique of Pure Reason*), he appears to have changed his mind to some extent over the matter. He does not, indeed, withdraw the contention that thinking involves other presuppositions than those based on the categories: on the contrary, he strives to reinforce it by considering two special classes of judgement not previously examined, judgements ascribing beauty to natural objects and judgements about organisms. But he now says that the principles involved in such judgements, as well as the principle that Nature is (in his own phrase) 'formally purposive' (such that it can be understood through a system of laws discoverable by scientific investigation), belong not to reason but to the faculty of reflective judgement. Judgement, which contains no special concepts of its own,[1] is said to be either *determinant*, when it argues from universal principles to particular cases (i.e. when it is *applying* universal principles), or *reflective*, when it begins from particulars and tries to discover the general laws they involve. And it is *qua* reflective that judgement is compelled to make the assumptions ascribed to reason in the first *Critique*, as well as others not treated of there.

The change of terminology, and slight shift of emphasis, here involved seem to have been introduced by Kant to underline his lesson that, whatever the proper account of them, the special ideas presupposed by aesthetic consciousness on the one hand, and the biological sciences on the other, cannot be given the same status as the categories.[2] Though they give rise to *a priori* principles, these cannot be said, as the principles of the understanding can, to be prescribed by the mind to all experience. Their function is regulative only, not constitutive. Thus Kant maintained the claim, basic in his philosophy, that fundamentally there is only one form of experience which yields knowledge, namely sense-experience as investigated by the physicist. Whether we can follow him in this is a matter to be discussed in a later chapter.

[1] The concept of purpose is itself a concept of reason, but belongs to the faculty in its practical (moral) aspect.

[2] I am ignoring the famous passage in the *Critique of Judgment* (§ 70) where Kant puts the principles of mechanical and teleological causality on the same level. Whatever the merits of this view, it seems quite inconsistent with the main principles of his philosophy. (See further below, Chapter X, § 3.)

VIII

REASON AND IMAGINATION

§ 1. We have now stated the case for the Kantian view of knowledge at some length. Our aim in doing so has, as we have said, been expository rather than critical; yet we can perhaps claim that a number of objections to the theory have received some sort of answer in the course of the discussion. In particular, we can argue that the fundamental empiricist criticism set out on pp. 112–13 above has been considered at least implicitly at several points. The argument for a distinction between immediate and developed experience has grown stronger as we have proceeded, and the view that *a priori* must accompany empirical thinking has at least become more clear.

Nevertheless, even if the reader is willing to agree that we must recognize the existence of categories as well as empirical concepts, and to accept the view that they must be *a priori*, it does not follow that this conclusion is necessarily to be interpreted in favour of rationalism. For it is possible, as I have more than once pointed out, to follow Hume and produce what is in effect an empiricist doctrine of categories. And this, it should be noted, does not mean that we must argue that the categories are after all empirical concepts: we can recognize their *a priori* character, do full justice to their special status, and still interpret them in an empiricist way. What we have to do to achieve that result is to show that, contrary to first appearances, there is nothing particularly *rational* about the categories. There is nothing that makes us use one set of categories rather than any other; or if there is, it is only a matter of convenience or at most of human nature. In short, though the categories, on this interpretation, function in experience in the way we have described, they originate not in reason but in imagination; and imagination is a faculty with far less philosophical pretensions than intelligence, and, therefore, more acceptable to the plain men that empiricists are.

In considering this thesis it will be as well to start with an examination of Kant's own views, which are in some respects rather surprising.

1. There can be no doubt that Kant's *fundamental* outlook was rationalist. We can see this by reflecting that it was his consistent doctrine that the categories were by no means peculiar to human

nature, but were involved in discursive thinking as such. The categories of the *Critique Of Pure Reason* descend from the 'pure intellectual concepts' of the inaugural *Dissertation*, a work in which Kant took up an avowedly rationalist position. And in the *Critique* itself he argued, in a way which we shall examine presently, that we can arrive at a complete list of the categories by considering an activity whose intellectual nature is not in doubt, namely, judgement. It is in and through judgement that the categories are applied. To discover *what* categories function in developed experience it was thus not enough, as Hume had suggested, that we should undertake a psychological or historical survey of our own mental activities; we must take the matter deeper and have recourse to 'transcendental logic'. This science could not only assure us whether any particular concept was a category; it could produce a complete list, based on an *a priori* principle, of all possible categorial concepts. By drawing up such a definitive list, Kant thought, we should solve all the problems of metaphysics at a single stroke.

All this sounds uncompromising enough; yet there were important qualifications, even at this level. The categories belonged to discursive intelligence as such, and were indispensable to any such understanding. But it was a contingent fact that our human intelligence was discursive: we might, after all, have been endowed with intellectual intuition. And again, there could be no explanation, in the last resort, of our thinking in terms of the categories we in fact used. For though we could show that they were involved in judgement as such, judgement itself might have proceeded on quite different lines, just as the forms of our sensible intuition might have been quite other than space and time.[1]

2. Kant's rationalism was further qualified by his doctrine of *a priori* imagination, to understand which we must touch on the very difficult subject of the Schematism of the categories. We have seen earlier (pp. 132 ff.) how the problem of the objectivity of *a priori* concepts was for Kant a problem of showing that they relate to sensible intuitions (sense-data). But in the case of the categories, he thinks, we have the difficulty that there seems to be nothing in common between the category on the one hand and sense-data on the other. Categories, involved in the nature of discursive intelligence as such, are the product of understanding; sense-data come from sensibility, a wholly separate faculty. To

[1] The *locus classicus* for this subject is *Critique of Pure Reason*, B 145–6.

ensure that the categories can be applied to the manifold of sense we need to find some third thing, homogeneous with the category on the one hand and the manifold on the other, which will help bridge the gap between them. We find that something in the schemata. The schemata, described by Kant as 'transcendental determinations of time', are products of the faculty of *a priori* or (as he sometimes calls it) 'productive' imagination, and their purpose is, as it were, to fertilize the pure concepts of understanding and make them fruitful in human knowledge. And if we turn from these difficult generalities to the particular examples Kant gives, we are not likely to underrate the importance of the whole doctrine. Thus we learn that the schema of substance is the permanence of the real in time, while that of causality is 'the real which, whenever posited, is always followed by something else'.[1] It requires only a brief glance at our last chapter to see that these schemata come near to constituting the whole content of the categories of substance and cause as they actually function in human experience. Substance as vindicated by Kant is the conception of the permanent which underlies change, while causation is a relation of events as necessarily preceding or following one another. It is true that Kant is always ready to say that substance is not *merely* the conception of the permanent, nor causation that of necessary precedence and succession in time: he continues to maintain that, even in their concrete form, the categories have about them something of the logical content from which they started, and that they signify respectively that which is always a subject and never a predicate, and that which is the ground of the existence of some other thing. But this logical aspect of the 'schematized' categories is, if present, far from prominent; and it is difficult, when we go into the detailed arguments of the Analogies, to know how Kant could justify its presence at all. But if we do abstract from it we leave ourselves with nothing but the schemata. Is not this to dispense with the understanding as a source of pure concepts and to put our trust in imagination instead?

It can scarcely be denied that an interpretation of Kant on these lines, in which we emphasize the part of imagination and play down that of understanding, is not only possible, but may

[1] Ibid., B 183 = A 144. Besides the chapter on Schematism (B 176 = A 137 ff.), § 24 of the 2nd edition Transcendental Deduction (B 150–2) should be consulted for Kant's doctrine of the imagination.

even be necessary, at least if we are interested in bringing out the element of truth in his theory. Certainly the wise empiricist would incline to such an interpretation. But it must be made quite clear that Kant himself would have no sympathy with it. We can see this if we look at one or two typical passages in the *Critique* itself. Thus at an early stage of the argument (B 103 = A 78) we are told that 'synthesis in general is the mere effect of the imagination, a blind though indispensable faculty in the soul, without which we should have absolutely no knowledge'. But, Kant adds, 'to bring this synthesis to concepts is a function belonging to understanding; knowledge in the strict sense is produced only when understanding exercises this function.' And much the same doctrine appears in the Transcendental Deduction, where we learn that the transcendental synthesis of imagination must be related to the unity of apperception if it is to result in objective knowledge. As Kant says in one passage (A 119): 'The unity of apperception in relation to the imaginative synthesis *is* the understanding.' But it is perhaps on his argument that the categories are involved in judgement that Kant rests most weight in believing them to have an intellectual origin, and it will perhaps be worth our while to examine this in some detail.

The problem of providing what is technically called a 'metaphysical deduction' of the categories, i.e. of making a list of them which depends on a principle, was one which long exercised Kant.[1] Already in his famous letter to Marcus Herz of February 21st, 1772, in which the problem of the *Critique of Pure Reason* was first formulated, we read of his ambition to construct a list of the categories not like that of Aristotle, who put together categorial concepts just as he happened on them and in no sort of order, but 'as they divide themselves into classes according to some few fundamental principles of understanding'.[2] Later, it became clear that it was not a plurality of principles but a single 'clue' for which Kant was seeking. He solved the problem, and at the same time justified his fundamentally rationalist conception of the categories, by connecting them with formal or, as he himself called it, 'general' logic. It was the business of this science to give an account of 'the absolutely necessary rules of thinking, without

[1] For the history of his attempts to solve it see Vleeschauwer, *La Déduction transcendentale*, t. i, pp. 217 ff. and Kemp Smith's commentary on the *Critique*, pp. 186 ff.

[2] Berlin edition of Kant's works, vol. x, p. 132.

which no employment of understanding whatever takes place';[1] and to achieve its ends it considered the forms of thinking only, abstracting from the content thought through them. Not only did Kant consider logic as thus described an *a priori* science; he held further that it had, for all practical purposes, been brought to completion by Aristotle, and stood in need of no further improvement. The doctrines of formal logic were thus fixed and certain, and any of them could in consequence serve as the sort of principle for which Kant was looking.

Now among the topics treated of by formal logic was that of judgement. Logicians classified the forms of judgement, distinguishing them as, e.g., universal and particular, positive and negative, categorical, hypothetical, and disjunctive. Thanks to the *a priori* character of formal logic, we could make a complete list of such forms.[2] But the list became of something more than ordinary interest when we realized the identity of the act of judging with that of categorial thinking. The categories, as we have seen, were concepts of the ultimate ways in which we gave unity to our experience: they expressed the basic rules in accordance with which different sense-particulars were united as belonging to a single objective world. But judgement, according to Kant, was itself essentially a way of uniting particulars: every judgement contained at least one concept, and every concept might be said to embrace in a unity all those particulars which fell under it. What Kant seems to have been suggesting was that these two types of unity were imposed in a single act of thinking, and therefore that any account of the one, such as that given by formal logic, would tend to illuminate the other.

The argument is difficult to state with any plausibility, since it seems to be plainly fallacious. Kant is saying that formal or general logic, the study of thinking as such, contains the key to transcendental logic, the study of synthetic *a priori* thinking. And the nerve of his argument is to be found in his conception of judgement. Judgement, as he quite rightly sees, is not to be regarded as the mere uniting of two concepts or ideas, nor is it an academic exercise, the entertaining of a proposition for its own sake. As Hume puts it in an interesting passage in the *Treatise*,[3]

[1] *Critique of Pure Reason*, B 76 = A 52.

[2] For some of Kant's difficulties in compiling such a list, and his differences from contemporary logicians, see Vleeschauwer, op. cit., t. i, pp. 244 ff.

[3] p. 108, ed. Selby-Bigge.

judgement 'peoples the world', enabling us to extend our experience to embrace things, persons, and events with which we were never actually acquainted. But it must be remembered that though this sense of judgement, described in Kant's technical language as 'the way of bringing given cognitions to the objective unity of apperception',[1] is a perfectly legitimate one, it is not that presupposed by the formal logic Kant had in mind. It would seem rather that that discipline, concerned as it is to consider the forms of thinking as such, without regard to the nature of the objects thought about, takes precisely the view of judgement which Kant repudiates in the passage from which I have just quoted. A judgement, for formal logic, is a proposition, something which considered in abstraction may be true or false, but is not necessarily asserted to be so in any concrete piece of thinking. Formal logic is quite justified, in view of its entirely general nature, in taking this view of judgement; but for all that it seems quite illegitimate to argue from it, as Kant does, to judgement in the other and more special sense. For the latter involves not merely the general principles (expressed in the rules of logic) to which all consistent thinking must conform, but certain particular principles of its own as well. And no amount of scrutiny of the first set of principles, whether in the form in which Kant knew them or in any other, will throw any light on the second.

It is on this general point, rather than on defects in his conception of formal logic or difficulties in his particular arguments, that we must ground our criticism of Kant. He is, it would seem, attempting the impossible: to argue from general logic, which treats of consistency, to transcendental logic, which treats of truth. No such transition can be made, and in consequence the metaphysical deduction of the categories, with its corollary that they originate in understanding, breaks down. Certainly the deduction contains an element of value in connecting the categories with judgement; it is perfectly true that it is in and through judgement that they are applied in experience. But the judgement here spoken of is an activity which involves synthetic *a priori* principles; and to think that one can discover what those principles are, and even prove that they originate in the understanding, by contemplating the bare forms of propositions as studied by general logic, is surely absurd. For anything that Kant has proved of it in this part of his argument, judgement

[1] *Critique of Pure Reason*, B 141.

might be just the sort of thing which Hume in effect says it is, an activity involving *a priori* principles indeed, but principles which spring from the non-rational part of our nature. Even if we correct Hume and insist, as we well may, that it is a genuinely intellectual activity (and not an odd species of sensation), we may still have to accept the fundamentals of his account. Viewed as a 'logical' activity, in the sense distinguished in Chapter III, judgement is certainly intellectual; but in its 'real' aspect, which is after all the vital point at issue, it may be nothing of the sort. We shall have to discuss these questions again at a later stage in the chapter.

§ 2. These considerations appear to dispose of Kant's main argument for the view that the categories are the product of reason in the broad sense of that term. But before we ask whether this entails our acceptance of the semi-empiricist interpretation of his position given above, we shall do well to consider another rationalist account of categorial thinking. It was the boast of Hegel[1] not only to have improved on Kant by pointing out categories whose existence Kant had never suspected, but further to have done this by discovering the true key to a 'metaphysical' deduction of all such concepts. The key was to be found in the notion of dialectic. Categories, in Hegel's opinion, were one and all products of pure thought, ways in which thought strove to comprehend the Absolute. In actual fact Hegel seems to have taken this position largely for granted: he gives no hint in the *Encyclopaedia*, for instance, of even considering a view such as that we are attributing to Hume.[2] But he could, if confronted with Hume's sort of criticism, have defended himself by referring to the dialectical character of thought. The series of categories was, he held, self-generating, and this could be seen in the following way. Take any category (any of the Kantian examples will do) and reflect upon it. You will find that it displays certain inner contradictions and so tends to give rise to a further category, which is in effect its opposite or antithesis. But the second category is no more stable than the first: it passes in turn into a third concept, which unites what is of positive value in both its

[1] What follows is mainly based on Part I of Hegel's *Encyclopaedia of the Philosophical Sciences*, especially on what he calls the 'preliminary concept' (§§ 19–83).

[2] Imagination, for Hegel as for Spinoza, was simply a lower analogue of scientific or philosophical thinking: see p. 65 above for the developing series of which these three are members.

precursors.[1] Here we have an example of the familiar triadic relationship of thesis, antithesis, and synthesis of which Hegel was always talking. But we must not suppose any triad (save the highest of all) to be complete in itself. Every triad culminates in a synthesis, but this does not mean that the aspirations of thought are satisfied by a single triad. For the concept produced by the synthesis, if subjected to examination, will itself be found to contain inner contradictions, and so to become the thesis of a fresh triad, in which further categories are generated. The process continues until a truly adequate concept is reached, in the shape of what Hegel calls the Absolute Idea. And it can be traced backwards to its logical prerequisite the simplest category of all, called by Hegel pure Being. From pure Being to the Absolute Idea there is thus an unbroken dialectical progression, in the course of which reason generates or 'posits' the entire series of the categories.

Before we say anything about this remarkable theory it will perhaps be worth pointing out one of its corollaries. Because of his notion of dialectic Hegel disagreed with Kant not only about the number and inter-connexion of the categories, but further about their relation to experience. According to Kant categories are concepts of an object in general, ways in which unity is given to the manifold of sense. In theory they have a validity outside the range of human experience, since they refer to objects of 'intuition in general'; but in practice it is only in their schematized form (as they relate to a spatio-temporal manifold) that we can find any determinate content for them. Pure categories are altogether too vague to function in knowledge. Now Hegel will have none of this. For him categories can have phenomenal embodiment and be reflected, for instance, in the fields of Nature and history; but this does not mean that they are intelligible only in the concrete. On the contrary, the categories have, he holds, a content of their own, supplied to them by pure reason, and this enables us to study them in and for themselves. The study of logic, of which the pure categories are the true object,[2] is not only

[1] For example, Hegel thinks the three categories of substance, cause, and reciprocity are thus dialectically related: compare *Encyclopaedia*, §§ 150–6. The thought of substance and accident leads on by its own inner logic (cf. below, p. 172) to the thought of cause and effect, which in turn passes into the thought of reciprocity.

[2] Hegel's logic descends from the Transcendental Logic of Kant. On the relation of this to formal logic see above, p. 5, n. 1. It should be mentioned that Hegel uses the term 'dialectic' in a way quite different from that of Kant. For Kant a dialectical argument is a particular sort of bad argument; for Hegel

possible in itself but is indeed the culminating point of philosophy, the branch of it which illuminates all its other parts. And it is because of their internal content that the Hegelian categories serve, as those of Kant emphatically could not, to determine the unconditioned which lies beyond the range of any possible sense-experience. Because they proceed from reason, and because the real is the rational, they can be held to give us insight into the essential nature of reality. It requires little reflection to see that Hegel was here stating a view not basically different from that which Kant put forward in the 1770 *Dissertation* (pp. 130–1, above). He had abandoned Kant's mature conception of the categories as concepts of rules of synthesis and had reverted to the notion, at once more primitive and more congenial to the rationalist mind, that they enabled us to know intelligible 'things or relations'.

So much by way of summary statement of the theory. Now it might be thought possible to produce a very simple refutation of it. Hegel supposed, as we have seen, that the series of categories was self-generating: that we could start from pure Being and proceed to the Absolute Idea, passing *en route* through every category that the wit of man can devise. But this, we shall be told, is surely an all or nothing theory. If it is agreed to, we ought to accept not only the principle of the Hegelian dialectic but the Hegelian logic in its detail as well. And conversely, if we reject the details of Hegel's theory—if we think him wrong over this category or that —we are in effect denying the whole dialectical principle. For the principle says that from any given category we can construct the entire series, and if there is anything in it we really ought to be able to carry out this programme. But in fact there are few or none, even among professed followers of Hegel, who would declare themselves satisfied with every detail of his doctrine of categories. Is not this to confess the bankruptcy of the whole theory?

Despite its plausibility, the objection is not really valid. It owes its apparent success most of all to Hegel's personal conceit. The shortcomings he found in the work of his predecessors did not deter Hegel from claiming something like infallibility for his own writings. Certainly his confidence in the correctness of the main principles of his philosophy was such that he did not stop, as a less rash man might have done, at enunciating the notion of the dialectical nature of thought and illustrating it by one or two

all reasoning is dialectical. Aristotle's use of the term is different again, though Plato's use of it in the *Republic* goes some way towards anticipating Hegel's.

obvious examples; he went on to trace the march of reason, as he thought it, through all the stages of its weary progress. But this heroic (or, if we like, quixotic) course was scarcely necessary in the interests of the theory. For that it was enough to argue that the categories were discoverable in principle, not that a full list of them could be constructed by any particular philosopher. And it is interesting to notice that something like this line was taken by Hegel's sceptical English follower, F. H. Bradley. In the first part of *Appearance and Reality* Bradley takes up a number of familiar ideas and shows, quite in the manner of Hegel, that they break down through inner contradiction. But he makes no attempt to arrange these ideas on a scale, nor to demonstrate how one passes into another.[1] Bradley's procedure is perhaps too negative for a true Hegelian, but his example shows that something like the dialectical principle can be accepted without our being committed to any detailed doctrine of categories.

Whether our criticism of this anti-Hegelian argument is right or not, it is clear enough that the important thing in Hegel from our point of view is not so much his actual list of categories as the way in which he claims to arrive at it. What we need to investigate is dialectic itself. Many philosophers would say that it was the function of reason to discover truth about the universe, and that anything short of absolute truth and complete explanation will fail to satisfy it. What distinguishes Hegel from others is not this general assumption (which he shares), but the view that reason is impelled *by its own inner logic* to proceed from one position to another. With one exception, any principle we adopt in explaining the universe and any concept we form to characterize it as a whole will break into contradictions. It is on this contention that thought is dogged throughout its course by impending contradictions, and produces one idea after another in an unceasing effort to avoid them, that the general plausibility of the theory turns.

In what sense can a category or categorial principle involve inner contradictions? The whole idea is far from precise. In the first place it is not obvious how any concept or principle can be self-contradictory unless it is complex. A complex idea or proposition can indeed be shown to involve contradictions: pointing to inconsistencies of this kind is one way in which we seek to dis-

[1] He does, however, imply that they do form a scale—in the doctrine of degrees of Truth and Reality.

credit our opponents in everyday life. But does Hegel think that the categories *are* complex concepts? It is difficult to pin him down on the point, but in general his view would seem to be that the antithesis of simple and complex cannot be precisely applied to philosophical ideas like the categories.[1] Every category has a content of its own: it is an attempt to provide a definition or characterization of the Absolute, to say what reality is as a whole. So regarded, every category is a simple or single idea. But every category contains, despite this, the seed of its successor, and so is complex. And the contradiction which breaks out inside any given category arises from the fact that no two concepts of this kind can in the last resort tolerate each other's presence. Each category is a partial definition of the Absolute, and so must clash with all other categories. So far as they (or any of them) are right, it is wrong.

To guard himself against the charge that this is to play fast and loose with the rules of formal logic, Hegel goes out of his way to stress that in his opinion the type of thinking investigated by that logic is inferior or abstract. Formal logic is concerned with the thinking of understanding, whilst philosophy is the product of reason. Philosophy, the study of reality in its concrete detail, cannot be bound by rules formulated for the proper conduct of understanding, which studies only certain abstract aspects of things. Such rules govern the thinking of the scientist and even that of the historian; but they clearly cannot lead to ultimate truth. For they depend on holding, with Bishop Butler, that 'everything is what it is and not another thing', when this, in Hegel's view, is palpably untrue of concrete fact.

Hegel's position thus involves (i) a peculiar attitude to the principle of contradiction, (ii) a special conception of the categories, and (iii) a belief in a faculty of philosophical reason quite separate from that of understanding.

(i) As we have seen, thought is impelled onwards in its restless course by its desire to avoid contradiction. It aims at achieving

[1] Compare Professor Collingwood's view (in his *Essay on Philosophical Method*) of the 'overlap' of philosophical concepts. Philosophical concepts do not exclude each other precisely, but are dialectically related; they can be identified as philosophical by being seen to display this relationship. Collingwood was clearly much influenced by Hegel in writing this essay. For examples of Hegel's own view of the relationship of philosophical concepts the reader may be referred to the details of his two works on logic, the *Science of Logic* (1812) and Part I of the *Encyclopaedia* (first published 1817). The triad Mechanism, Chemism, and Teleology (ibid., §§ 194 ff.) is a suitable example to start from.

ultimate truth about the universe, and the one thing it feels justified in taking for granted throughout the search is that reality is not self-contradictory. This is to accept the principle of contradiction as valid of philosophical thinking. But we are also told that reason is the faculty which overcomes the abstractions of understanding, and that it does it by refusing to submit its concepts to precise qualification. Sharp alternatives, such as are postulated by formal logic, will not apply to concepts like the categories. This seems equivalent to rejecting the principle of contradiction.

Here one can only say that Hegel is not entitled to have it both ways. If he asserts that reality is not self-contradictory, then he ought not to go out of his way to abuse formal logic. He should accept the rules of formal logic for what they profess to be, as valid of all sorts of thinking. Alternatively, if he denies them universal validity on the ground that they do not apply to philosophical thought, philosophy itself should not be based on one of them. In philosophy, as in politics, there is such a thing as fair play.[1]

(ii) The special feature of Hegel's conception of the categories is that he regards each of them as, in a sense, in competition with all the others. The proper way of expressing them is in the formula 'the Absolute is *a*, *b*, or *c*,' where *a*, *b*, and *c* are categories. And when we take any particular category and apply it to the Absolute, we automatically exclude all similar predicates. We are putting forward a complete philosophy, as is shown by the fact that we can find separate stages in the history of speculation corresponding to some of the individual categories. Parmenides, for example, based his philosophy on the idea of pure Being, Heraclitus his on the category of Becoming. If Parmenides is right, Heraclitus is wrong, and vice versa.

This sounds plausible enough, so far as Parmenides and Heraclitus are concerned; but the crucial question is whether it can be justified as a general rule. Is there the inevitable clash of categories which Hegel supposes? Certainly Kant never seems to have thought there was anything inherently impossible in providing a

[1] For a defence of Hegel's view of the principle of contradiction see G. R. G. Mure, *An Introduction to Hegel*, pp. 139 ff. The real difficulty is perhaps to know how the principle, which is taken by Hegel as valid at the level of understanding, can be destroyed yet preserved ('sublated') in the higher thinking of philosophy. The same problem appears to arise in the philosophy of Bradley, for whose views on contradiction the reader may be referred to Mr. R. W. Church's book *Bradley's Dialectic*.

plurality of criteria of objectivity. The categories, in his view, each give rise to a principle which is of universal application in the world of experience; but there is no suggestion that each principle exhausts the nature of that world. Because we think in terms of causality there is no reason why we should not go on using the principle of substance. Hegel would have been on better ground had he confined his clashes to whole sets of categories. The conflict between materialism and idealism is, if we like, a conflict between two sets of categories. But can we be sure that inside each set there are inconsistencies of the same sort as we find between one set of categories and another?[1]

(iii) But the basis of Hegel's whole theory is to be found in his conception of reason, a subject we have already discussed at some length. He held, as we saw, that the last word about human thinking cannot be said by examining the procedure of understanding, which operates pre-eminently in the natural sciences. Over and above this is a more concrete form of thinking, the thinking of philosophical reason. Reason contrasts with understanding by containing an intuitive as well as a discursive factor; its universals are not abstract but concrete. Now it is clear enough that it is reason in this technical sense which functions in dialectic: dialectical thinking, for Hegel, is rational thinking *par excellence*. But the difficulty, here as before, is to know just what sort of a thing reason is supposed to be. Is it, like the intuitive understanding whose nature Kant analysed, a faculty which knows the particular in the general, whose thinking is automatically a knowing of individual facts? Much of Hegel's language (in particular his use of the term 'concrete universal' and his ascription of 'immediacy' to the thinking of reason) suggests that some such idea was at the back of his mind, though the paradoxes the view involved clearly deterred him from any open adhesion to it. The difficulty of holding that the philosopher can deduce the empirical nature of reality in advance of experience (a difficulty of which Hegel was fully aware) induced him to fall back on a theory which was essentially hybrid. It began from the Kantian position that reason cannot be the source of *a priori* intuitions but at most of *a priori* concepts, but went on to qualify this by arguing that

[1] Hegel, it should be noted, felt bound to maintain that there were, because otherwise he could not have held that a dialectical transition from one type of philosophy to another was possible. We shall encounter the problem of conflicting philosophies again in Chapter X.

reason has a peculiar insight into the (dialectical) relations of its own ideas, which, unlike the Kantian categories, have a content of their own. To justify this contention Hegel relied on the element of intuition which, as we saw before (pp. 56 ff.), is involved even in formal inference. But such intuition, though undoubtedly genuine, belongs, unless I am mistaken, to the 'logical' side of the human intelligence, and cannot be appealed to as the basis of a 'real' activity. Formal inference is a purely analytic procedure, whereas dialectical thinking, as one of Hegel's commentators has said, is synthetic and analytic at once.[1]

I conclude, then, that Hegel's attempt to evolve, if not the detail of experience, at any rate the categories from the depths of rational consciousness, is a failure. His 'metaphysical deduction' is, in the end, no more successful than Kant's, though its defects are by no means so patently obvious as those of Kant's argument. Neither Kant nor Hegel has succeeded in discovering a truly rational basis for the categories, and the way is accordingly still open to an empiricist interpretation of them. I do not say here that we need in the end accept any such interpretation; but I do suggest that it would be well worth our while to consider it in detail. Accordingly I shall proceed next to a short study of the views of Hume on this topic.

§ 3. To suggest that Hume has a theory of categories of any sort will come as a surprise to many students of his writings. And indeed it can scarcely be doubted that his own attitude to the suggestion would have been hostile, if not contemptuous. Like his followers the modern Logical Positivists, Hume has no use for the conception of synthetic *a priori* thinking. But his practice, as we shall see, does not always square with his professions.

I shall begin by trying to sketch what may be called his official account. 'All reasonings', says Hume in a passage in the *Enquiry*,[2] 'may be divided into two kinds, namely, demonstrative reasoning, or that concerning relations of ideas, and moral reasoning, or that concerning matter of fact and existence.' These two different sorts of reasoning give rise to two fundamentally different types of knowledge. Knowledge of relations of ideas is arrived at by intuition or demonstration, and is confined, if Hume is to be believed, to the sciences of geometry, algebra, and arithmetic.

[1] J. M. E. McTaggart, *Studies in the Hegelian Dialectic*, chap. ii.
[2] p. 35, ed. Selby-Bigge.

These sciences are through and through analytic: propositions in them 'are discoverable by the mere operation of thought, without dependence on what is anywhere existent in the universe'. Their principle is the principle of contradiction. But it is quite otherwise with our knowledge of matters of fact. There the principle of contradiction no longer holds sway, except as a formal condition of our thinking, and intuition and demonstration in the strict sense do not function. Our knowledge of matters of fact is, in Kantian language, synthetic not analytic.

Now Hume's interest in these two types of reasoning was by no means equal. He has little to say, either in the *Treatise* or in the *Enquiry*, about our knowledge of the relations of ideas, appearing to think that the account of it given by Locke was correct in essentials.[1] It was over knowledge of matters of fact that Hume showed his true originality. He saw, as Locke and Descartes had not seen, that 'moral' was not reducible to demonstrative reasoning, and he realized that it was most important to investigate its nature. His own suggestion was that it approximated far more closely to sensation than to demonstration. Thinking about matter of fact and existence was just not thinking in the rationalist sense at all: it was not an activity involving rational insight, but something much more passive, dependent on habit and, in some respects, best describable as a way of behaving. Hume argues for this view in the central sections of the *Treatise* (Bk. I, part iii) dealing with causation, belief, and probability. The important thing to notice here about his theory of causation is that he denies that we attain by causal reasoning to any knowledge of the *intrinsic* relation of one event to another: we merely connect events in our own consciousness, passing from one to another by a purely subjective necessity. It is thus custom, and not reason in the formal sense, which governs all causal arguments. And Hume supports this conclusion by his theories of belief and probability. Belief, by which Hume means what other writers call judgement, just *is* 'a lively idea associated with a present impression', and so 'more properly an act of the sensitive, than of the cogitative part of our natures' (*Treatise*, p. 183, ed. Selby-Bigge). Probable reasoning, again, 'is nothing but a species of sensation' (ibid., p. 103). It appears, indeed, from Hume's detailed discussion that

[1] Hume, however, rejected Locke's suggestion (*Essay*, IV. iii. 18) that ethics might become a demonstrative science. On Locke's theory generally see pp. 78–81 above; compare also pp. 43–4 (on Hume and his predecessors).

this statement can only be accepted with modifications, for the sort of probable arguments we use in attempting to establish either a scientific law or an historical fact are extremely complex; but Hume would none the less hold to his conclusion, maintaining that the principles to which we appeal are none of them rational in the strict sense and that our final conclusion is a belief determined, like any other, by the liveliness of the ideas to which our present impressions relate.

This account of what we have called in previous chapters 'empirical' thinking is presented by Hume within the framework of a theory of knowledge whose leading principle is not in doubt. The contents of the mind, which constitute the materials of knowledge, can be divided exhaustively into impressions and ideas. And philosophical reflection establishes the general proposition that 'all our simple ideas in their first appearance are derived from simple impressions, which are correspondent to them, and which they exactly represent' (*Treatise*, p. 4). When confronted with any idea we are accordingly entitled to ask for its origin; and if this cannot be traced to an actual impression or impressions, we can (and should) treat it as worthless, since it lacks all objective reference. This may be called Hume's principle of radical empiricism.

It is clear enough that such a principle is quite inconsistent with any view like Kant's which holds that certain peculiar *a priori* concepts function in (developed) experience. Officially, the possibility that *a priori* might lie behind empirical thinking is ruled out by Hume at the start. Nevertheless, he shows himself sensitive to the special character of some of our ideas. He is puzzled, in particular, over the concepts of causation and thinghood, and it may be worth our while, even at the cost of repeating what is generally familiar, to explain very briefly how he deals with them.

1. Causation sets Hume a problem because the relation of cause and effect carries with it a necessity which we cannot observe in immediate experience. We find ourselves asking from what impression the idea is derived, and are at first at a loss for an answer. But there *is* an answer, as Hume points out: the necessity lies not in the objects connected but in ourselves who connect them. Thus the idea of cause and effect turns out to be empirical after all.

Unfortunately, this solves only half the problem. The puzzle about causality is not simply that of knowing what connects cause with effect, but also that of why we say that every event has a cause. Hume points out brilliantly that we cannot intuit or demonstrate the general causal principle, but his own final attitude to it is obscure. He treats it as if it were not a factual but a prescriptive principle, valid of all possible objects of experience. But it is not clear how he is entitled to do this on the empiricist premisses from which he sets out.

2. Hume's treatment of the idea of thinghood is strikingly different. Confronted by a series of impressions which either closely resemble one another or exhibit a coherent rhythm of change, we postulate objects which continue to exist when we are not there to observe them. But this, though a natural, is none the less an unwarranted procedure. What we are doing, as Hume shows, is mistaking closely similar for precisely identical situations. Our inference arises from imagination, but cannot justify itself at the bar of reason.

Here Hume treats an ostensibly categorial concept as, in the end, no better than a fiction. He admits that the vulgar make constant use of it, and that even philosophers have recourse to it at all times except when they are explicitly considering the question in their studies. Nevertheless, he persists in believing such use to be without justification, and recommends 'carelessness and inattention' as the only escape from the theoretical difficulties it involves.

But this, as we have said before (p. 121), is surely a counsel of despair. A concept so universally appealed to cannot be dismissed quite so simply; even if fictitious, it is at the least a most important fiction, and some further account of it needs to be given, in which it is distinguished from fictions of a more common and altogether less reputable sort. Hume's sceptical temper, which leads him to reject as illegitimate any idea which originates neither in sensation nor in (demonstrative) reason, has here clearly overreached itself. If imagination cannot be allowed to produce legitimate ideas, by what title can it govern empirical thinking? 'Moral' reasoning, for Hume, reduces to a form of imaginative association; but unless imagination has a respectable side, this only seems to make out that such reasoning is totally irrational: a serious conclusion to come to when we reflect that 'moral' reasoning includes the greater part of the thinking of history and natural science.

The truth is that Hume needs for his own purposes a conception somewhat like that of Kant's synthetic *a priori* thinking. He was anxious, as we have seen, to limit the pretensions of reason, and to show that reasoning about matters of fact was altogether different from demonstration. But though he argued that belief and probable reasoning were akin to sensation, he wanted despite this to draw a clear distinction between rational and irrational belief. One of Hume's most cherished convictions was that human beings can be divided into two classes, the Vulgar and the Philosophers. The Vulgar, plain men that they are, are governed by prejudice and superstition; they jump to conclusions in the teeth of all the evidence. Philosophers, by way of contrast, are at any rate capable of regulating their thinking by scientific principles; their beliefs can be reasonable and their inferences just. But if thinking about matters of fact, whichever party carries it out, is only imaginative association, and imagination is itself dismissed as a source of fiction, there seems nothing to choose between them.

Hume recognizes this difficulty himself in more than one passage in the *Treatise*. He tells us at an early stage that 'as all simple ideas may be separated by the imagination, and may be united again in what form it pleases, nothing would be more unaccountable than the operations of that faculty, were it not guided by some universal principles, which render it, in some measure, uniform with itself in all times and places'.[1] And in the section on 'unphilosophical' probability, one of the most interesting in the whole work, he takes up the problem again in talking of general rules.

'When an object appears, that resembles any cause in very considerable circumstances, the imagination naturally carries us to a lively conception of the usual effect, though the object be different in the most material and most efficacious circumstances from that cause. Here is the first influence of general rules. But when we take a review of this act of the mind, and compare it with the more general and authentic operations of the understanding, we find it to be of an irregular nature, and destructive of all the most established principles of reasoning; which is the cause of our rejecting it. This is a second influence of general rules, and implies the condemnation of the former. Sometimes the one, sometimes the other prevails, according to the disposition and character of the person. The vulgar are commonly guided by the first, and wise men by the second.'[2]

But it is quite late in the *Treatise* that we find Hume's best exposition of his view, from which I will quote at length.

[1] p. 10, ed. Selby-Bigge.

[2] pp. 149–50.

By what right, Hume asks, can he condemn ancient philosophers for having recourse to imaginative fictions when he himself says that imagination is the ultimate judge of all systems of philosophy?

'In order to justify myself, I must distinguish in the imagination betwixt the principles which are permanent, irresistible and universal; such as the customary transition from causes to effects, and from effects to causes: and the principles which are changeable, weak and irregular; such as those I have just now taken notice of.[1] The former are the foundation of all our thoughts and actions, so that upon their removal human nature must immediately perish and go to ruin. The latter are neither unavoidable to mankind, nor necessary, or so much as useful in the conduct of life; but on the contrary are observed only to take place in weak minds, and being opposite to the other principles of custom and reasoning, may easily be subverted by a due contrast and opposition. For this reason the former are received by philosophy, and the latter rejected.'

And he adds an example.

'One who concludes somebody to be near him, when he hears an articulate voice in the dark, reasons justly and naturally; though that conclusion be derived from nothing but custom, which infixes and enlivens the idea of a human creature, on account of his usual conjunction with the present impression. But one, who is tormented he knows not why, with the apprehension of spectres in the dark, may, perhaps, be said to reason, and to reason naturally too; but then it must be in the same sense, that a malady is said to be natural, as arising from natural causes, though it be contrary to health, the most agreeable and the most natural situation of man.'[2]

The problem with which Hume was dealing in this passage, as his example shows, was the familiar one of separating the objective from the subjective elements in experience. And in suggesting that in objective thinking the imagination is ruled by 'permanent, irresistible and universal' principles Hume was offering a solution very much on Kantian lines. It is true that this solution, even if we interpret it in the most Kantian manner possible, must be admitted to be different from Kant's in important particulars: it derives the categories, so far as it recognizes them, from human

[1] i.e., the principles appealed to (or alleged to be appealed to) by the ancient philosophers.

[2] *Treatise*, pp. 225–6, ed. Selby-Bigge. Compare also Hume's footnote on p. 117 (on two senses of the term 'imagination').

nature rather than human reason, and it is the work of a man anxious, at every turn, to strike down undue intellectual pretensions. But these are not necessarily defects. Indeed, it may be argued that Hume's theory leads, with very little revision, to an interpretation of the facts to which Kant called attention which can commend itself to all intelligent empiricists. It is a matter for regret that Hume himself did not see the full force of his own arguments, and that his conception of empiricism was unduly narrow. His sensationalist account of empirical thinking errs because he failed, here as over the problem of universals, to recognize the compatibility with empiricism of the intellect's having a 'logical' function; and his official hostility to synthetic *a priori* thinking led him into weaknesses, as we have seen, in his treatment both of causality and of material thinghood. These weaknesses could have been overcome had he recognized, what his theory demanded, that imagination as he conceived it has and must have an *a priori* as well as an empirical side. The notion of an *a priori* imagination, prescribing to experience principles which originate in human nature, is never attained to by Hume; but it is none the less one which is required if we are to do full justice to the lessons of his philosophy.

§ 4. After this long historical survey it remains to attempt some independent conclusions. The question which confronts us is to know whether a theory of categories, which we hold to be indispensable for objective knowledge, is to be interpreted naturalistically or rationalistically: whether, in less clumsy terms, such concepts spring from the rational or the non-rational side of our nature. And here we can begin with a point which stands out clearly from our examination of the classical theorists of knowledge. If by reason we mean *demonstrative* reason, the intellect as it functions in formal thinking, then we cannot ascribe a rational origin to the categories. Hume's distinction of 'moral' from demonstrative reasoning is surely sound, and it is in the former that the categories operate. The failure of Kant's attempt to derive pure concepts of the understanding from the judgement forms of formal logic serves only to reinforce the value of Hume's doctrine. Kant was quite right to connect the categories with judgement, but not to think that formal logic could throw light on them. And we can call on Hegel as well as Hume in support of this conclusion, since the reason which, in his view, elaborated the categories was emphatically not conceived as a purely formal faculty.[1]

But to deny that the categories originate in reason strictly so called is not necessarily to assign them a non-rational origin. Here we must be careful with our terms. We saw that, even on a theory like Hume's, it was necessary to distinguish between rational and irrational belief. Rational belief is arrived at in accordance with the 'permanent, irresistible and universal' principles of the imagination; irrational (or, as Hume calls it, 'unphilosophical') belief depends on others which are 'changeable, weak and irregular'. What this comes to, in the Kantian language we have adopted in this book, is that rational thinking is governed by the categories, whilst irrational thinking is not.[2] But on this conception of rationality, which applies peculiarly to 'moral' reasoning, the categories themselves cannot be pronounced either rational or irrational. They are the ultimate concepts by which we estimate rationality, and clearly cannot be used to measure themselves.

All this suggests that there is at most a difference of emphasis between the Kantian understanding and the Humean imagination. That there is such a difference cannot, of course, be denied. Kant connects the understanding with rational consciousness as such, while Hume is defiantly anxious to draw attention to the continuity between the reason of men and the reason of animals.[3] Hume lacks the conception of the 'logical' activity of the intellect,[4] and so tends to hold that empirical thinking is not really thinking at all, a proposition which Kant very properly denies. Again, Kant thinks that an *a priori* imagination is not intelligible save in relation to the transcendental unity of apperception, an entity (or function) of which Hume shows no explicit awareness. But for all these differences there is a substantial area of agreement between the two philosophers. Both argue, in effect, that

[1] Hegel himself would not have accepted the ultimate validity of Hume's distinction, just as he could not agree to Kant's separation of analytic from synthetic judgements. In his view it is the same reason which functions in 'moral' and demonstrative reasoning alike. It is interesting to notice, however, that in marking off the abstract thinking of understanding from the concrete thinking of reason proper, Hegel was offering his own interpretation of Hume's distinction, and that he believed that the concrete illuminated the abstract, not vice versa.

[2] The categories do operate in irrational thinking (e.g., there are causal connexions in dreams), but they are applied without due regard to the full circumstances of the case, i.e. their application is only partial.

[3] Cf. *Treatise*, Bk. I, part iii, § 16; *Enquiry*, § ix.

[4] Though he does of course ascribe *analytic* powers to the pure intellect—in mathematics.

objective experience cannot be understood unless we suppose that in it the human mind proceeds in accordance with synthetic *a priori* principles; and Kant, for all he has to say about discursive intelligence as such, agrees with Hume that in the last resort we cannot show why we have recourse to the particular principles we do use. That we think in terms of these and no other categories is a contingent fact, which we can describe according to taste as a truth about human nature or a truth about human reason. And unless we are prepared to subscribe to some such view as Hegel's, it is difficult to see how we are to get beyond that position.

It thus seems as if we might solve the problem of the rational or non-rational origin of the categories, the question whether reason or imagination governs our thinking about matters of fact, by a compromise satisfactory to both parties. The categories, on this view, are the ultimate concepts determining rational judgement as such; and to ask whether they are themselves rational is to ask a question which cannot be answered. We can agree with Kant, if we choose, that the principles based on these concepts should be associated with understanding because it is empirical *thinking* that they determine; or we can emphasize, with Hume, that because they are neither self-evident nor demonstrable by formal reasoning they should be connected with an altogether different faculty, invoking here the notion of an *a priori* imagination as their source and habitat. But each of these statements, though justified in its own way, is misleading in its implications. To connect the categories with understanding suggests that they are rational in a sense in which they cannot possibly lay claim to rationality; and to connect them with imagination implies that empirical thinking is a piece of passive behaviour rather than a rational activity. It is accordingly better to refuse the dilemma with which we have tormented ourselves throughout the discussion; to emphasize the unique status of categories among our concepts and of categorial principles among our judgements, and to point out that even if their removal would not entail, as Hume thought, that 'human nature must immediately perish and go to ruin', it would at least involve the destruction of all organized knowledge as we now know it.

§ 5. But before we accept this conclusion there is a further point to be considered. When Hume wrote his *Treatise of Human*

Nature and Kant his *Critique of Pure Reason* they supposed that they were analysing, respectively, human nature and discursive consciousness *as such*. And the conclusions to which they came were, they believed, valid timelessly as are the truths of natural science; applicable to all men, or again to every discursive intelligence. Thus Hume believed his universal principles, and Kant his categories, to govern all empirical thinking: not just the thinking of men in the eighteenth century, but that of all men at all times. But this, we are told by some recent writers, was a gross mistake. It is not in fact true that a principle such as that of causality has always been an absolute presupposition of objective thinking, nor is it true that it will always remain such: indeed, some say that it has already been given up by natural scientists. There are no universal principles of the kind for which Hume and Kant were looking, for the simple reason that the categories have a history. Their validity is limited to a certain age and a certain group of thinkers; and when they have served their purpose they are discarded in favour of fresh concepts of the same kind.

The arguments for this point of view have been effectively put and illustrated by Professor Collingwood in his *Essay on Metaphysics*, a book to which we have more than once referred. But to see the full relevance of the theory to our present subject we shall do well to examine it as it appears in the work of another modern writer. In *Mind and the World Order* (1929) Professor C. I. Lewis of Harvard argued not only that categorial concepts do in fact change in the course of time, but further that we can change them at will. Starting from Kant's position that *a priori* thinking is necessary if we are to delimit the real from the unreal, the objective from the subjective, Professor Lewis proceeded to turn its flank by maintaining that such thinking has no roots either in rational consciousness or even in an unchanging human nature. Knowledge, he held, certainly demands that we organize the given, and in such organization categories have their part to play; but what categories we bring to bear is entirely a matter of choice. Our use of this set of categories rather than that is purely arbitrary: in the last resort we could apply to experience any set of categories whatever. It is true that we should find some sets extremely cumbersome and inconvenient, since if we thought according to them we should have to reject an unusually large part of our experience as unreal; but apply them we could, if we were so minded.

It is clear enough that the theory in this form can give little comfort to rationalist philosophers. Certainly it recognizes that rationalists are right against empiricists of the more literal sort in asserting that judgement rests upon *a priori* principles; yet it rapidly takes away with the left hand what it has conceded with the right by insisting on the arbitrary character of those principles. And in fact it is not difficult to see that Professor Lewis's whole theory is conceived in the interests of empiricism. This comes out in his view of what may be called the unitary character of *a priori* thinking. To understand the nature of the *a priori*, Professor Lewis argues, we have only to look at the case of geometry, a science whose postulates are, as its development has shown, entirely a matter of convention, and whose truth is none the less quite independent of the truth of any factual judgements. A plurality of geometries is possible because we can take any set of primary geometrical propositions we please and develop their logical consequences; nor is our choice of propositions determined in any way by the empirical nature of reality. And just as we can set up a plurality of geometries, so we can set up a plurality of categorial systems. In each case it is only a question of supplying definitions of basic concepts and fundamental rules of procedure, and these, provided we take care to be consistent, we can choose entirely at will.

Professor Lewis's theory is conceived in the interests of empiricism because he denies, in effect, the existence of any separate class of synthetic *a priori* judgements. Besides truths of fact he recognizes only definitions, which he thinks entirely arbitrary, and the analytic truths which follow from them. The originality of his point of view is seen in his extension of this theory of analytic *a priori* thinking, which, as we have noticed before, is the distinctive feature of modern empiricism, to the case of categorial thinking. Empiricist philosophers, apart from Hume, seldom have anything convincing to say on the subject of *a priori* concepts: they mostly tend to discount their existence on the simple ground that it would be inconsistent with empiricism to accept it. Professor Lewis cannot be accused of this faint-hearted policy. Not only does he admit that his opponents have produced not a monster but a real animal; he undertakes further to show that it is after all tame, and can be led quietly to the empiricist stable.

Is he right in all this? I shall start by making the preliminary point that his theory offers one more instance of the fascination of mathematics for philosophers. We have seen already the way in which rationalists of the Cartesian school looked on mathematics as the type of all knowledge, and used the certainty of mathematical propositions as a yard-stick by which to measure truth of every kind. This policy was, in fact, a failure, if only because of the distinction, pointed out by Hume, between 'moral' and demonstrative reasoning. But though modern philosophers have been forced to recognize that thinking about matters of fact is a very different thing from mathematical thinking, mathematics, as Professor Lewis's example shows, has not lost its influence over some of them. And we may perhaps be permitted to wonder whether, just as the rationalist exploitation of mathematics broke down because it blurred the distinction between analytic and synthetic knowledge, so this empiricist appeal to mathematics as the type of the *a priori* may not turn out to be unsuccessful in the end. We have seen already (pp. 95 ff.) the difficulties of the application of the theory to the sphere of logic: can we expect better results in the sphere of categorial thinking?

Whatever we expect, it is by its consistency with the facts that the theory must be tested. We must accordingly inquire into the question how far the content of the categories is arbitrary and changeable.

That there is change in the explicit content of the categories can scarcely be denied. The principles that determine the judgement of a primitive savage are different from those governing the thinking of a civilized man, though there is some ground for regarding the second set as a development of the first. But it is one thing to believe that the categories do in fact change in the course of history, and another to argue that we can change them at will and indeed as often as we please. In fact it would seem that writers like Professor Lewis exaggerate both the instability of the categories and the element of choice which enters into their imposition.

1. There are some categories which in name at least appear to be of a singularly persistent nature. Thus the ideas of thing and property, of substance and of causal connexion, have a history which goes back to the beginnings of European speculation. It seems to be somehow natural to interpret our experience along certain lines: to think of events as occurring through the causal interactions of things, themselves believed to be manifestations or determinations of a permanent substance or substances. And when we attempt to discard this way of thinking—when we say,

for instance, that the principle of substance is no longer appealed to in natural science—we get an uncomfortable feeling and wonder whether we are really justified in believing that scientists have spoken their last word on the subject.

There is perhaps a parallel to the situation here described in the sphere of ethics. A certain school of moral philosophers, whose ideas, familiar in ancient Greece, are extremely influential to-day, holds that moral principles rest on convention rather than moral insight. The case for this view is that the content of the moral law varies from society to society and, inside any society, from one age to another. But the view runs into difficulties when we consider that there are some moral principles, such as that we should tell the truth or keep promises, which seem to be recognized as valid in all societies. A society which did not recognize such principles would perhaps not be a moral community at all.

2. Professor Lewis meets this objection by protesting that it is only in name that the categories persist. My conception of thing and property is different from that of a native of Polynesia. This is no doubt true, but it may be only that I am thinking clearly what he thinks confusedly. And here we should notice a more general point. Those who affirm the arbitrary character of categorial principles speak as if the giving up of one category or set of categories and the adoption of another were a matter of sheer substitution. But is this really true? Must we not recognize that, sometimes at least, new categories arise out of the criticism of old categories, which they do not so much suppress as modify, and that there is a great deal more continuity in our categorial thinking than the theory we are examining suggests?[1] Indeed, it would seem that only if such continuity is presupposed can we speak of a history of the categories in the strict sense; failing any such connexion, all we could have would be a chronicle recording that men thought in one way at one time and later gave it up in favour of something quite different. There could be no suggestion here that the later view was any more true or adequate than the earlier.

3. This brings us to a final point. Professor Lewis's theory rests on the notion that categorial thinking is like geometrical thinking in so far as both are independent of the particular nature of fact. But this is not quite true. Categorial principles are not, of course,

[1] Compare the changes in cosmological presuppositions between the time when Greek philosophy began and the present day, as recorded (for instance) in Professor Collingwood's *Idea of Nature*.

drawn from immediate experience; yet they refer to it in a peculiarly close way. And here they differ from the principles of geometry. In pure mathematics our object is solely to discover the logical implications of the premisses we adopt; we are not concerned, as pure mathematicians, with the question whether our results can be applied empirically. But there is no pure science of categorial thinking. The categories are concepts which govern our judgements about matters of fact, and unless they can be applied in the empirical world they are useless. Hence the nature of the given does exercise an influence, though an indirect one, on the categorial concepts we choose; hence, too, there is a test of one set of categories in comparison with another, for a set which covers more facts, and covers them with more precision, is better than one which is narrower and vaguer in its application.[1]

For these reasons we may agree that to say that the categories change in the course of history is not necessarily to believe their imposition arbitrary; and in fact there are good grounds for thinking it is not. Our earlier conclusion that the categories are involved in rational judgement as such, but should not themselves be pronounced either rational or non-rational, can accordingly stand. As for the fact that the content of the categories does change, the most convincing explanation of it I can think of myself would run on rationalist rather than empiricist lines.[2] On this view we should say, when we give up one categorial principle in favour of another, that we do it to attain a fuller understanding of the true principles of judgement, and so, indirectly, of the reality we construct or elaborate in judgement. Categorial change would here be interpreted as development, development towards a more adequate comprehension of the world of facts. And unless some such theory is adopted I do not see how we can justify the common belief that the progress of learning leads not merely to the extension of the field of knowledge, but also to a truer and deeper understanding of the field already before us.[3]

[1] See Chapter X, § 6, for further discussion of this point.

[2] Something like it appears in Hegel, and may be retained even if we reject the main principles of his philosophy.

[3] Although, if the argument of this chapter is right, it is wrong to describe categories and categorial principles as either rational or irrational, we can ask which set of such concepts it is most rational to accept. As explained in Chapter X, to answer this question is the proper business of metaphysics.

IX

SELF-KNOWLEDGE

§ 1. We are now in a position to state the conclusions of our main inquiry. They can be put very briefly as follows:

1. Because intellectual intuition is impossible for human beings, the contention of the rationalist school that knowing at its best is a strictly intellectual activity cannot be defended. If truths of reason are taken to be nothing but bigger and better truths of fact, there are no truths of reason. All reasoning about matter of fact and existence must start from empirical premisses, i.e., depends in the first place on what is given in sensation, and cannot legitimately proceed beyond the boundaries of possible experience. This means that metaphysics in the traditional sense, a science professing to set forth the necessary nature of the reality which lies beyond sensible appearance, and to arrive at its results by pure thinking, is impossible. The only conclusions to which we can come by pure thinking are analytic; and analytic judgements tell us nothing about the structure of fact.

2. These criticisms of rationalism would all be endorsed by empiricists; but it does not follow that in making them we commit ourselves to the support of empiricism as it is normally stated. For the view that knowing is primarily and properly an affair of pure sensation is just as erroneous as the view that it is primarily and properly an affair of pure intellection. Sensation in itself can afford us no knowledge; for that we must not merely be acquainted with a manifold of sense-data: we must also conceptualize and judge it. But this means that while the intellect is not in itself a source of cognition, there can be no truth without an intellectual activity. Moreover, if we are to know a common objective world we need agreed principles by which to interpret the given, principles which, because they express our fundamental conception of what it is to be objectively real, cannot themselves be derived from immediate experience. We can, if we like, describe these principles as 'truths of reason'; but we must remember, if we do so, that the term itself stands in need of analysis. For while it is possible to maintain that principles of the type in question are rational in so far as they function in all rational thinking about matters of fact, that is not the same as showing that they proceed from reason. Our principles could only be truths of reason

in the strict sense if we could demonstrate that they are somehow involved in reason as such; but despite the attempts of some eminent philosophers, this is a task which has yet to be accomplished.

The position here set out can be characterized, according to choice, as moderate rationalism or modified empiricism. It is rationalist in so far as it calls attention to the very important part played by the intellect in knowledge: that faculty is needed, if the arguments we have put forward are correct, in both its 'logical' and its 'real' capacity. Unless we could form concepts our knowing would be mere feeling, beyond description or communication; and unless we could form *a priori* concepts organized learning itself, the study of the objective world of experience, would be ruled out. But because we hold, despite this, that concepts are themselves of significance only when they are referred to particulars, and that the intellect cannot produce particulars from itself, our rationalism rests on an empiricist basis. It preserves all the essential contentions of empiricism, but contrives also to do justice to factors which are normally neglected by philosophers of that way of thinking. In particular, by its double doctrine of analytic and synthetic *a priori* knowledge, it allows the rationalist claim that some truths are necessary truths, and so opens the way to a resurrection of metaphysics understood in the modest sense of a science of the presuppositions of experience.[1]

But before we can regard these conclusions as established there are certain major objections to be considered. Among the stock criticisms of empiricism mentioned in our preliminary survey in Chapter II were two which can be brought equally against the theory advocated in this book. These are the criticisms (1) that whilst offering a plausible account of knowledge of the external world it is far from satisfactory over the problem of self-knowledge, and (2) that, like other philosophies based on or closely influenced by empiricism, it starts from a dogmatically narrow conception of experience. I shall devote this chapter to discussion of the first of these objections, and consider the second in Chapter X.

§ 2. The problem of self-knowledge has many interesting aspects, but it cannot be dealt with exhaustively here. We must confine ourselves to those points in it which are relevant to the empiricist-rationalist controversy. A very brief statement of the history of the problem was included in Chapter II (pp. 20–3),

[1] See further, Chapter X, § 5 below.

at the end of which I suggested that it was necessary to concentrate on two main questions: whether introspection is in fact the same in nature as external sensation, and whether knowledge of the self is exhausted by what we know in introspection. I will begin by summarizing the opposing answers to these questions.

Empiricists have no doubt that the answer to both questions is in the affirmative. It has been a principle with the empiricist school since Locke that there is a faculty of reflection which is precisely parallel to external sensation. Reflection is a kind of internal sensation, and the results it produces are epistemologically on the same level as those of the five outer senses. By reflection I know such things as that I am feeling angry or bored, just as I know by sensation that this is hard or that tastes sour. And just as the data of the external senses provide raw material for sciences such as physics, chemistry, biology, and physiology, so the data of inner sense provide raw material for the psychologist. Psychology is the science of the self, and reflection is its indispensable instrument. It is true that psychology is a more difficult study than physics and the rest, a science in which it is altogether harder to reach agreed conclusions; but that fact can be explained simply enough. Because every self is directly accessible to a single observer only, whereas objects in the material world can be observed by as many people as like to look,[1] the psychologist faces problems, both in collecting his material and in testing his conclusions, which are unknown in the physical sciences. But empiricists would hold that though these difficulties have impeded the progress of psychology, they are far from showing that it is an inherently impossible discipline. The success of psychologists in devising experimental methods, and the practical results they have produced, would seem to be clear testimony to the contrary.

Empiricists combine with this positive doctrine of self-knowledge a polemic directed against any suggestion that we know ourselves in any other way than by reflection or inner sense. In the case of the classical exponents of empiricism this polemic took the form of an attack on the conception of rational psychology

[1] There is a sense in which *all* sense-data are private to a single percipient, since every act of sensation is an act of a self. But in the case of the external senses we find that one man's data correspond to, or cohere with, another's; and when this happens we say that they are observing the same object. There is no corresponding phenomenon in internal sensation: even when my feelings are sympathetically like yours, I do not suppose that we are both aware of the same self.

put forward by the Cartesian school, an attack which began, moderately enough, when Locke pointed out that we have no more grasp of the true substance of the self than we have of the true substance of the material world, and which was pressed home by Hume in a famous passage from which I have already quoted (p. 21 above). The self, for Hume, was a 'bundle of perceptions', just as external objects were bundles of perceptions; it was absurd to regard it, in the manner of Descartes, as a substantial unity whose nature could be grasped in a series of rational intuitions. In modern versions of empiricism there is less emphasis on the confutation of rational psychology, a discipline now generally abandoned (except in the official philosophy of the Roman Catholic church) as impossible. But the hostility to any non-psychological doctrine of self-knowledge survives in an interesting way in the denial that philosophy can give us any special insight into the nature of mind. The propositions actually discussed by philosophers, we are now told, include, besides nonsense statements of the old-fashioned metaphysical type, many empirical hypotheses, among them some which belong properly to the science of psychology. Philosophy thus appears to afford us a kind of self-knowledge, but the impression is, in fact, entirely erroneous. For the only genuine philosophical propositions are one and all analytic: philosophers are concerned not to state or explain facts, but to elucidate the proper use of symbols. Any suggestion that there can be such a thing as philosophy of mind must accordingly be dismissed as absurd.[1]

The rationalist answer to our questions is not so easy to state clearly, if only because of internal differences within the school. In general, however, we may say that rationalists are inclined to be sceptical about the view that introspection is adequately described as a form of internal sensation; and even when they admit that it is, they do not attach any very high value to the resulting science of psychology, which they believe to give only a partial view of the mind and its workings. In addition, they lay great stress on the fact of self-consciousness, a fact which (they think) is left out of account altogether in the theories of their opponents.

To illustrate the first of these points it may be instructive to consider briefly the views of Berkeley on the subject. Berkeley's account of our knowledge of the physical world is, of course,

[1] See A. J. Ayer, *Language, Truth and Logic*, chap. ii, for an excellent exposition of the modern empiricist view of the function of philosophy.

largely empiricist: he holds that we know external objects by way of ideas furnished by our senses. But he refuses to give an analogous account of self-knowledge. The self is a spirit, and a spirit is above all an active agent. To know the self we must grasp it in its activities; but that we cannot do if we are confined to knowing it by way of ideas, which are passive and inert.

'If any man shall doubt of the truth of what is here delivered, let him but reflect and try if he can frame the idea of any power or active being; and whether he has ideas of two principal powers, marked by the names *will* and *understanding*, distinct from each other as well as from a third idea of substance or being in general, with a relative notion of its supporting or being the subject of the aforesaid powers, which is signified by the name *soul* or *spirit*. This is what some hold; but so far as I can see, the words *will, understanding, mind, soul, spirit*, do not stand for different ideas, or in truth, for any idea at all, but for something which is very different from ideas, and which being an agent cannot be like unto, or represented by, any idea whatsoever.'[1]

How then, we may ask, do we know the self at all, if we do not know it by way of idea? The question evidently occurred to Berkeley, and he made some attempt to answer it, particularly in the second edition of the *Principles*. Thus he added to the passage just quoted the statement that 'it must be owned at the same time, that we have some notion of soul, spirit, and the operations of the mind, such as willing, loving, hating, inasmuch as we know or understand the meaning of those words'. And elsewhere he wrote that 'I have some knowledge or notion of my mind, and its acts about ideas, inasmuch as I know or understand what is meant by those words. What I know, that I have some notion of.'[2] But this language about notions is not elaborated, and we do not know precisely what Berkeley intended by it. All we do know is that he held knowledge of spirits to be quite different from knowledge of material things, and thought this was due to the fact that the essence of spirit is activity.

The point which gives plausibility to Berkeley's doctrine is the important one that there is a sense in which we seem to know ourselves from within rather than from without: as experienc*ing* rather than experienc*ed*. In the words of Samuel Alexander, we 'enjoy' ourselves and 'contemplate' objects. All rationalist theories of self-knowledge rest in the last resort on this awareness, or

[1] *Principles*, § 27 (first edition text).

[2] Ibid., § 142 (second edition text). (Berkeley's account of spirit, so far as it goes, is to be found in ibid., §§ 27 and 135–44.)

supposed awareness, of the self as subject: the *cogito* of Descartes, the Hegelian philosophy of spirit, the theory of mind as pure act of Gentile, are alike grounded in it. It is thought to be a form of knowledge more direct and intimate than any other, and for that reason to provide a model of what all knowledge should be. But it must be admitted that to lay exclusive stress, as Berkeley seems to do, on this aspect of the self as activity leads to paradoxical results. For, after all, there are many situations in which we seem to be not so much 'enjoying' as 'contemplating' the self, regarding it not as subject but as object. If I sit down and try to determine my precise feelings, for instance, I make myself my own object; and the 'reflection' by which I pursue my inquiries seems to be closely akin, if not to sensation itself, at least to sense-perception. Nor is there any obvious reason why I should not advance from such perceptual knowledge to a systematic study of the self as object, i.e. elaborate a psychology of the scientific type. But once that is admitted we seem to be saying that there is a good deal in the empiricist account of self-knowledge after all.

In actual fact most rationalists try, in these circumstances, to have the best of both worlds. Because of the existence of self-consciousness they are reluctant to identify introspection as such with inner sense, or, if the identification is made, to allow that inner sense is the only direct source of self-knowledge. But every-day experience constrains them to admit that the self can be an object to itself, and thus that the psychology of the empiricists is a legitimate undertaking. They qualify their approval of it, however, by maintaining that it is an 'abstract' form of knowledge; that, in considering content apart from act, the psychologist necessarily distorts his subject-matter; and that his results must accordingly be supplemented and corrected by self-knowledge obtained from within. And if they are asked where that knowledge is to be found, they refer to history, polite literature, and the writings of their fellow philosophers.

§ 3. The aspect of the self on which rationalists lay stress is, as will be apparent from the above, its being a subject aware of its own activities. The self is essentially an active being, and its true nature can be grasped only in self-consciousness. Against this empiricists make the point that in introspection and systematic self-knowledge (i.e. in psychology as it is normally understood) the self we are knowing is an object like any other. Now there seems no reason why this controversy should not be settled to the satisfaction of both parties, if only it can be agreed that the self is to be viewed as subject and object at once. Each side would then be right in what it affirmed and wrong only in what it denied. A solution on these lines was attempted by Kant, whose views on the matter I now propose to examine. It may be remarked in advance that his solution has, in fact, pleased neither party, and that it contains certain obvious difficulties of its own. Nevertheless, a study of it seems essential to any discussion of self-knowledge.

The following passage from Kant's lectures on 'Anthropology' (popular psychology) is perhaps as full and clear a statement of his position as can be found:

'Distinguishing as reflection the inner act of spontaneity which makes possible a concept or thought from apprehension, the receptivity which makes perception, i.e. empirical intuition, possible, and considering both acts as conscious, we can divide consciousness of ourselves (apperception) into consciousness of reflection and consciousness of apprehension. The first is a consciousness of understanding, the second of inner sense; the first is pure, the second empirical apperception (it is wrong to call it inner sense). We investigate ourselves (*a*) in psychology, using as material the representations of our inner sense; (*b*) in logic, using what intellectual consciousness provides. This seems to make the self double, which would be contradictory: (1) there is the self as subject of thinking (in logic), i.e. there is pure apperception (the merely reflective self). About this we can say no more than that it is a quite simple representation. (2) There is also the self as the object of perception, i.e. of inner sense. This self contains a plurality of determinations, through which an inner experience is made possible.

'The question may be asked whether, in view of the variety of changes of mental state, changes in what he remembers or in the principles which he accepts, a man can be conscious of these changes and still say that he remains the same man (has the same soul). The question is absurd, since consciousness of such changes is only possible on the supposition that he consider himself in his different states as one and the same subject. The self is therefore formally but not materially double: double with reference to the way in which it is represented, but single in regard to its content.'[1]

Whatever the difficulties of this passage, it is clear that Kant

[1] *Anthropologie in pragmatischer Hinsicht*, footnote to § 4 (Berlin edition of Kant's works, vii. 134 n.). These lectures were published by Kant himself in 1798. The quotation given is hardly a fair specimen of the difficulty of this 'popular' course.

is trying in it to do justice to both the empiricist and the rationalist accounts of self-knowledge.

(A) His doctrine of inner sense, and his view of psychology, are both fundamentally empiricist. The self, he affirms, can be known as an object, and it is the business of the psychologist to investigate this aspect of it. Inner sense, the basis of psychological knowledge, is precisely parallel to outer sense, which provides the raw material for those sciences which deal with the external world. This is exactly the view of Locke. It is true that Kant goes beyond Locke by distinguishing empirical apperception from inner sense; but the distinction, unless I am mistaken, is only parallel to his general separation of sensation from sense-perception. I derive the raw material for knowledge of myself as an object from inner sense, but it is only in empirical self-consciousness that I can know my feelings precisely. It is true, too, that Kant sometimes expresses considerable scepticism about the prospects of a scientific psychology, and that in the preface to *Metaphysische Anfangsgründe der Naturwissenschaft,* where the whole subject of what constitutes a science is discussed, he contrasts psychology most unfavourably with physics, ending by suggesting that the most we can hope to get out of it is a natural history of the human mind.[1] But the objections he there brings up against psychology —that mathematics cannot be properly applied to psychological data, that we cannot carry out experiments with them because they do not exist in separation, and that they are inevitably distorted in the act of introspection—do not spring from the systematic hostility to the whole idea of such a discipline which we find in some rationalist writers. They reflect rather a conservatism which is common in scientifically minded persons, and which has its parallel to-day in the attitude many scientists take up to the results of psychical research.[2]

(B) But if Kant agreed with the empiricists that we can have knowledge of ourselves through inner sense, he also agreed with the rationalists that that does not end the matter. Besides the object self we must recognize the self as subject; and this, as the rationalists saw, must be conceived in terms of spontaneity or activity. The second paragraph of our quotation from the

[1] Berlin edition, iv. 471.

[2] Kant must in any case be given the credit of having clearly seen that empirical psychology is a branch of natural knowledge and not a part of metaphysics. For his views on this subject see *Critique of Pure Reason,* B 876–7 = A 848–9.

Anthropology shows the sort of argument Kant himself produced in support of a subject self: it is a presupposition of our having any sort of diversified experience that the self for which the experience exists should be thought of as a subject persisting unchanged through it. And this is, of course, in line with the general doctrine of the Kantian philosophy that the reality we know in everyday experience and investigate in history and the sciences stands in essential relation to a self which elaborates it in judgement. The notion of the self as an active agent plays as important a part in the Kantian scheme of things as it does in the metaphysics of Berkeley.

What is interesting about Kant's view, however, is not so much his admission of a subject self as his conception of its nature and of our knowledge of it, for it is here that he makes his distinctive contribution to the problem. Experience, he says, certainly involves the notion of a unitary self; but it is wrong to think of that self as having a content of its own, or as knowable by some form of rational intuition. To explain how knowledge of objects is possible the subject self we require need not be conceived as a substantial entity at all: it is sufficient to think of it as a formal unity preceding experience as its *a priori* condition and capable of knowing its own identity in its different acts. What we require, in fact, is the notion of a unity of apperception which is (*a*) transcendental, and (*b*) synthetic.

Few ideas in the history of philosophy have caused so much difficulty as Kant's idea of the transcendental unity of apperception; yet the thought behind the tortuous language in which it is expressed is comparatively simple. It is a presupposition of experience, as we have seen, that every object should relate to a subject, and that this subject should be aware of its own identity. But, Kant argues, we have no right to claim that we know such a subject as it is in itself, since in fact all we know of it is that it is what is formally identical in our various acts of cognition. If we abstract from these acts of cognition, taking away the content which the senses, external and internal, provide, we are left with nothing but a bare unity of consciousness, i.e. with no content at all. That is why Kant says, in the passage quoted above, that all we can say of the subject self is that it is a 'quite simple representation'. To think we can go beyond this—to think we can qualify our subject as something more than an activity which gives unity to all our knowledge—is to fall into the paralogisms of rational psychology, the futile quest for a rational doctrine of the soul which exercised Descartes and his followers. The self can and must be *thought* as subject, but it can only be *known* as object; and for that we require data from inner sense.

This point about the subject self being not so much known as thought is obviously a crucial one for our purposes, and deserves careful consideration. Before going into it, however, we must mention a complication so far passed over in silence: the distinction Kant draws between the 'real' and the phenomenal self. The distinction is important both for Kant's theory of knowledge and for his moral philosophy. It arises in theory of knowledge from Kant's desire to maintain a parallel between internal and external sensation. In external sensation, he holds, we are acquainted not with things as they exist in themselves but rather with such things as they affect our sensibilities, i.e. with appearances. Similarly, we must say that in internal sensation we intuit ourselves not as we are but only as we appear to ourselves. This gives a straight distinction between the self as phenomenon (as object of inner sense) and the noumenal reality which lies, or is thought to lie, behind that appearance; and the distinction is widely drawn on by Kant in his moral philosophy, more particularly of course in his discussion of the problem of freedom.

Now it seems natural, once we make this distinction between the 'real' and the phenomenal selves, to hold that, while the phenomenal self is known in introspection and investigated in psychology, there is also awareness of the 'real' self in self-consciousness. This is the line taken by some of Kant's successors, and it obviously fits in admirably with the requirements of the rationalist theory. But we should notice at once that Kant will have nothing to do with the suggestion. 'In the original synthetic unity of apperception', he says in a well-known passage,[1] 'I am conscious of myself neither as I appear to myself, nor as I am in myself; I am conscious only that I am. This representation is a thought, not an intuition.' He goes on to explain the point in a note, in which he argues that while apperception involves the existence of a self, it does not itself present that existence in determinate form. I am conscious of myself as an active being, and for that reason am entitled to call myself an intelligence; but to *know* myself in that capacity I should require a special intuition, 'giving me acquaintance with the determining element in me, of

[1] *Critique of Pure Reason*, B 157.

whose spontaneity I am conscious, prior to the act of determination, just as time [the form of inner sense] presents me with the determinable element prior to the act of determination'. Unhappily no such intuition is forthcoming, and I must conclude that my existence is determinable only through inner sense, i.e. as appearance. The same doctrine appears in the Paralogisms, though the wording there is somewhat different. The 'I think', we are told, which accompanies all the contents of my consciousness and itself represents the fact that I am a self-conscious being, 'expresses an undetermined empirical intuition, i.e. perception. . . . An undetermined perception means here only that something real has been given, given to thought in general, not however as appearance, nor yet as thing in itself (noumenon), but as something which in fact exists and is indicated as such in the proposition "I think".'[1] In other words, the fact of self-consciousness is itself enough to establish the existence of a self: 'I am' is already contained in 'I think'. But the self whose existence is 'indicated' by the 'I think' is not thereby known determinately, as Descartes supposed: the existence we ascribe to it is not existence as a category. It is a problem rather than a true datum, a problem which can be solved only if we have recourse to inner sense.

Kant puts his main position in the same context by saying that the 'I think' is always an empirical proposition, though he adds that the phrase should not be misunderstood. The unity of apperception is, of course, the ultimate presupposition of experience, and it is absurd to regard it as empirical. Again, the 'I' in the proposition 'I think' is to be taken as purely intellectual, since it belongs to thought in general. But 'without some empirical representation providing the matter for thought the act "I think" would just not take place':[1] the intellectual faculty comes into operation only on the occasion of experience. This is, of course, Kant's consistent doctrine, and it serves to explain his whole conception of the subject self. By the subject of thinking he means no more than the faculty of thought itself. Thought, as we have seen in previous chapters, is for Kant an empty form without content of its own: it is to be conceived in terms of activity, spontaneity, or function, but can lead to results only if brought to bear on data which some other faculty provides. And this account applies to all intellectual acts and all forms of thinking: not only to empirical thinking, which must obviously start from what is given in experience, but

[1] *Critique of Pure Reason*, B 422–3 n.

to *a priori* thinking too. It is not surprising, in these circumstances, that Kant describes the subject self, the supreme condition of all thinking, as a 'mere form of consciousness', capable of accompanying the representations of inner and outer sense,[1] that he denies that it is identical with the 'I in itself', and that he maintains that we cannot know but only think it. His view is that it is not a substantial entity at all, but merely a separate aspect of the reality which we know from another point of view (as object) in inner sense. An intelligence like ours necessarily conceives the self in this dual way, as subject and object, but it does not follow that it is 'really' double. An intuitive intelligence would make no such distinction.

§ 4. Kant's account of self-knowledge has met with severe criticism. It is attacked in the first place by empiricists who propose to define the self, as Hume did, entirely in terms of 'perceptions'. On this view there is no subject self, and the problem of what we can know of it does not arise. Nor is it thought, by those who support this analysis, that the phenomenon of self-consciousness is of special interest to the philosopher. In Mr. Ayer's words, 'all that is involved in self-consciousness is the ability of a self to remember some of its earlier states. And to say that a self A is able to remember some of its earlier states is to say merely that some of the sense-experiences which constitute A contain memory images which correspond to sense-contents which have previously occurred in the sense-history of A.'[2]

I do not propose to discuss this empiricist criticism at length here. I will say only that it seems to ignore the obvious fact that, when introspection takes place, there is a self which is introspected and a self which introspects. To say that all that happens in such a case is that one set of sense-contents confronts another is, at the least, very paradoxical. Nor do I find the equation of self-consciousness with memory at all plausible. It might, indeed, be held that the contents of inner sense, or if we like the objects of *empirical* apperception, include our own past acts of awareness.[3]

[1] e.g., A 382.

[2] Op. cit. (first edition), p. 195. Mr. Ayer refers his readers to Mr. Russell's *Analysis of Mind*, chap. ix, for an elaboration of the point. For arguments against an account of cognition in terms of subject and object see chap. i of that work.

[3] Mr. T. D. Weldon (*An Introduction to Kant's* Critique of Pure Reason, pp. 154 ff.) has even argued that Kant could find no content for inner sense except such past acts of awareness.

But there is a world of difference between empirical and pure self-consciousness, and it is in the second that the philosopher is interested. What he wants to account for is the direct awareness of our own activity which we appear to have when we are actually performing a mental act, not the reflective awareness we can get if we give our attention to the act a moment later.

It seems strange that empiricists are not generally inclined to look on the Kantian theory of self-knowledge with a more kindly eye, since it is clearly more favourable to their point of view than it is to that of the rationalists. Kant is just as severe on the notion of rational psychology as is Hume, and his careful exposé of the pretensions and paralogisms of that 'science' has, in fact, proved quite unanswerable. Kant's subject self is, most emphatically, not a 'pure ego', yet it contrives to do justice to those facts which lead rationalist philosophers to invent 'pure ego' theories. Why then, we may ask, is it not taken more seriously by empiricists? Partly, no doubt, the reason is to be found in the unfamiliar and, indeed, repulsive terminology which Kant adopts, here as elsewhere. Expressions like 'transcendental unity of apperception' have an air of mystery about them, and one suspects that some empiricists, feeling rightly that philosophical theories ought to be expressed in clear language, are inclined to ignore or unduly neglect those which are not. But there is a more important reason. The Kantian subject self, despite its apparent harmlessness, is looked on by many empiricists as the thin edge of the rationalist wedge; and confirmation is found for this interpretation of it in the fact that it was so treated by Kant's immediate successors. The unity of apperception, regarded by Kant as a mere form without content of its own, became a very different thing when criticized and developed by Fichte and Hegel, and one can scarcely expect empiricists to welcome the change. If it is true that Kant's doctrine is capable of the extravagant interpretation put upon it by his immediate successors, one cannot really be surprised at the common empiricist attitude to it. Whether it is true is what we must now attempt to determine.

I propose to deal briefly with three rationalist criticisms of Kant's account of self-knowledge: (1) that the 'I' of apperception cannot be regarded as an empty form without content of its own; (2) that Kant's so regarding it depends on his erroneous belief that the real self which is the subject of knowledge must, if we are to know it at all, itself be determinable as an object of knowledge, and (3) that the Kantian theory must be wrong because it fails to provide any explanation of the peculiar self-knowledge we have in philosophy.

1. The first of these criticisms is in line with views we have considered more than once in this book already. The 'I' of apperception is looked on by Kant as an expression of that spontaneity in virtue of which I am entitled to call myself an intelligence. It is because I am a thinking being that I am capable of self-consciousness. But the faculty of thinking cannot, in human beings, lead to knowledge, since it is in no sense intuitive: it needs data given from without to work upon, and its essential function is to impose form on such material. Now this whole account of thinking has been strongly disputed, as we have seen. It was held by Hegel, for instance, that thinking cannot be thus regarded as a purely formal, discursive activity, but must rather be supposed to contain an intuitive element of its own, an element whose importance is increasingly apparent the more we give our attention to the higher forms of thought. And it is in accordance with this doctrine that Hegel refuses to regard the unity of apperception, the condition of all thinking, as nothing but an empty form. Even in Kant the unity of apperception is thought of as in some sense the source of the categories, and is described as synthetic just because of that fact. It is Hegel's contention that we cannot distinguish sharply, as Kant does, between the material of knowledge and the form imposed on it by the knowing mind. And the implication of his position seems to be that the 'I' of apperception is the source not only of the categories but indeed of the material of knowledge, too, an implication which, if not explicitly drawn by Hegel himself, is to be found quite plainly in the writings of his modern follower Gentile.

About this I can say only what I have said before, that it rests on a confusion between human thinking and the thinking we may suppose to characterize an intuitive understanding. Such an intelligence would indeed produce the materials of knowledge from itself, and impose form upon them in so doing. But that our understanding is not of this nature is clear from many considerations. To describe human experience we need, in Kantian language, concepts and intuitions; but there is no one faculty from which we can get them both. Our knowing thus appears to involve a dualism which no amount of reflection can transcend. Hegel, of course, did try hard to overcome this dualism, attempting to meet it by such devices as his theory of concrete universals and his conception of reason as a speculative faculty distinct from understanding. But just as these doctrines can clearly not be derived from anything asserted by Kant, so it cannot be shown that the Hegelian view of self-consciousness is a necessary development of the Kantian. Indeed, the two philosophers, in this as in so many other matters, stand poles apart from each other.

2. The second criticism of Kant may be thought to depend on the first, and to fail if the first fails. Yet it is perhaps worth some independent consideration. Hegel is always saying that what was wrong with the rational psychology of the pre-Kantians was that they took the self as a thing (i.e. as an object), and tried to discover its proper predicates.

'But if we propose to think the mind, we must not be quite so shy of its special phenomena. Mind is essentially active in the same sense as the Schoolmen said that God is "absolute actuosity". But if the mind is active it must as it were utter itself. It is wrong therefore to take the mind for a processless *ens*, as did the old metaphysic which divided the processless inward life of the mind from its outward life. The mind, of all things, must be looked at in its concrete actuality, in its energy; and in such a way that its manifestations are seen to be determined by its inward force.'[1]

Now it may be argued that the mistake of the old metaphysicians was repeated by Kant, despite his exposure of the paralogisms of rational psychology. To know myself as active, Kant says in a passage already quoted, I should need a special intuition of myself *qua* determining, just as I need a special intuition of myself *qua* determined to know myself as object. This suggests that he tended to think of the two sorts of knowledge as identical in kind, i.e. that he believed that to know the self as subject we should have to have some means of making it an object. And the impression is confirmed by the passages[2] where Kant argues that we cannot know the self which thinks in us since the only concepts we might invoke for the purpose are the categories, and these, since they spring from the unity of apperception, cannot themselves be used to determine it.

The impression is, in fact, a perfectly just one. Kant did hold, officially at least, that there was only one kind of knowledge, namely, knowledge of objects. To know the subject self we should

[1] Hegel: *Encyclopaedia*, § 34 (*Zusatz*), translated by W. Wallace.
[2] Compare, e.g., *Critique of Pure Reason*, A 401–2.

have to make it an object, and this, of course, we cannot do. The most we can do is think the self as subject, not know it. And this, we may be told, is a definite defect in Kant: if the self is an essentially active agent, we must try to know it from the inside. But Kant's point is that the immediate awareness we have of the subject self in pure self-consciousness is not sufficient to give us knowledge of it. To be that it would have to be a form of intellectual intuition, which it plainly is not. And the onus of proof here is surely not with Kant but with his critics.

It may be objected that, despite his theory, Kant did make some attempt to characterize the self as an agent: in his moral philosophy. There, as is notorious, he uses the antithesis between the 'real' and the phenomenal selves to which we have drawn attention, and contrives to say a good deal about both. But it may be questioned whether he would, even there, claim to be offering *knowledge* of the 'real' self. The main aims of Kant's moral philosophy are two: first, to provide an analysis of the nature of moral action, bringing out its special character and distinguishing it clearly from all other action; and second, to explain under what conditions we might regard ourselves as moral agents. The first of these involves nothing more than, in Kant's own words, 'a development of the universally received notion of morality',[1] and does not so much as presume that a moral action has ever been done. Moral action, we are told, would, if possible, involve determination of the will by pure reason; but whether it is in fact possible is not in question. It is only in the second part of his moral philosophy, where he discusses the concept of freedom and asks under what conditions we can regard ourselves as free, that Kant makes extensive use of the contrast between the two sorts of self, putting forward his famous theory that though phenomenally determined we are noumenally free. But even here he does not say that we *know* ourselves as noumena: to make moral action conceivable we have only to *think* ourselves as free of the conditions of sensibility. That is indeed why Kant's solution of the problem of freedom is, in effect, that the problem is insoluble. It would not be so if we had insight into our 'real' selves, but moral philosophy gives us no more insight of that kind than any other inquiry. It rests on the deliverances of the moral consciousness, which are accessible to reflection and in no other way.

3. Now it may be held that this explanation is plausible only

[1] *Grundlegung zur Metaphysik der Sitten*, section ii, last paragraph.

because of an important ambiguity in the word 'reflection'. 'Reflection' may be used, as it was by Locke and as it has been earlier in this chapter, as a general synonym for introspection, with the implication that it is nothing more than a kind of internal sensation (or internal sense-perception). But it may also be used to refer to the act by which reason reflects on its own operations and obtains knowledge of them. Reflection in this sense seems to be indispensable to philosophy, or at least to parts of it such as theory of knowledge and logic. But how it could be regarded as a source of cognition on premisses of the Kantian type is not by any means obvious.

We come here to the last and most difficult of the three objections which were to be considered. It raises a problem which is by no means peculiar to the philosophy of Kant, but is urgent for all philosophies of the empiricist type too. Every philosophy must explain, among other things, its own existence; or, to put it another way, among the types of knowledge which the philosopher has to consider is philosophical knowledge. A theory which produces what purports to be a comprehensive account of knowledge and yet says nothing about the status of its own propositions cannot claim to be complete. Now rationalists have no special difficulty with this problem, because they identify knowing as such with intellectual intuiting: that reason should be able to intuit its own nature seems to them far from surprising. But this solution is not, of course, open to empiricists, nor, one would suppose, to Kantians either, since both deny that intellectual intuition is possible for human beings. Yet if we refuse to admit that reason can have any special awareness of its own operations, it looks as if we must assert the fundamental propositions of theory of knowledge, for instance, to be propositions in psychology—a result which few philosophers would welcome.

I propose to confine myself here to the problem as it arises for Kant, reserving some more general remarks for the next section. Kant has a good deal to say about the nature and aims of philosophy, but he is silent, as we shall see, at the crucial point. His views can be summarized as follows:[1]

1. Philosophical knowledge is all rational knowledge, i.e. it is cognition by reason, where 'reason' is understood in a general

[1] For Kant's views on philosophy see especially *Critique of Pure Reason*, B 860 = A 832 ff.; *Logik* (ed. Jäsche), Introduction, i, iii; *Grundlegung zur Metaphysik der Sitten*, Preface.

sense. There are two sorts of philosophical knowledge, pure and applied. Pure philosophy is made up entirely of *a priori* propositions, and sets out what reason can attain when taken entirely on its own account. Applied philosophy does not confine itself to investigating *a priori* principles for their own sake; its business is to examine the concrete world in the light of such principles. Applied philosophy amounts, in fact, to the study of certain empirical questions from a philosophical point of view, and doubtless owes its place in Kant's system to the tradition that philosophy is an all-embracing discipline. It is pure philosophy which gives life to it, and on which we must concentrate our attention.

2. Pure philosophy divides into three parts, metaphysics, ethics, and logic, and each of these is made up, as we have seen, entirely of *a priori* propositions. Now if we ask Kant how reason can have *a priori* knowledge in metaphysics his answer is not in doubt. Metaphysics in the only sense in which it can be regarded as a legitimate inquiry is made up of the principles which reason prescribes to experience, and indeed must prescribe if objective knowledge is to be possible. Principles of this sort, though not derivable from sensation, have none the less an essential relation to sense-experience. Nor does the synthetic *a priori* knowledge we have in ethics present any major difficulty to Kant. Ethics deals not with statements of fact but with assertions of what ought to be; and the reason with which it is concerned is accordingly practical reason. In Kant's view it is quite wrong to think that ethics gives us any theoretical knowledge of ourselves. But what of logic? In the passage from the *Anthropology* quoted on page 196 above we have seen Kant saying that in logic we know ourselves 'using as material what intellectual consciousness provides'; whilst in the lectures on logic published in Kant's lifetime by Jäsche we find logic described as the 'self-knowledge of reason and understanding'.[1] Does not this suggest that in logic we have to deal with a form of self-awareness of a special kind, and if so how is Kant to account for it? Should he say, in particular, that logic enables us to know ourselves as we actually are, in contrast to psychology, which tells us only how we appear to ourselves? That he ought to have drawn this conclusion was certainly urged by Kant's successors, and we may well think their point here a sound one.

Now Kant himself was quite clear that logic does *not* give us knowledge of our 'real' selves. The business of the logician, he

[1] Berlin edition, ix. 14; cf. *Critique of Pure Reason*, B ix.

held, was to reflect on concrete examples of thinking, and elicit the rules to which it conforms when true to its own nature. In formal logic we are concerned with the most general of all such rules: with the laws that govern correct thinking of any kind. But it is wrong to suppose that, when we discover those rules, we are knowing ourselves as noumena. All we are doing is bringing out a certain truth about the subject of thinking: that it must, if it is to think at all, comply with certain formal principles. But the subject of thinking, as we have seen many times already, is not for Kant a substantial self. It is only a formal unity to which all our knowledge must relate, a mere aspect of the concrete self we know in introspection. To put logic alongside psychology as a source of knowledge of the self is thus, at the least, highly misleading.

Yet, even if we accept the principles of this defence, we may well ask whether Kant is entitled to his main assumption. It seems undeniable that he thought that, in logic, reason does have insight into its own nature. He believed the laws set out by the logician to be involved in discursive thinking as such; that human reason, if it is to think soundly, must think in accordance with these and no other laws. The suggestion, favoured by some later writers on the subject, that the laws of logic are true only by definition or arbitrary convention, does not seem to have been even considered by him. The alternative to that view which Kant accepts is to say that logical laws express necessary truths about the nature of human reason (or perhaps about discursive reason as such); but how is he to explain our knowledge of such truths? He can only say that we know them because we *see* them to be involved in all thinking. If such 'seeing' is not intellectual intuiting, what is it?

Nor is this all: if we leave the consideration of formal and pass to that of transcendental logic, further difficulties arise. Transcendental logic has to deal with our *a priori* thinking of objects, and it forms part of that propaedeutic to a true metaphysics which Kant calls 'critical philosophy'. But though Kant thought hard and long about how to validate the propositions which transcendental logic establishes, propositions such as the general law of causality, he does not appear to have given any thought to the question how it is itself possible. That there could be such an inquiry as critical philosophy, that reason could reflect on its own operations and discover the limits of its proper employment, are things which he just takes for granted. Here again he appears to have assumed that reason in a broad sense is capable of intuiting its own nature, and it is upon such an intuition that he would presumably base such a fundamental proposition as that sense and thought must co-operate in human knowledge. But it is not clear that we can admit both the intuition and the proposition it is alleged to establish: one of the two must go, yet both seem to be indispensable to Kant's thinking.

We must conclude that Kant has not sufficiently considered the sense in which some parts of philosophy seem to depend on our ascribing to reason a power of self-awareness, in virtue of which it is able to discover truths about its own nature. He recognizes, indeed, as the passages we have quoted show, that logic is, in a broad sense, a form of self-knowledge; and he should have seen that the same is true of critical philosophy itself. But his insistence on the important point that the self we illuminate in logic and theory of knowledge is really only the subject of thinking, and therefore not a substantial entity, causes him to overlook the fact that, in assuming that reason can know itself at all, he is breaking with the main principle of his philosophy. In so far as this is true, we must admit that the Kantian philosophy is self-contradictory; and there are some who would give it up just because of that fact. But it is perhaps fairer to say that Kant leaves us with a puzzle: the puzzle of knowing in what sense philosophy can throw light on the nature of mind. That there is a sense in which the study of some philosophical disciplines adds to our grasp of the nature of the self is hard to deny; but what that sense is, and how philosophical knowledge of mind relates to psychological, remain to be determined.

§ 5. At this point it may be helpful to put together what seem to be the main lessons of the foregoing discussion.

(A) There can be little doubt that a satisfactory account of the self must do justice to its dual character as both subject and object. What has been called the paradox of self-knowledge arises from the fact that 'we' are said to intuit 'ourselves': a proposition which suggests that the self is at once united and divided. The paradox has proved a source of inspiration to exponents of the Hegelian philosophy, with their dogma that identity is nowhere to be found apart from diversity; but even plain men must recognize that it has a certain foundation in fact. Whatever explanation we give of the duality which characterizes our conception of the self (and it may be, as Kant said, that no explanation of it is possible), conceive it as dual we must. To try to suppress the subject self altogether, as some empiricists would like to do, is as absurd as to attempt to characterize the self as pure spontaneity, and deny that we can know it as object at all.

(B) The strength of the empiricist view of self-knowledge lies in the undoubted fact that we can make the self an object of knowledge, and that when we do so our experience of it is in some ways akin to our experience of external objects. In both cases we have to deal in the first place with a manifold of intuition or stream of feelings, which subsequent reflection transforms into a more or less orderly world. Our acquaintance with our own inner states is sufficiently like our acquaintance with external reality to justify us in calling it inner sensation. And just as the data of the external senses form the raw material for sciences like physics, so do those of internal sensation provide the basis for a science of psychology. This does not mean, of course, that the psychologist must conceive the self precisely on the lines on which physicists conceive their objects: clearly there are fundamental differences between the two. The phenomena of the self are not localized in space; and again they display a unity and a continuity which are without parallel in the world of inanimate objects: in their investigation we cannot (or should not) lose sight of the fact that they belong together as constituents of a single person. But though this is no doubt important if we are considering the methods the psychologist should follow in his studies, it casts no doubt on the legitimacy of his whole undertaking.

(C) The strength of the rationalist conception of self-knowledge lies in our being subjects as well as objects of introspection. That there is a sense in which we know ourselves from within, 'enjoy' ourselves as active agents, seems hard to deny. It is when we attempt to cash in on this fact, if a crude metaphor can be forgiven, that difficulties arise. What are we to make of the active self, and how are we to know it? The first answer to these questions was that given by the old-fashioned metaphysical psychology, which claimed that we could know by rational intuition the properties of the active self, which thus turned into the soul of theological discourse. The fallacies of this point of view were exposed once and for all by Hume and Kant, whose criticisms were endorsed here by Hegel. The self as subject was not to be thought of as a superior kind of object. What then was it? Kant himself made out that it was nothing more than the transcendental unity of apperception, a mere formal identity which accompanies all our thinking and as it were stamps it all as ours. About such an entity (if entity it should be called) nothing significant can be said: it is the absolute subject which admits of no predicates. But this view is not one which has carried complete conviction. Kant seems to have overlooked (or understressed) the fact that his own philosophy presupposes in human reason a power of self-awareness, and that thanks to this power we do seem able to formulate certain important truths about the knowing subject. The criticisms of his successors, in particular of Hegel, who strove to interpret the self in terms of pure spontaneity, are by no means all justified; yet over this point at least they seem to be well-founded. Philosophy does appear to shed light on the nature of the self, and Kant has not accounted satisfactorily for its doing so.

The problem of self-knowledge is thus, as we saw at the end of the last section, in essentials a problem about the relation between the knowledge of the self provided by psychology and the self-knowledge, if any, which philosophy provides. It can be put, if we like, in the question how far we can draw a legitimate distinction between introspection, where that term is taken to signify a kind of internal sense-perception, and what might be called rational reflection. It is closely bound up with the questions what philosophy aims at and how philosophical knowledge is itself possible.

Let us take two representative views.

(I) Modern empiricists, confronted with the sort of argument we have considered in this chapter, would deny that there is any problem on the ground that philosophical judgements are all analytic. Philosophy, they say, tells us nothing about the world of fact. Every factual statement is capable of translation, in principle, into sentences which record actual or possible sense-experiences or introspections; and all such statements are the object of some science or other. Philosophy is like grammar in so far as its concern is not with the factual content of sentences, but with the formal relations of the symbols they contain. There can accordingly be no clash between philosophy and the sciences, and so no possibility of there being a philosophical knowledge of mind to supplement or rival that provided by psychology.

The theory is worked out in a series of arguments which are now generally familiar. With some of these—for example, with those which profess to demonstrate the impossibility of metaphysics—

we need not concern ourselves here. We should, however, notice the view of logic taken by the school. Logic is said, as it was by Kant, to be a purely formal science; but the forms which it investigates are not specifically forms of thinking. The logician's business is to examine the types of relation which hold between propositions, in virtue of which we are justified in passing from one to another.[1] Given any proposition or set of propositions, we can pass by logical inference to further propositions; and what the logician does is to investigate the principles on which our argument proceeds. But there is no single set of principles to which we are bound in formal reasoning, no group of logical rules which constitutes the laws of thought as such. On the contrary: just as we can take what symbols we like for the objects of which we are thinking, so can we devise rules for their transformation at will. No set of rules (including those we follow in everyday discourse) has any absolute validity, nor is any involved, as earlier logicians thought, in the nature of reason. Rather we must say that every logical law owes its 'truth' to our determination to follow it, and holds good only so long as that determination is maintained.

It is clear enough that, if this view of logic is correct, the suggestion that logic throws light on the nature of mind is a false one. Now it certainly is the case that modern logicians recognize far more principles as involved in formal reasoning than did their predecessors in the science, and that they have succeeded in grouping these principles in a plurality of logical systems. But, as we saw in discussing this point in an earlier chapter (pp. 95 ff.), it is by no means obvious that these different systems are genuine alternatives to each other. When we compare one system of formal logic with another, or when we say that inside any given system there must be no inconsistencies or that the consequences deduced must *follow* from the original premisses, we appear to be appealing to a more fundamental logic which they all presuppose. Such a logic might well be taken as concerned to define what is meant by

[1] What *is* a proposition? Here we get divergent answers from different exponents of formal logic. One group, now rather outmoded, thinks of propositions as in some sense objective constituents of the universe, constituents which exist whether or not anyone takes up a mental attitude to them. Seeing that one proposition entails another, for this group, is to discover something important about the nature of fact. But the empiricist school whose theories are discussed in the text is far more inclined to identify propositions with sentences rather than facts, and to look on formal argument as a means of transforming one sentence or set of sentences into another. Logical argument is, in this interpretation, purely tautological.

logically possible, and this subject at least is not unconnected with the nature of our minds. For, as Kant pointed out, only minds of a certain sort would draw the distinction between the possible and the actual that we draw. Leibniz said that the truths of logic were true for all possible worlds, but he should have added 'as conceived by *discursive* consciousness'. The notion of logical possibility, which logic is concerned to elucidate, is one which to a different sort of understanding from our own would be entirely without meaning. An intuitive intelligence would neither need nor show interest in any system of logic.

It appears from this that the form of empiricism we are considering has not succeeded in making out its contention that the study of logic throws no light on the nature of mind. But there is a further difficulty in which it is involved. We have seen that its official view of philosophical propositions is that they are all analytic. But though this account can be applied with fair plausibility to a good many philosophical statements, it is not clear how it would apply to the fundamental principles of theory of knowledge. If we say, as supporters of this view do, that every significant (synthetic) statement must be, in principle at least, verifiable in some sort of sense-experience, is that to be taken as an analytic or a synthetic proposition? Certainly if someone asked why he should accept such a criterion of significant statements, it would not be enough to reply that it was a matter of definition and nothing more; he would want to be shown that no other criterion was, in the nature of things, appropriate or even possible. But a demonstration of that sort could only proceed by pointing to the *facts* about human knowing as revealed in philosophical reflection, i.e. by taking account of the constitution of our intelligence. Is this not to admit that theory of knowledge is a study which both issues in and depends upon our knowing certain *synthetic* propositions, and if so how are empiricists to explain that knowledge?

Probably the best line for them to take in this difficulty would be to admit that epistemology does involve factual knowledge of the constitution of the human intelligence, but to say that such knowledge is psychological. This would preserve their main contention, that philosophy can contribute nothing to the study of mind, at the cost of transferring part of it to another discipline. And it would be in accordance with the tradition of empiricism as represented, for instance, by Hume, whose philosophy of human nature was quite openly a psychological study.[1] But there are, of course, objections to any such procedure. In the first place (though this is far from decisive) one would expect, if epistemological questions did fall within the province of psychology, that their solution would present less difficulties than it in fact does. Like other empirical inquirers, the psychologist has a means of checking his theories, by referring to the facts they are alleged to explain. But if philosophical theories depend on facts, they are not facts of the same easy and obvious kind. And there is a second and more serious difficulty. Psychology is a first-order study, concerned to reflect on the phenomena of mental life and discover the laws they embody. But theory of knowledge is a second-order discipline, which comes into existence only when first-order studies like psychology already exist. This seems to imply that the facts which theory of knowledge elicits are on a different level from those established by the psychologist. Because theory of knowledge is concerned, not with knowing about any particular department of reality, but with knowing as such, there is a sense in which the truths it formulates are prior to those discovered in other branches of learning. It is therefore paradoxical to lump theory of knowledge in with psychology, which is, after all, a special science like any other.

These considerations suggest that the attempt of the modern empiricist school to dispose of our problem by denying its existence is not likely to be successful. In theory of knowledge, at least, there is a sense in which we are exploring the nature of the human intelligence, and so attaining a species of self-knowledge. But we are still without any satisfactory account of the relationship of this knowledge to that provided by the psychologist, our only clue being the statement that theory of knowledge is a second-order and psychology a first-order study. Let us therefore turn to a different view of the matter.

(II) We might expect an intelligent rationalist, confronted with the actual development of a science of psychology, yet anxious to maintain that philosophy throws light on the self, to argue on the following lines.[2] There can be philosophical knowledge of the self,

[1] Compare the way in which Hume establishes, in the first section of the *Treatise*, his own version of the main principle of empiricism, that every simple idea must be derived from some precedent impression.

[2] In what follows I have had in mind particularly the views of Professor R. G. Collingwood, though I have not set them out in detail, as I do not wish to discuss here his contention that all philosophical knowledge is historical. For Colling-

and there can be psychological knowledge of it. When we investigate ourselves in philosophy it is the self *qua* rational, the activities of reason and understanding, that we make our object. This is the part of the self which is often called the mind, and if we adopt this designation we must say that philosophy alone can give us organized knowledge of mind. And an indispensable condition of our being able to acquire such knowledge is that we should have a faculty of rational reflection, a power of turning our attention to our own thinking and considering questions about its formal nature and presuppositions. Rational reflection here is a form of self-awareness which is *sui generis*; it is quite different from the introspection of the psychologist. Introspection is akin to sense-perception, and in it we can distinguish two factors: the apprehending of a content and the characterizing of it in judgement. Rational reflection appears, by way of contrast, to be single rather than double, intuitive rather than discursive.

But, of course, the activities of the self are not all rational, and indeed it might be true to say that singularly few of them are. Rational thinking (and rational willing, too, if there is any such thing) is conditioned throughout by the presence of non-rational factors in the self, factors which are responsible for the constant discrepancy between thinking as it is and thinking as it should be. And this leaves room for a further study of the self over and above that of the philosopher. If it is the business of philosophy to consider the self *qua* rational, it is for the psychologist to investigate the non-rational background to our rational activities—to give an account of what Professor Collingwood called 'the blind forces and activities in us which are part of human life as it consciously experiences itself, but are not parts of the historical [rational] process: sensation as distinct from thought, feelings as distinct from conceptions, appetite as distinct from will'.[1] A study of these blind forces is clearly indispensable if we are to say anything about ourselves in the concrete, since they make up a very real and important part of human nature. But just as it would be wrong to neglect them, so would it be improper to equate them with the self as such. Whatever the importance of psychology, it cannot be held to be the sole science of the self. Psychology can tell us nothing about the higher forms of human activity, just as

wood's opinion of the province of psychology see especially *The Principles of Art*, p. 171 n. and *The Idea of History*, pp. 230–1.

[1] Ibid., p. 231.

it cannot explain how we ought to act and think if we are to be rational beings. It is to philosophy that these tasks belong.

What this comes to, put very broadly, is that philosophy studies the higher self, psychology the lower. Now it may be objected that this sharp division does not square with the facts, and would be disputed by philosopher and psychologist alike. It is not true, in the first place, that the philosopher is silent about the non-rational part of the self. Any theory of knowledge must clearly have a good deal to say about sensation, just as any theory of morals must discuss the nature of appetite. Nor again would the psychologist agree to leave what we are calling the higher activities of mind out of account—to abandon all consideration of the phenomena of religion and the moral life, for instance. He would argue that the influence of the factors in which he was interested could not be confined to any particular sphere, but might be seen in any department of experience, and would accordingly claim that there was no branch of human activity which his study might not illuminate.

The objection is a perfectly just one; yet it is perhaps possible to meet it without making any substantial change in the theory. Instead of saying that philosophy and psychology study different *parts* of the self, we should say that they study different *aspects* of it. The self is to be regarded as containing two sets of factors, rational and irrational, and we can direct our attention to whichever we choose. The influence of both sets can be seen throughout our mental life: we are constantly thinking and acting as rational beings, yet we are also constantly failing, through the operation of non-rational factors in ourselves, to live up to the standards we set ourselves. To give a complete account of the self we must hence undertake both a philosophical and a psychological study of it. We cannot fuse the two, though it has often been proposed that we should, since the self *qua* rational differs fundamentally from the self *qua* non-rational. To consider myself as a thinker, or again as a moral agent, I must make use of methods totally different from those I should adopt in investigating myself psychologically. And it seems hard to deny that the difference is connected with the fact that I have a kind of insight into my rational nature which I do not have into the phenomena of the non-rational self.

§ 6. This theory of the relationship between psychology and what may be called, very generally, philosophy of mind, presents an account which, as it seems to the present writer, is not only intelligible but also substantially correct. It has the solid merit of doing justice to all that is important in the rationalist tradition, whilst at the same time retaining some central features of the empiricist view; and for that reason might be expected to commend itself to philosophical moderates of all kinds. But it cannot be denied that, as here expounded, the view contains certain obscurities, and that in particular the notion of rational reflection which it involves stands in need of further clarification. I will end this chapter with some remarks on that notion and on the consequences its acceptance entails for theory of knowledge.

In the first place, it seems important to point out a sense in which every philosopher ought to agree that rational reflection is possible. To see that sense we have only to take some ostensible example of thinking or rational action and (in a broad sense of the term) reflect upon it. If we do that, we find that there are two quite different questions we can ask about it. First, we can inquire whether it is in fact a genuine act of thinking or an action in the true sense. What troubles us here is the possibility that we might not be thinking or acting at all, but only behaving in an automatic way, as of course we often do. Our way of answering the question is to examine our behaviour, as revealed in introspection, closely, and apply to it such tests as the psychologist may devise. But once we have convinced ourselves that we are really thinking or acting, there is a further question we can go on to ask: what is the content of our thought, or the purpose to which we are striving to give effect? It is here, I think, that rational reflection comes in. Reflection on our rational acts enables us to grasp the content of those acts: to find out what we are thinking, or what we are trying to do. It is true that reflection on any one act will not answer all questions about it: it will not enable us to connect it with previous acts, to get at the premisses or motives which lay behind our thought or actions. To discover those an extensive inquiry may be needed. But that we can grasp what it is we are thinking when we think, and do so by rational reflection, seems obvious enough.

However, to say that rational reflection is possible in this sense is not to say anything exciting. It amounts to no more than the assertion that human beings have a faculty of abstraction, and can consider the content of their thinking in separation from its psychical background. The theory we are considering would certainly claim that this was true, but it would also claim something more. It would claim that rational reflection gives us insight of a special kind into the nature of reason. Thanks to this insight the philosopher is able to discover certain truths—indeed, certain necessary truths—about the human mind, and so to provide an important form of self-knowledge. It is on the possibility of rational reflection in this wide sense that the whole theory turns. What are we to say about it?

Here I think we should do well to take the cases of logic and theory of knowledge separately. Let us take first the logician reflecting on his own acts of thinking and seeking to establish the formal principles to which they conform. Aristotle said long ago that we could be led by rational reflection to see that our thought embodies certain formal principles such as the law of contradiction. His own explanation was that the law is a necessary truth about the world of fact, discoverable by intuitive induction. In criticizing this view in an earlier chapter we pointed out that the true concern of formal logic is not with the actual but with the possible, and that the laws it establishes are prescriptive rather than factual in character. But it may be asked here whether we should not say that they are both prescriptive and descriptive: prescriptive to whatever falls within experience, but descriptive of the essential nature of the experiencing subject. To this we can certainly answer that they are not descriptive of mind in the way the old rational psychology purported to be, since if anything is clear it is that the logician has no direct intuition of his own thinking self. Yet it seems perverse to deny that, in knowing that the mind, if its thinking is to be effective, must conform to certain principles, we are discovering something important about it. The logician, though unable to study the subject-self directly, is none the less able to bring out some aspects of it quite clearly. What he does can be compared to what, on a Kantian view of the science, the Euclidean geometer does about space. According to such a view, there is an essential connexion between geometry and space, yet space itself cannot be intuited.[1] We find, however, that when we construct figures in space, or consider the geometrical properties of objects in space, we can discover certain *a priori* principles to which all such figures and objects conform. These principles, if Kant is right, depend on the necessary nature of

[1] Kant himself frequently says that space *can* be intuited; but it is not clear that he ought to do so, for the purposes of his philosophy of mathematics at least.

space itself, and in knowing them we are thus gaining insight into that necessary nature. Similarly with logic: unless we adopt the modern empiricist account of them, it seems that we must agree that logical principles depend on the nature of the knowing subject, and that in establishing them the logician gains insight into that nature, knowing it not directly but obliquely.[1]

But if we accept this conclusion, as I think we must, it is only right that we should be clear that it does involve a most important concession to rationalism. We are allowing that, in logic at least, mind can know its own nature, and can do this by what is, in fact, a species of intellectual intuition, though a rather odd one. It is true that all that emerges from a logical study, even on this account, is knowledge of the most general principles by which we are bound in our thinking. If reason knows itself in logic, such knowledge is, as Kant was never tired of saying, of a purely formal character. But whether formal or not, it is knowledge which none the less deserves its name, and for that reason excites the interest of the philosopher.

Now let us turn to theory of knowledge and consider whether we can give the same account of that discipline. At first sight it appears that we can. If the task of the logician is to discover the principles which govern valid thinking as such, the epistemologist may be held to consider thinking of a special type—namely, *a priori* thinking of objects—with the aim of eliciting its special principles. But when we examine the way in which this task is carried out, we cannot avoid seeing an important difference between logicians and epistemologists. The difference is that while the logician seems to have intuitive insight into the principles of formal reasoning, the epistemologist must have recourse to an elaborate proof to establish his conclusions. We cannot just *see* that the law of causality is involved in objective thinking as we can see that the law of contradiction is involved in formal thinking.

And there is a further difference. The business of theory of knowledge does not end with the establishment of the *a priori* principles governing objective thinking: it has also to consider in virtue of what we need to apply those principles, and this is indeed its central problem. Here reason does truly seek to elicit its own

[1] I am, of course, disregarding here the third possibility that logical laws might be laws of things and not of thought: on this see p. 98 above. On my own view, logic must apply to whatever exists, since the minimum prerequisite of what we take to be fact is that we should be able to think it.

nature and bring out the properties of the subject of knowledge. But though the procedure of reason in solving this problem is without doubt to reflect on examples of knowledge and consider what is involved in them, it would be absurd to claim that the result of the process is a flash of intuitive insight. What does result is a *theory* which seeks to do justice to the facts of consciousness and must be tested by reference to them. It is the facts which are known by rational reflection rather than the theory about them. And just how much argument may be needed to establish any set of conclusions we can see by considering any of the classical writings on the subject: Hume's *Treatise*, Kant's *Critique*, or Hegel's *Logic*.

I conclude that, though in theory of knowledge our aim is to throw light on the knowing subject, we cannot claim any special intuition to help us in the search or to guarantee our results. Our procedure, here as in the positive sciences, is to review particular cases in the hope of finding a theory which will fit them all. The more complex our facts, the more argument we need to ground our conclusions, and the less certain we can be of them. But if I am asked whether this does not show that theory of knowledge should be considered a positive science like any other, I can answer only by pointing to the difference between first-order and second-order inquiries, and by saying that there is a sense in which epistemology presupposes the positive sciences rather than is co-ordinate with them. It seems to me, indeed, that theory of knowledge occupies a peculiarly ambiguous position in the world of learning: that it is neither an ordinary empirical discipline, because it is concerned with the presuppositions of experience itself, nor yet an *a priori* one, since there is no insight to which we can appeal for a definitive solution of its problems. What status its propositions have, and how they can be tested, seem accordingly to need careful discussion. But I have not found any such discussion in the main authorities I have consulted, nor can I supply one myself.[1]

[1] Perhaps I should mention that Kant was led to overlook the need for such a discussion by considering critical philosophy a part of metaphysics, and so making the answer to the question 'How is metaphysics possible as a science?' also answer 'How is critical philosophy possible?' But to show that metaphysics can consist of valid synthetic *a priori* judgements is not to show that critical philosophy consists of propositions of the same kind.

X

EXPERIENCE AND METAPHYSICS

§ I. *Nur in der Erfahrung ist Wahrheit*: all genuine knowledge rests on experience. The truth seems so obvious as scarcely to need enunciation, much less the elaborate discussion and defence it receives from writers on theory of knowledge. Yet controversy on the subject continues, and the partisans of experience, for all the initial plausibility of their point of view, by no means enjoy an undisputed triumph. One reason for the doubts felt about their fundamental contentions we have been at pains to stress in the present book: an ambiguity which infects the term 'experience' itself. Speaking roughly, we may say that the term is used indiscriminately to designate two quite different levels of awareness: the stage which Bradley calls 'feeling' and the stage he calls 'relational thought'.[1] At the level of feeling we seem to have immediate contact with reality, to grasp the real in its individuality and to possess it without question or doubt. It is to the satisfaction this state involves that empiricism owes its perennial appeal: here, at least, we believe, is something palpable and beyond cavil, a sure foundation for all our knowledge. But the satisfaction is scarcely a lasting one. For if feeling is certain, it is also dumb: to say what it is we are feeling we must pass beyond the feeling state itself to the level of judgement or relational thought. Here we move to an experience of a very different type, an experience in which the intellect as well as the senses has its part to play, and in which, though we have advanced to the apprehension of truth, we have also laid ourselves open to the possibility of error. Experience at this new level, of which we may take sense-perception proper to be typical, clearly provides a very different basis for knowledge from that offered by simple feeling, more particularly if we press the arguments which show that it involves not only thinking but *a priori* thinking too; and we can scarcely wonder that strict empiricists look on it with suspicion. But, unless I am greatly mistaken, the initial plausibility of the whole empiricist case depends on a tacit confusion between these two types of experience; and some of the most interesting questions in theory of knowledge arise out of the attempt to specify their exact relations.

[1] The corresponding terms in Kant are *Empfindung* and *Wahrnehmung*.

But though this contrast between immediate and developed experience is undoubtedly of major importance, it is not necessarily the only ambiguity which the term conceals. All synthetic knowledge, we say, rests on experience; but can we be sure that there is at bottom only one *kind* of experience—that we call sensation in its immediate and sense-perception in its developed form? Writers on these questions who have been brought up in the empiricist tradition tend to assume dogmatically that this is the case, and their example is often followed by those who draw their inspiration from Kant. But it is by no means obvious that they are right in this assumption. There is at any rate a *prima-facie* case for the view that there are several fundamentally different kinds of experience: that the experience of the mystic, to take one example, is different in kind from that of the rest of us, or again that aesthetic and religious and scientific experience are not reducible one to another. No investigation of the basic problems of knowledge can afford to pass over this claim in silence, since it is clear enough that our answers to epistemological questions will vary greatly according to our attitude to it. To deal with it adequately—to attempt to specify in detail the relations of the different spheres mentioned—would doubtless require a book in itself, and a long book at that. But a shorter examination, in which we concentrate on questions of principle and consider details only in so far as they serve to illustrate these, may none the less have its uses. It is such an examination that we shall undertake in the present chapter.

I must begin by making a point which I take to be of some importance. When we say that there are fundamentally different kinds of experience open to human beings we may mean one of two things. We may mean that there is more than one kind of immediate experience, i.e. that sensation is not the only primary source of knowledge; or we may intend to assert that, though immediate experience is single, developed experience is not. On this second view we should hold that the element of thought which developed experience involves varies according to the different sorts of data we are sensing; that when we are dealing with living things, for example, or with the actions of human beings, we need different categorial principles from those we invoke to explain the movements of dead matter. Where different categories can be pointed to, there we have to do with different kinds of experience. And it may be remarked at once that the second of these alternatives is far more favourable to rationalism than the first. The only form of immediate experience in which rationalists are specifically interested is intellectual intuition; if this is denied them, they can draw no comfort from a proof that sensation is not the only primary source of knowledge. The situation is, however, entirely altered when it is maintained that there are different forms of developed experience, varying according to the fundamental ideas they involve. For the rationalist can—and does[1]—turn this position to his advantage by arguing that these forms of experience can be arranged on a scale according to the purity or adequacy of the thought they contain. The thought in some forms of experience—for example, ordinary sense-perception—may be poor and abstract, whilst that in others—for example, in philosophical experience—may be rich and concrete. If we are to speak of experience as such, the rationalist will argue, we should take it not at its lowest but at its highest level, the level at which the thought it involves is most explicit and free. This is clearly an important argument, whose possibilities we must examine with care, more especially since, as we shall see, it is closely bound up with the question of the sense in which metaphysics is a legitimate study. But before we deal with it we must say something on the subject of immediate experience.

§ 2. Leaving aside intellectual intuition, which I do not propose to discuss again, can we point to any other form of immediate experience besides sensation? An answer which will occur to many readers is that we can find such a form in the experience of religious men generally and of mystics in particular. There is and has been a widespread conviction, common to many nations and manifested by believers in very different faiths, that immediate experience of the supersensible is possible in moments of religious ecstasy at least; that in such moments we can penetrate the veil of phenomena which constitutes our object in ordinary sense-perception and gain direct insight into reality, seeing or rather experiencing God face to face. It is not maintained, of course, that this sort of experience is open equally to all men in the way sensation is; it should rather

[1] For an example cf. Collingwood's early work *Speculum Mentis* (1924), where art, religion, natural science, history, and philosophy are compared and contrasted. Mr. Michael Oakeshott's *Experience and its Modes* is another instance of the same sort of thing, though its conclusions are more sceptical, as might have been expected in a follower of Bradley. This sort of philosophizing goes back, I think, to Hegel's *Phenomenology*.

be regarded as analogous to the insight of the poet or the artist, whose powers are looked on as a divine gift and their exercise as inspiration. Yet it would be wrong to suggest, in the case of the mystic as in that of the artist, that whether or not they have these peculiar powers is a matter of good fortune and nothing more. The religious man, in particular, will urge that experience of the supersensible is most commonly found among those who have led, or are living, an intensely religious life; that the insight they gain should be thought of as the culmination of a long process of spiritual activity rather than as an isolated phenomenon unconnected with the rest of their personality. We may not be able to *induce* mystical experience in ourselves; whether we have it or not is in the last resort not of our own choosing. But we can, by following a particular regimen, put ourselves in a position in which we are at any rate *disposed* to have the experience. Hence the description of the mystic way, with its three stages, purgative, illuminative, and contemplative, which is given in many books about mysticism.[1]

It is difficult to say in a short compass anything at all satisfactory about a subject so vast as this, with its close bearing on the whole question of religious truth. The following remarks should be taken as no more than notes on some points of particular interest for theory of knowledge.

(i) Despite the claim set out above, it is not clear whether mystical experience should be interpreted as 'immediate' or 'developed' according to the distinction made in this book. Perhaps it will be said that the distinction just does not apply. In the immediate experience we call sensation we find ourselves aware of a manifold of sense impressions, which we proceed to judge and characterize in the developed experience of sense-perception. But the mystic, we may be told, has no need to go through separate stages like this. The vision, if vision it can be called, which he has of the true nature of things is at once intuition and interpretation; if we like to put it so, it bears its meaning on its face. There is no question of the mystic's first having certain experiences and then reflecting on their significance: what he has is rather an immediately significant experience. In this respect mystical experience is akin to the knowing of an intuitive understanding rather than to anything with which we are familiar in everyday life.

The difficulty about this is that it is possible, particularly for

[1] Compare, e.g., Dean Inge's *Christian Mysticism*, pp. 9 ff.

persons not much given to reflection, to think that an experience is free of interpretation when it is in fact nothing of the kind. That mystical experience is unusually intense, and that it carries with it an overwhelming conviction of its being genuine, is clear enough from all accounts we have of it. But it does not follow from this that it is altogether independent of subjective considerations. And in fact there is evidence to suggest that it does contain an element of interpretation. We can see this by considering the accounts of their experiences given by mystics brought up in different religions. The content of the religious experience of Christian mystics, though not entirely different from that of non-Christians, is none the less coloured throughout by the fundamental doctrines of Christianity, e.g. that of the Trinity.[1] And indeed it would be surprising if this were not the case. Beliefs such as those we hold as a matter of religious conviction penetrate the whole of our minds, with the result that we find it overwhelmingly difficult to abstract from them. There is no reason to suppose that the mystic is any better off than the rest of us in this respect.

The conclusion to be drawn from these considerations must be that the phrase 'mystical experience' is itself ambiguous. We have to reckon, in fact, with two possibilities: first, that the actual *data* with which the mystic is acquainted when he has his special experience are entirely *sui generis*, i.e. that they are other than the data of sensation and introspection; and second, that the *categories* which the mystic brings to bear in the interpretation of his experience constitute a special set of their own, into whose validity we ought to inquire. It is only with the first of these possibilities that we are concerned in the present section; but we should not allow our preoccupation with it to make us forget the second, for when we speak of mysticism as a philosophy it is evidently to this that we refer.

(ii) What are we to make of the claim that mystical experience is a primary form of awareness, entirely distinct from sensation? It is widely held in the literature of mysticism that there is spiritual as well as physical seeing; that the soul as well as the body has its

[1] Cf. G. Dawes Hicks, *The Philosophical Bases of Theism*, pp. 119–20: 'When, for example, some of the mystics declare that in the stage of what they call "contemplation" they have been able to "see" how God can be three Persons, or in what wise the Virgin Mary had been assumed into heaven, nothing can be more obvious than that they "see" what they have been by training and teaching predisposed to see. Had they been nurtured in the faith of Buddhism or of Taoism their mystic visions would unquestionably have been entirely different.'

eye. This is figurative language, but the intention behind it is clear enough. Yet we may well feel scruples about accepting it. What makes us hesitate about it most is that we cannot be certain whether the mystic has an experience which is really unique or whether he is only having very peculiar sensations. We have seen that the central experience of mysticism is alleged to supervene on an elaborate course of preparation, which includes a disciplining of the body as well as of the mind. It would be a perfectly possible, though perhaps a cynical, interpretation of this situation to suggest that the experience can be explained in terms of the physical conditions to which the mystic subjects himself, when these are considered along with his peculiar state of mind. The mystic sees visions, on this view, simply because he is physically and mentally disordered, and his doing so is a matter of interest not to the philosopher but to the physician and above all the psycho-analyst.

Without accepting this extreme view as accounting for the whole of mystical experience (which would amount in effect to judging mysticism by the metaphysical preconceptions of natural science), we may none the less agree that mystical experience is throughout conditioned by the physical and psychical background against which it takes place. That the mystic should be in a certain emotional and volitional state seems to be a necessary if not a sufficient condition of there being mystical experience at all. This does not mean, of course, that we can dismiss such experience without further ado, any more than pointing out that our dreams are conditioned by physical factors means that we can argue that there is nothing in, say, a Freudian analysis of them. But it does suggest that at least part of the content of the mystic's experience is his having sensations of a strange and rare order. And we may perhaps wonder whether the essence of mystical experience cannot be found to consist in the having such sensations, together with the intense conviction that they are the effect of a cause which lies beyond the sensible sphere altogether. This would explain the mystic's assurance that he is in contact with the supersensible without entailing the assumption that he has a peculiar faculty of knowledge all his own.

(iii) Suppose, however, that we take the mystic at his word and allow that he has an experience different in kind from the rest of us: the problem then arises how we are to know that the content of that experience is objectively valid. One of the things which mystics stress most about their experiences is that strictly speaking they are ineffable:[1] they could not be properly described or communicated to non-mystics for the simple reason that the latter could have no idea of what was being described or communicated. The most that could be done is that the mystic should find some situation in the sensible world which bears a remote analogy to what he has seen 'on the other side of being', and use this to convey, however inadequately, some notion of the nature of reality. Hence the profusion of metaphors which characterizes all mystical writing, and the vague language in which mystical doctrines are apt to be expressed. Now there are some empiricists who have a short way with mystics in this situation. The mystic, they say, is welcome to his experiences; but if they are really ineffable, that is the end of the matter. There can be no obligation on anyone constructing a system of knowledge which professes to be common property (and philosophical knowledge would clearly fall within such a system) to take account of what is, by definition, a purely private insight. But we may well question whether this attitude is not, like some others adopted by empiricists, a trifle dogmatic. We have, after all, to face the empirical fact that the phenomena associated with mystical experience are both widespread and well documented. It is not as if we had to deal with some isolated claim to special insight, but rather with a whole series of recognizably similar claims. In these circumstances it is at least worth asking whether means could not be devised for testing the objective validity of mystical experience and separating true 'visions' from the products of idle imagination and morbid conditions.

It is possible to imagine one such test which might conceivably be of use. Let us suppose that some mystical experiences are genuine, and ask what we should expect about their communicability. We may agree that to non-mystics[2] they are strictly incommunicable, for the reason given above; but it is not clear that the same would be true if we asked whether one mystic could convey his experiences to another. If mystical experience is truly cognitive, we should expect those who have it to find ways of

[1] Ineffability is noted as the first of the characteristics of mysticism by William James in his *Varieties of Religious Experience*, p. 380. See also p. 405 of that work.

[2] I assume here a sharper distinction between mystics and non-mystics than some would be ready to admit. It might be argued that mystical experience is far more widely distributed than it appears at first sight to be, though in most people at most times it is only faint and feeble. But even if this is correct, it makes no difference to the argument. It is in those in whom mystical experience is urgent and intensive that we should expect to find a special vocabulary developed.

referring to different parts or aspects of it which would be intelligible to other mystics at least. There ought, on this hypothesis, to be a special mystical language, a set of symbols expressly devised to enable mystics to compare their experiences. It is true that everyday speech would be useless for this purpose, since the symbols it contains can be cashed only in terms of sense-experiences; but that would not prevent the invention of a special vocabulary to suit the mystics' needs. And, conversely, if we found such a vocabulary in existence we could take it as evidence (though not, of course, as proof) that mystical experience is genuinely cognitive.

Do we in fact find a special terminology of this kind in use among mystics? This is a question which I do not feel myself at all competent to answer. But there are one or two points in connexion with it on which I will venture to remark. In the first place, it is a fact that the actual language used by mystics shows recognizable similarities the whole world over. Differences of religious upbringing are doubtless responsible for important divergences, but the similarities which remain are none the less striking. It is true that what we meet with is not so much a recurring technical vocabulary as a recurring set of metaphors and similes, in which an attempt is made to extend the resources of everyday language to cover the needs of mystical experience. By stressing the inadequacy of all such metaphors the mystics seem to go out of their way to underline their failure to invent a special vocabulary of their own. But in fact some metaphors, such as that of the blinding light seen at the moment of mystic union, are so frequently met with that they have almost become technical terms in themselves. And, secondly, it is surely a point of importance that while mystical writing is usually regarded by persons of non-mystical temperament as tedious and even nonsensical, it produces quite a different effect when read by other mystics. Symbols which to the one party seem empty or vague to a degree evoke an immediate response in the other: it is as if they really did stand for an experience which writer and reader had in common. One cannot help being reminded here of the similar case of art criticism. Disputes about, e.g., painting or music are meaningless to those who can make nothing of these arts; but that does not imply that they are absolutely nonsensical, and indeed to many people they mean a great deal.

The foregoing discussion, brief and imperfect as it has been, will perhaps suffice to make clear that, in the opinion of the present writer, the philosophical issues raised by mysticism cannot be regarded as anything like settled. Probably no one would deny that consequences of the greatest importance for theory of knowledge would be entailed if we agreed that mystical experience deserved to rank alongside sensation as a primary source of knowledge. This is the rock on which theologians, and idealist metaphysicians too, would be well advised to build. But it cannot be said that at present it affords an altogether sure foundation. What is needed most of all is, I think, a clear statement of the case for mysticism from someone who, whilst himself having some share of mystical experience, possesses also a critical temperament and the ability to do justice to the arguments against mysticism. Such a statement, in which the philosophical claims of the mystics were set out and defended against attack, would be of real benefit both to supporters and to opponents of mysticism, to say nothing of students of theory of knowledge. Unfortunately, mystics with critical minds are as rare as critically minded persons with mystical experience.

§ 3. I come now to the problem of developed experience. To make clear what that problem is, it will perhaps be best to start from a familiar criticism of the philosophy of Kant. We are often told that though Kant professed to set out in the *Critique of Pure Reason* the presuppositions of experience as such, he succeeded only in elucidating the first principles of Newtonian physics. He proposed to take all knowledge for his province, to discover the *a priori* principles involved in all objective thinking; but in fact the only knowledge he really considered was that we have of objects in space and time, i.e. the scientific knowledge available in his own day. This gave an altogether one-sided twist to his conclusions, and necessitated a good deal of correction of them by his successors.

It is perhaps worth noting as a preliminary point that the criticism appears to contain two charges rather than one. The first is that Kant considered only perceptual or scientific experience, to the neglect of other forms of knowledge or human activity, such as history, moral action, and artistic experience. The second is that he interpreted perceptual experience itself in a particularly narrow way, in fact equating it with the experience of the (Newtonian) physicist. It may be useful to keep this distinction in mind in the sequel.

What are we to say about the criticism, and what answer, if any, can Kant make to it? I think it can scarcely be denied that, so far as the *Critique of Pure Reason* is concerned, the criticism is valid in its more general form at least. There Kant does set out to investigate the fundamental principles of objective thinking, and he understands by objective thinking the thinking of a world of objects united in one space and one time. It is true that the problem of the work is stated in a wider fashion. Kant asks how pure science of Nature is possible, and he takes Nature to include minds as well as bodies. But though this means that in theory he is asking after the first principles of psychology as well as those of physics (or rather after the principles presupposed by both sciences), he is in practice far from certain whether psychology can become a science in the strict sense,[1] and his conclusions are not affected by the results of that study in the way they are by the results of physics. As a result Kant's concept of possible experience becomes identical with the notion of experience as interpreted in the physical sciences: a fact which goes some way to justify the criticism in its narrower form too.

All this sounds dogmatic to a degree; yet Kant's position is not as absurd as it may seem. We should never forget (though it is all too easy to leave it out of account) that the *Critique of Pure Reason* is only part of the great critical edifice, the first volume of a trilogy which was completed by the *Critique of Practical Reason* and the *Critique of Judgment*. And if we turn to those works we find that while the doctrines of their predecessor are presupposed without substantial change or fresh direct argument, the case for our acceptance of them is incidentally reinforced by the raising of questions not previously considered. Among these questions are that of the cognitive value of forms of experience other than sense-perception, and of whether perceptual experience can always and everywhere be interpreted by reference to the categories of the first *Critique* alone. I will say a little about each of these.

(A) The first question arises because of Kant's recognition of other forms of judgement besides the normal judgement of sense-perception. On this point there is no excuse for misinterpreting him. He was just as alive as his successors to the fact that men engage in other activities besides the acquiring of knowledge in natural science, and just as clear that these further activities

[1] On this point see p. 197 above.

deserve philosophical examination. He does, in fact, agree that there are forms of experience other than perceptual or scientific experience. But he will not draw the conclusion that by analysing the thinking involved in these other forms of experience we can acquire fresh sets of categories to complement or challenge the categories of the scientific understanding. He believes, indeed, that both moral action and aesthetic judgement depend on principles of their own, and that these principles are *a priori*; but he denies that they are *cognitive* principles. They are not cognitive because moral and aesthetic judgements are not cognitive. Reason, Kant holds, is most certainly operative in moral judgement, but it is reason in its practical rather than its theoretical aspect. The moral agent is interested in acting not knowing, and the assumptions he makes are to be judged by their relevance to the ends he sets himself. There is no sense in looking to an analysis of moral conduct to provide us with ideas in terms of which we may hope to understand what actually exists. And fundamentally the same thing is true of aesthetic judgements. When we make a judgement ascribing beauty to a natural object we are not learning anything fresh about that object. All we are doing is giving expression to the fact that it affects us in such a way that there results a certain harmony between our imagination and our understanding, a harmony derived from the circumstance that the form which imagination grasps is such that we feel it to be orderly without being able to bring it under any general concept. If such a judgement were cognitive a special theoretical principle would be implied, the principle that Nature displays in some of its products what Kant calls *Zweckmässigkeit ohne Zweck*, purposiveness without purpose; but in fact to assert that principle is beyond the powers of theoretical reason. It is an assumption made for the purposes of aesthetic judgement, and nothing more.

It would obviously be absurd to attempt to criticize these views at all seriously in the present context. Whether we can distinguish sharply, as Kant did, between theoretical and practical reason, whether we can be content to regard aesthetic experience as being, fundamentally, a state of feeling rather than cognition, are questions which we cannot raise. But we may, for all that, regret certain omissions in Kant's account. In particular we may regret the fact that he confines his study of action to the examination of moral judgement in the strict sense, without inquiring at all into the principles we use in trying to understand action in everyday life and in history. Kant was one of the pioneers of speculative philosophy of history,[1] but he seems to have been quite unaware of any need to consider the nature of historical knowledge itself. Yet there is at least a case for the view that history is a study involving a special type of judgement and special ideas of its own; and some of these ideas—the ideas of purpose and personality, for instance—seem to be derived from the study of moral experience. Had Kant considered these facts his account of the cognitive value of that experience might well have been different.[2]

(B) Of even more interest than his theories of ethics and aesthetics are the remarks Kant makes in the second half of the *Critique of Judgment* about teleology. Here he faces the question whether the account of perceptual experience given in the first *Critique* can be regarded as final. Thinking in accordance with the categories of the *Critique of Pure Reason* gives us a world whose different parts are in thoroughgoing causal interaction. But it does nothing to explain how some of those parts can co-operate intimately as they do when they are members of an organism. For anyone who confines himself to the view of causality as a relation of events in necessary precedence and succession, i.e. to the mechanical causality of the first *Critique*, the fact that there should be organized beings is incapable of explanation. As Kant puts it in one passage: 'It is quite certain that we cannot ever come to a satisfactory knowledge of, much less explain, organized beings and their inner possibility according to mechanical principles of Nature; so much so that we may boldly assert that it is absurd for human beings even to attempt any such thing, or to hope that one day perhaps there may arise another Newton capable of making intelligible the production of a single blade of grass in accordance with laws of Nature which no design has ordered.'[3] Yet obviously we do make constant use of the concept of an organism to elucidate certain parts of our experience, and the questions arise to what principles we appeal in doing so, and with what justification we use them.

[1] His essay *Idee zu einer allgemeinen Geschichte der Menschheit in weltbürgerlicher Absicht* appeared in 1784, about the same time as the first part of Herder's *Ideen*.

[2] It should be mentioned that Kant thought the fact that we have moral experience could be used to disprove a philosophy of materialism: it showed that explanations in naturalistic terms could not be taken as ultimate. But he did not, apparently, think that reflection on it could provide any alternative account of the facts.

[3] *Critique of Judgment*, § 75.

Kant's answer is that we certainly do resort to a special principle in making judgements about organisms, namely, the principle of teleology, and this is something he had not made clear in the *Critique of Pure Reason*.[1] But he will not agree that the admission entails any real break with his earlier conclusions. The concept of purpose is not one we can apply to the whole of Nature: for that we should need to have insight into the supersensible substrate of phenomena. It serves only to render coherent a particular part of our experience, and its status is, in the terminology of the first *Critique*, not constitutive but regulative. In the language Kant used in the *Critique of Judgment* the teleological principle belongs to reflective, not determinant, judgement:[2] it is a principle we must adopt for heuristic purposes (i.e., for the practical ends of scientific investigation), but which we cannot hope to deduce or prove in the way we can deduce the principles of the understanding. To put the concept of purpose as used in the explanation of experience on the same level as the categories would accordingly be a grave mistake.

This is Kant's official doctrine. But there is a curious and interesting divergence from it in one passage of the *Critique of Judgment*. In § 70 of that work Kant sets out what he calls the antinomy of the faculty of judgement. How, he asks, are we to reconcile the two statements: (A) Production of material things (natural objects) is possible only according to mechanical laws; (B) In some cases we cannot understand such production if we use mechanical laws alone. His answer here is to treat *both* the mechanical and teleological principles as belonging to reflective judgement: to say there is no real clash between them because they are both no more than heuristic maxims elaborated to further the understanding of the given. This is, of course, a possible view, and a tempting one too; but it is quite inconsistent with the general principles of Kant's philosophy. For it amounts to an assertion that the analysis of perceptual experience given in the *Critique of Pure Reason*, an analysis in which Kant had professed to show that the human intelligence must order the data of the senses in certain specifiable ways, is not to be taken as final; that alternative sets of ordering principles are possible, and that the principles of the understanding cannot claim any privileged position among them. Such a conclusion may be in accordance with the spirit of Kant's

[1] Some points about teleology are, however, discussed in *Critique of Pure Reason*, B 714 = A 686 ff.

[2] For this language see p. 162 above.

earlier doctrine, but it is most certainly not in accordance with what he actually asserted.

In the end, however, Kant does not himself stand by the suggestion he makes in this particular section. He goes on to argue the less controversial point that neither the mechanistic nor the teleological hypothesis can be taken as explaining the constitution of ultimate reality (a view entirely consistent with the anti-metaphysical tendencies of the *Critique of Pure Reason*); but he does not again stress the epistemological equivalence of the two principles. His view seems rather to be that an explanation in teleological terms is always to be looked on with suspicion and resorted to only if all else fails, whilst an account of Nature in the language of mechanism remains everywhere normal and proper. Thus, he preserves his original conviction that for a true understanding of the empirical world we must go to the science of physics. The categories of the first *Critique* are not indeed thought by Kant to be derived from physics: they can be shown (or so he thinks) to be inherent in the nature of reason itself. But it is in the sphere of physics that they find their most ready application, and one feels that Kant had at least half an eye on that science when drawing up the list. This would account, as we suggested before (Chap. VII, § 4), for his omission of the concept of thinghood from it. But if Kant did thus equate empirical thinking as such with the thinking of the physicist, he clearly was seriously mistaken. No doubt it is easy to see why a philosopher in his time should have taken that view: physics was then the only branch of empirical inquiry with substantial achievements to its credit, and chemistry and biology (to say nothing of history and its cognate studies) had not yet attained a level of development entitling them to be regarded as well-founded disciplines with methods and principles of their own. But none of this can be of more than historical interest to us, who are confronted by a diversity of empirical studies, and must consider whether separate categories are not involved in each (or at least in each group of them). We cannot assume cheerfully, as Kant could, that there is no difficulty about developed experience because it can mean one thing, and one thing only; we have to take account of more than one claimant to the title. And in fact we shall find, as the sequel will show, that the conflict between different systems of philosophy, or of metaphysics if we prefer the term, takes its rise out of this diversity of claimants, and can be regarded as, in one of its aspects at least, an argument about what set of concepts we are to accept as definitive of reality as such.

§ 4. Now the suggestion that metaphysics might, despite all that has been said against it, be found to be a legitimate undertaking will strike many as nothing more than a deplorable attempt to revive outworn superstition; and before we commit ourselves to it we should consider carefully whether there is not some alternative to it. To this end let us imagine the comments which an intelligent empiricist might be expected to make on our present position. 'In the course of this book', such a critic might say,

'you have accepted from Kant the view that a distinction must be drawn between immediate and developed experience, arguing that the latter includes thinking as well as sensing, and in fact depends in the last resort on the mind's bringing to the interpretation of the given certain *a priori* concepts or categories. But you find yourself unable to accept the particular list of categories Kant produces, partly because you are dissatisfied with his formal "deduction" of it, partly on the more serious ground that it rests on too narrow a conception of developed experience itself. You suggest that a modern philosopher, confronted with a diversity of empirical inquiries, may have to admit that different *a priori* principles function in each of them; and this you think an argument for the view that, so far from there being only one set of categories, there might well be several. Metaphysics, you hint, would then be concerned to adjudicate between these different sets. But why need you proceed to any such conclusion? Why should you not be content to agree that different empirical studies do proceed on different assumptions (which, by the way, it would be better to call arbitrary definitions or methodological postulates than synthetic *a priori* "truths of reason"), and leave the matter at that? Why not give up the useless search for a unitary interpretation of "experience", and recognize the simple fact that the word means one thing to the physicist, another to the biologist, another to the historian, and so on? Why talk in terms of a single reality and a single basic set of categories, when the senses present us with phenomena of such variety that the attempt to bring them under a uniform formula seems absurd from the first? No purpose is served by this intellectual *Gleichschaltung*; it does not advance our knowledge of matter of fact and existence in any way. Would it not be better to recognize the autonomy of the various empirical inquiries and to confine philosophers to the useful, if unexciting, task of analysing their fundamental concepts and principles?'

The answer to this empiricist (or positivist) criticism is that it is not enough to recognize the autonomy of the different empirical studies and to analyse their presuppositions; we need also to consider their relations. We have to do this because the fields and problems of those studies have an unfortunate habit of overlapping. That is not to say, of course, that there is any persistent conflict between, for example, the physicist and the historian: each has a subject-matter of his own and a special technique for dealing with it. But it remains true none the less that situations arise in which two or more departmental inquirers are interested in the same phenomena; and when that happens the outside observer is liable to be confronted with conflicting explanations of them. Suppose, for instance, that the subject of study is a series of human actions. The physiologist will explain them in his own way as the effect of physical influences, whether in the body of the agent or in the environment. The psychologist will trace them to the working of non-rational forces in the mind. The historian may refer to the past events which preceded the actions in question, with a view to showing how they developed out of these, or he may invoke a general conception of human nature which clarifies the different ways in which men respond to different kinds of challenge. The moralist (who after all is also entitled to be heard) will insist on the factor of choice which the agent exercised and argue that an action, whatever its other qualities, is the giving effect to a certain idea or purpose. In any particular case such explanations may not, of course, conflict: it may be possible to produce out of them a view which does justice to them all. But in some instances—for example, if we are treating a case of juvenile delinquency—we find ourselves compelled to make a choice between interpretations which are clearly not reconcilable with one another. And when we make such a choice we no longer, I think, pay exclusive attention to the immediate facts we are trying to explain: we attempt to face the much wider question of the value we are to attach to the principles which lie behind the different interpretations before us. We consider which hypothesis will account not only for a single limited experience, but for experience taken in an altogether broader way. In a word, it is the *general* validity of each *type* of explanation that we are trying to assess. And this is a problem to be tackled not by any departmental inquirer, but by someone who looks at things from a wider point of view; in fact, by the philosopher.

The same point can perhaps be put in another way as follows. We tend to think of the main branches of human study as each concerned with a particular part of that totality of phenomena which is all that some empiricists will agree to understand by the word 'reality'. Thus there is one sphere for the physicist to investigate, another for the historian, a third for the student of religion. But in fact we find that the different studies refuse to stay within bounds in the way we might perhaps like. Each of them spreads itself over the spheres of all the rest, claiming implicitly to offer an interpretation not of a part of reality only, but of everything that is. And this movement towards universality starts, I think, within the departmental studies themselves. No self-respecting scientist will allow himself to be told in advance that there are some things which he can and others that he must not investigate; on the contrary, he will try to push his principles for all they are worth, with the aim of extending his province to the maximum extent. But this demand for scientific *Lebensraum* is very easily converted into a claim to possess the whole world. What seems to happen is that the physicist or the historian or the religious man becomes so convinced of the efficacy of his leading ideas that he assigns them categorial status: he comes to think of them as definitory of reality itself. It is at this point that the empirical investigation of a particular set of data passes into the advocacy of a whole philosophy or metaphysical system; at this point that physics, for instance, becomes mechanistic materialism, or history historicism. And however much we may denounce the transition as improper and unempirical, it seems to be one which it is altogether natural to make.

If this is at all right, the philosopher cannot stop, as the positivist would have him do, at the recognition of a number of basically different types of empirical inquiry, nor can he confine his activity to questions of analysis. However hard he may find the task, he has to undertake a work of synthesis when the analysis is finished; he has to assess the relative value of the philosophies based on different sides of human experience. And this, I suggest, is the proper subject of metaphysics. Metaphysical systems arise when we take the ideas which function in any particular type of departmental thinking and give them unrestricted validity, converting them into concepts which define what it is to be real, i.e. into categories. And as a plurality of such systems is possible, because of the plurality of kinds of departmental thinking, there must be an inquiry, itself metaphysical, into the value of different systems of metaphysics. Contrary to what some may suppose, this inquiry does not aim at overstepping the bounds of possible experience and laying bare the secrets of a supersensible reality; its purpose is rather to produce a unitary interpretation of experience itself. In the language of this book, it is concerned with developed experience, and hopes to find the final and proper meaning of that term. Whether it can achieve its ambition, and how it should set about the task, are, of course, questions in themselves. But that there is a problem here is a conclusion to which I hope the reader will now agree.[1]

§ 5. Before asking to what tests we might appeal to enable us to judge the merits of conflicting metaphysical systems, it might be as well if we said something at this point on the general question of the possibility of metaphysical knowledge. A brief examination of this problem, one of the most frequently discussed in contemporary philosophical literature, would not in any case be out of place in a study of this kind. Its relevance in the present context is that many readers may well feel confused at finding that there is a sense in which we stand committed to metaphysics, after virtually ranging ourselves on the anti-metaphysical side throughout the book. The only way to dispel this confusion is to discuss the different senses of the term 'metaphysics' itself.

The origin of what may be called the classical sense of the word has already been indicated briefly in an earlier chapter.[2] Aristotle, who was the first to discuss the nature of metaphysics (though not, of course, the first metaphysician), argued that the subject might be conceived either as a doctrine of being as such (the science of *τὸ ὂν ᾗ ὄν*) or as an account of the most real of all things, i.e. as *θεολογική*. In the rationalist tradition of western Europe, these two views became combined in the theory that metaphysics was a study with different parts, embracing on the one hand ontology, 'scientia entis in genere seu quatenus ens est,' as Christian

[1] It may be remarked as an *argumentum ad hominem* that the history of positivism itself confirms the need for a metaphysical study of the type argued for in the text. Comte and the nineteenth-century positivists were advocates of the exclusive validity of the principles recognized by natural scientists as criteria of empirical truth, and their programme included the reduction of historical to scientific knowledge. The logical positivists of the present century have in effect the same outlook, though they appear to be quite unaware of there being any special problem about history and its associated studies. It is in this sense that positivists are, as Bradley said, metaphysicians in disguise, with a theory of first principles of their own.

[2] See p. 130 above.

Wolff defined it,[1] on the other rational cosmology, rational psychology, and natural theology. The object of this study, in all its parts, was reality as opposed to appearance; it claimed to be able to say something of the inner essence of things, as opposed to their surface show. It was accordingly a doctrine which professed to take its adherents beyond the common-sense world known in sense-perception altogether, giving them insight into the general nature at least of the supersensible or intelligible sphere which lay behind it.

Now there seems to be little difficulty in showing that metaphysics in this sense is an impossible undertaking. To have knowledge of the supersensible we should either have to have some direct acquaintance with it, or we should require to be endowed with concepts specifically known to be valid of supersensible reality. But can we show that either of these conditions is fulfilled? The case for there being some form of intellectual intuition of the supersensible world is one which we have discussed exhaustively, and we need not revive the topic again. It is true that we have not ruled out the possibility that mystical experience might afford a form of immediate awareness entirely different from sensation, though this would not, of course, be *intellectual* intuition. But though the experience of the mystic may thus become the sheet-anchor of the metaphysician, there is little sign of its actually doing so; nor indeed is it wholly clear that it will in fact afford the sort of support the metaphysician needs. And as for the second alternative, we have seen that while there is a constant temptation to believe that *a priori* concepts like cause and substance can be applied to objects of all kinds, sensible or supersensible, the truth is rather that they can only be shown to have precise significance when referred to space-time experience. Concepts of this kind are bound up, as Kant pointed out, with those processes of synthesis which are a necessary part of the thinking of a discursive intelligence; and to understand them we must consider what it is they synthetize. If we take the categories and ask if they afford us insight into the general nature of a supersensible world, the answer must accordingly be that they do not. They serve as combining concepts for a manifold of sensible intuition, and cannot be shown to be valid except in reference to such a manifold.

[1] *Ontology* (1729), § 1. See also § 73 of the 'preliminary discourse' prefixed to Wolff's *Logic* (1728).

Thus the case for metaphysics in its classical form is one which cannot be defended. But to agree that there can be no science of the supersensible is not to abandon metaphysics as such, though many modern philosophers seem to imagine that it is. We can see this from a brief consideration of the theories of Kant. If any one philosopher is to be credited with having overthrown the classical conception of metaphysics, Kant is the man. Yet it is notorious that Kant conceived his mission as being not to abolish but to reform metaphysics: he proposed to put that study on the 'sure path of a science'. And the way in which he did this was to suggest that metaphysics should cease to concern itself with the supersensible and become instead a doctrine of the necessary nature of the sensible world. The sensible world had a necessary nature because we in our thinking of it made use of necessary principles. The metaphysician, Kant believed, could discover these principles by reflecting on the conditions of objective thinking, and to do that was his proper task.

The most remarkable point in this Kantian theory is undoubtedly its author's belief that the metaphysics of sense-experience he proposed to set up was capable of completion once and for all. Human reason, he held, was so much a unity that the knowledge of any part of its workings would lead inevitably to knowledge of the whole. Thus we must either claim to have produced a final and comprehensive list of the categories, or admit that our arguments were seriously wrong at some point or other. We have already had occasion in Chapter VIII to notice the theory, developed in opposition to this view of Kant's, that the categories have a history and are in fact constantly changing. The theory, which is fundamentally sceptical in character, can take one of two forms. On the one hand we have the version of it which appears in Professor Collingwood's *Essay on Metaphysics*, where it is argued that the absolute presuppositions of scientific and historical knowledge do in fact vary from age to age, and that metaphysics must confine itself to recording the history of these changes. This point of view is only one remove away from that of the positivists whom Collingwood denounces. The other version of the theory is that of Professor C. I. Lewis, who holds, as we saw, that the imposition of the categories is an arbitrary process. We can interpret experience according to any principles we choose, and it is convenience alone which leads us to prefer one interpretation to another. If we like to stick to our principles, however awkward they prove in practice, nobody can stop us and nobody can show that we are wrong.

The feature these two forms of the 'historical' theory have in common is that they both hold that categorial principles are neither true nor false. In Collingwood's language, they are suppositions, not propositions. Now, clearly there is something to be said for this point of view. As we saw in discussing the status of the Kantian principles of the understanding, the chief difficulty about them is to know in what sense they can be referred to as judgements, when they are themselves the basis of all objective judgement. Yet it seems unduly pessimistic, to say the least, to write them off as outside the sphere of truth and falsehood altogether. If absolute presuppositions are neither true nor false, but merely supposed, how are we to choose between accounts of experience given in accordance with alternative sets of them? Must we say, as the logic of Collingwood's argument requires him to say, that the progress of science cannot lead to a truer, but only to a different and more detailed, picture of the facts? Must we hold that when the materialist and his opponent offer conflicting explanations of our actions both must be accounted right, since the fundamental principles of each are equally arbitrary? Certainly the common man, if there be any such person, would revolt against this excess of conventionalism. He would say that those who held to it placed altogether too much emphasis on the subjective element in human thinking, and failed to realize that truth was determined by facts which were independent of human judgement. And with the spirit of this contention, if not with its letter, philosophers cannot fail to sympathize.

It seems, then, that once we admit the possibility of a plurality of categorial systems (and we cannot deny at least a *prima-facie* case for that possibility), we face the question which of those systems is true. And to answer this question (or at least to attempt an answer) is the primary purpose of metaphysics. What the metaphysician is concerned to do, if this is right, is to try to discover an interpretation of experience which does justice to all sides of it. Such an interpretation would clearly have to take account of man's moral, artistic, and religious nature as well as his strictly intellectual attainments. The aim of those who attempted it would assuredly be to frame a theory whose first requirement was to satisfy the intellect; but that need not make it a scientific theory in the narrow sense of the word. The scientific interpretation of experience is only one of a number of competing explanations, and it can claim precedence over the rest only if it can be shown to account for the facts more satisfactorily than any other theory. As our grandfathers knew quite well, good science may turn out to be bad metaphysics, though it is not of course necessary that it should.

It is perhaps worth emphasizing as one of the most important features of this conception of metaphysics that it presupposes a particularly close connexion between metaphysics and the departmental studies. Metaphysics, on the view here put forward, is not one of those studies itself; but it draws all its strength and all its ideas from them. To suggest that the metaphysician might produce an interpretation of experience out of the depths of his own consciousness, without reference to the work being carried on in natural science, history, and other particular branches of knowledge, is to suggest an absurdity. An interpretation of that kind could not hope to be anything but vague and unsatisfactory. The truth seems rather to be, as I have already tried to show, that it is in the departmental studies that metaphysical systems originate. A set of ideas which serves to co-ordinate a certain section of our experience is given unrestricted validity and made the basis of an interpretation of experience as a whole. What seems to happen here is that, in the words of a recent American writer,[1] we fasten on some 'root metaphor' and attempt to read all experience in terms connected with it. Thus we take the concept of personality as revealed in moral experience and make that central in our understanding of the universe, producing thereby a metaphysical theory of the idealist type; or again, we seize on the mechanical ideas used in classical physics and, extending the machine metaphor from inanimate Nature to the whole of reality, formulate the metaphysics of materialism. Unless the basic notions here appealed to had actually proved fruitful in the understanding of parts of experience, it would never occur to us to stretch them to cover the whole. Moreover, to apply them successfully the metaphysician must be familiar not merely with the general character of the departmental studies, but to some extent too with the detailed work being done in them. He needs this familiarity because, if we may put it so, the proof of every metaphysical pudding is in the eating: to test the validity of any suggested set of categorial ideas we must consider how far they illuminate the

[1] Professor S. C. Pepper in *World Hypotheses* (Univ. of California Press, 1942).

details of experience. Any metaphysical theory which is to merit serious attention must cover all the facts, and cover them adequately; and only a close acquaintance with the departmental studies will enable us to say whether or not it fulfils this requirement.

§ 6. This brings us to the question of metaphysical truth. To settle the disputes of metaphysicians (or, more modestly, to show that those disputes are capable of being settled in principle), we need a clear conception of what an ideal metaphysical explanation would be. Our answer to this question has so far been indicated only in the vaguest of terms: we have spoken of a serious metaphysical theory covering all the 'facts' and covering them 'adequately'. But facts, as we know, are slippery things, and what is fact for one theory is not necessarily fact for another. Adequacy, again, is a relative term, and we need to point to the standard in the light of which we are to judge it. These terms must clearly be improved on if we are to arrive at a satisfactory criterion of truth and falsehood in metaphysics.

Let us start with 'fact'. Every serious metaphysical theory, we say, must cover all the facts. Now this may seem the merest tautology, since we understand by metaphysics an attempt to give a comprehensive account of the whole of experience. But the matter is not so simple as this, as we can see by considering for a moment the procedure of the departmental inquirer. A physical scientist, if we can take an obvious example, starts by having before him certain ostensible experiences which he hopes to explain. But he does not attach equal importance to all these experiences. Some he ignores altogether (the emotional and aesthetic experiences of a scientific observer are cases in point), and others he will discard as irrelevant to the problem he has in hand (e.g., experience of secondary qualities in some cases). His explanation will therefore cover a selection of the available data only, and in making the selection he will in effect apply certain criteria of what he thinks is required to make an experience important and 'real' for the purposes of physics. And when, in the course of that natural extension of his province from part to whole of which I have spoken in § 4, the physical scientist becomes a materialistic metaphysician, these characteristics of his thought will remain with him. Certainly he will now have to deal with all ostensible experiences, and not be able to put some aside as outside his proper study. But he will continue to apply certain criteria of reality and importance to the given, and so allow far more weight to some experiences than to others. He will find it necessary to discredit certain apparent experiences, to say they are not what they seem, and, in extreme cases, to declare that those who think they have them are deluded. Thus we may expect him, when confronted with the testimony of mystical writers, to argue that their accounts are far from satisfactory, and that their experiences can be explained partly by reference to the physical conditions to which mystics subject themselves, partly as sheer hallucination. Towards the pronouncements of his fellow scientists, on the other hand, he will adopt a very different attitude, accepting them at their face value and asking only that they be made with due caution and in good faith.

Now the important point about this is that the tendency here shown to approach experience with definite preconceptions about what it should be like is by no means confined to materialism. On the contrary, it is a feature of every metaphysical system. All metaphysical theories aim at doing justice to all the evidence; but they each have their own criteria of what it is that constitutes evidence, and they all rule that some ostensible evidence is inadmissible or distorted. Nor should their doing so appear at all mysterious to those who have followed the argument of this book. The term 'experience', as we have repeatedly said, is itself ambiguous; and experience as we normally speak of it includes an interpretative as well as a given element. Pure or immediate experience, free of the contagion of interpretation, is an ideal to which we can approach only by stripping away the structure we have ourselves conferred upon it. That does not mean, as some rationalist writers conclude, that pure experience is a fiction, or that there is nothing in what empiricists say about the given. There is, indeed, a very great deal, and the given is something philosophers can ignore only at their peril. But it remains true that we have to establish what is given as well as interpret the given.

The conclusion I would suggest as following from this discussion is this: that metaphysicians should be ready not merely to interpret all the evidence they admit (that, after all, is their business), but to admit all the evidence they can. And I think that one test of a good metaphysical system is that it should have what Professor Pepper calls 'scope': it should cover as wide a range of experience as possible. What this means in practice is that metaphysicians should not be over-ready to use the veto which their office confers on them. They should avoid confusing the inconvenient with the unreal. The bad effect of a too liberal use of the veto is to be seen in metaphysical systems of an unsophisticated sort: in popular mysticism, which allows reality to a very limited proportion of ostensible experiences, and again in popular materialism, which shuts its eyes dogmatically to all evidence which cannot be readily interpreted in naturalistic terms. No metaphysical system will be able to avoid dogmatism altogether, since it is in the nature of metaphysics to be dogmatic. But a system which pursues its principles to the point of twisting or distorting the given (or, indeed, to the point of ignoring it entirely) cannot be anything but bad metaphysics.

So much for comprehensiveness in metaphysical systems: it seems clear that, despite the fact that every such system is, in its nature, an overall interpretation of experience, one system can be differentiated from another by the amount of ostensible data it is forced to discard or explain away. And this gives us one criterion by which to judge of the truth of metaphysical theories: a theory which covers more ground is, so far, preferable to one which covers less. But to the test of comprehensiveness that of adequacy must be added. It is no use for a theory to cover the ground but to do it in an unconvincing fashion. The metaphysician must not only explain his facts but explain them properly; and this, I think, means explaining them from the inside, explaining them in such a way that specialists in the several fields are satisfied by the explanations.

Let me illustrate what I mean by giving an example of an unsatisfactory explanation. In the latest version of naturalistic metaphysics which calls itself logical positivism we are treated, amongst other things, to an analysis of ethical and theological statements. The general line taken about both is that they cannot be regarded as expressing what is literally true or false, but rather as giving vent, in a more or less direct way, to our feelings. Now this theory has the merit of not discarding moral and religious experience altogether: it admits that there can be such things, and shows that they need not necessarily clash with scientific experience. But the explanation it gives of them is a bad one because it is such as no self-respecting moralist or theologian would accept. No religious man will purchase immunity from scientific criticism at the price of agreeing that his statements have no literal significance; yet that is what he is asked to do in this theory. Nor will any moralist be ready to admit that justice is done to the ethical life if it is said that ethical utterances are *sui generis*, but have nothing to do with the nature of fact whatsoever. No doubt it is true that ethics deals primarily not with what is but with what ought to be; it is concerned with practice, not with theory. But it is not clear from this that the study of morals can throw no light on the nature of reality. It seems to be an essential part of the moralist's claim that the world should not be entirely indifferent to moral demands; and if this is at all justified it is a fact of major importance for the philosopher. But this is a side of moral action which logical positivism leaves unexplained.[1]

By an adequate explanation in metaphysics, then, I mean one which allows for the diversity of different sides of human experience as well as the unity of experience as such; which attempts, indeed, to find a unity in diversity rather than a unity which cancels out all diversity. And I think that many famous metaphysical theories can be shown to fail by this test: not only philosophies of the materialist and naturalistic type, which tend to gloss over the special character of moral, artistic, and religious experience, but idealist theories, too, which frequently do less than justice to the strength of the naturalistic position and to the full significance of natural science. But it may be objected that the test here proposed is one by which all conceivable metaphysical theories must fall down. If the procedure of the metaphysician is, as has been suggested in this chapter, to start from familiarity with a particular branch of experience or of knowledge, and to give the concepts there used unrestricted validity, it looks as if the point of view of every metaphysical system must be partial and partisan. Each side of human experience, to put the argument in another way, will involve a metaphysics of its own, and explaining any of them to the satisfaction of its special exponents will

[1] As the reader will see, this criticism of logical positivism can be brought, with modifications, against the philosophy of Kant too. Kantian ethics, of course, differ *toto caelo* from the ethics of logical positivism, and nobody would say that Kant failed to recognize the autonomy of moral judgements. Yet some would claim, though not necessarily rightly, that he did not attach sufficient speculative importance to the facts of moral experience. Again, Kant's treatment of religion, though it contains features needed in any philosophy of the subject, may be criticized on the ground that it does not allow for the claim to true insight (and not merely sound practice) which the religious man implicitly makes. This is to say that Kant, like the logical positivist, does not offer an explanation of religious experience which does justice to it from the inside.

mean accepting that metaphysics. But how, on that basis, can there be a metaphysical theory which can claim to be adequate in the sense required? As soon as any theory passes beyond the sphere out of which it has arisen it will encounter another system, which it has the choice of accepting at the price of its own suicide or rejecting by simple annihilation. Can it be said that either course conduces to the sort of result we desire?

The answer to this objection is, I think, that it over-simplifies both metaphysics itself and the nature of metaphysical conflicts. It is true that metaphysical theories do arise, in the way described, when a particular set of ideas, found to be fruitful in the understanding of one department of experience, is put forward as capable of explaining the whole. It is true, too, that every major department of experience has its own metaphysical point of view; that art, the physical sciences and history, to mention three only, can be shown to involve distinct metaphysical positions of their own. But it does not follow that metaphysicians are confined to the blank acceptance of one of these points of view and the blank rejection of the rest. The possibility remains, after all, that conflicts between one type of philosophy and another are capable of resolution by some more civilized means than the staging of a stand-up fight. And the possibility would be fulfilled if, starting from the positions suggested by the different departmental studies, we could proceed to find a wider point of view which did not so much destroy as embrace its rivals, a system of principles which could be seen to contain all less satisfactory systems. A system of that kind might well claim to offer us a truly adequate metaphysics, since it would see things from the departmental standpoint as well as in their totality. And it is after some such ideal that all the great speculative philosophers of the past have striven, though their attainment of it has, of course, been no more than partial, and their emphases have inevitably been coloured by the departments of experience in which they were themselves best versed.

§ 7. The suggestion that we might be able to devise a comprehensive metaphysical system, which stood on a quite different level from all other systems and in fact contained everything of value in them, was originally made by Hegel; and it may be helpful in conclusion if I say a little about my attitude to Hegel's views on the question. This is the more necessary both because of the criticism to which Hegel has been subjected from time to time in this book, and because the Hegelian theory was the model for what has in fact become the standard rationalist interpretation of the different sides of 'levels' of experience.

Hegel made the astonishing claim to have produced an account of experience which was not only final in itself, but served to indicate the precise value of every other possible account. He was not content, as a more modest man might have been, to rule that a metaphysics based on physics, art, or religion must be defective because of the narrow range of experience from which its categories were drawn; he went further and undertook to show the relative adequacy of each of these imperfect systems. The basis of this view was his conception of philosophical logic. The task of logic, as has already been explained in a previous section (Chapter VIII, § 2), was, according to Hegel, to elaborate a doctrine of categories; and it was a task which, in principle at least, could be carried out completely, thanks to the dialectical relation by which all *a priori* concepts were linked. Possession of the Hegelian logic afforded a standard by which to judge of all other philosophies for the double reason that that logic contained a list, arranged in their proper order, of all categorial concepts, and that every other philosophical system (apart from some forms of empiricism, which in Hegel's view scarcely deserved to be called philosophy at all) was based on one or some of the categories. The concepts Kant had recognized as categorial in the first *Critique*, for instance, appeared somewhere in the middle of Hegel's list,[1] and the defects of the philosophy of that work could be indicated by stating that Kant failed to realize when he wrote it that there were any higher categories. He remedied the defect, Hegel thought, to some extent in the *Critique of Judgment*,[2] for the idea of teleology belongs to the logic of the Notion, the highest division of the Hegelian logic; but the remedy was only partial, thanks to the reservations with which Kant stated his doctrine.

I have already given reasons for doubting whether the Hegelian logic, which must surely be reckoned among the more remarkable achievements of the human mind, can in fact be regarded as soundly conceived. The notion of dialectic on which it rests seems to me

[1] The Kantian categories of Quantity and Quality appear in the first division of Hegel's logic, the logic of Being, and those of Relation and Modality in the middle section, the logic of Essence.

[2] Hence the popularity of this work with Hegelians, and the description of it as the 'crowning point of the critical philosophy'.

highly dubious, and the same must be said of the conception of philosophical reason to which Hegel appeals. Moreover, I believe there is a strong case for saying that, in thinking of his categories as specifications of the Absolute, Hegel was attempting to revive metaphysics in its traditional form, as a theory not of the unity of experience but of what lies behind and beyond experience; a task whose impossibility Kant had already shown. But despite all this I have more than a sneaking suspicion that modern philosophy has something to learn from Hegel. If we cannot follow him in detail, we can at least find in him ideas and suggestions which throw light on our own problems. I will mention two of these which concern questions discussed in this chapter.

First, I think Hegel was right in arguing that differences between speculative philosophies are to be understood by looking to the categories they embody. Every metaphysical system, if the arguments of this chapter are right, is in essence an interpretation of the whole of experience in the light of a certain set of guiding concepts; and to comprehend any system we must discover what its governing principles are. And I suspect that this method of treatment can be applied not only to philosophies like Kant's, which explicitly claim to be interpretations of experience, but to metaphysical systems of the traditional kind too. The speculations of philosophers like Spinoza and Leibniz, though their explicit aim was doubtless to transcend experience altogether, can none the less be regarded in a secondary sense as the extension to the whole of experience of conceptions derived from a part. Thus Spinoza's overwhelming conviction of the omnipresence of *Deus sive Natura* surely derives from some central experience of Spinoza's own, whilst Leibniz's conception of the monad as a true unity is to be connected both with his biological studies and with his grasp of the notion of personality. No doubt these references are insufficient in themselves to explain in detail why these philosophers wrote as they did: no account of Spinoza could neglect the importance of the mathematical method he inherited from Descartes, nor could any description of the views of Leibniz pass over the logical doctrines whose influence on his thinking modern scholarship has so clearly brought out. But the life which it is still possible to find in Spinozistic and Leibnizian metaphysics, despite the errors of their logic and doctrine of method, is to be traced to the fact that their fundamental conceptions do have a real metaphysical value.

Secondly, however shocking it may be to say it, I believe that Hegel was correct in principle in arguing for a hierarchy of philosophies. Some metaphysical theories must contain others; and, indeed, an adequate metaphysical theory must contain all the partial views it has refuted. Why this is so should be clear from the preceding sections. An adequate account of experience, we there saw, is one which does justice to all sides of it, explaining each department of human life to the satisfaction of experts in the particular field in question. But this means that the writer of such an account must incorporate in his thinking everything that is of positive value in the different departmental standpoints, i.e. that the categories he puts forward must *include* the concepts which more restricted views make central in their interpretations. And the same applies, again in principle, if we are trying to resolve a conflict between any two metaphysical systems, for example materialism and idealism. Unless we are content to let the conflict degenerate into a vulgar brawl, in which he who shouts longest and loudest is to be pronounced the victor, we must assume that one of the contending parties can be shown to have absorbed and gone beyond the other—that materialism can be stated in such a way that it is seen to contain the truth of idealism, or vice versa. How else one serious philosophy could refute another I do not see.

But though the Hegelian idea of a hierarchy of philosophies (and therefore of the categories on which they are based) is thus sound in principle, I feel very doubtful about whether it can be carried out in practice. That some sets of categorial concepts are inadequate to cover all sides of experience—the concepts of materialism, for instance—was, I should say, reasonably clear. But that we can actually arrange contending metaphysical theories on a scale, declaring, e.g., that a world-view based primarily on artistic experience is superior (or inferior) to one based primarily on religion, is a far more dubious proposition. And even if we do eventually find ourselves in a position to put some standard theories in an order of adequacy (as we may well hope to do), that can surely only be as a result of patient examination of the evidence they purport to cover and the explanations they give of it, and not, as Hegel believed, by having recourse to pure logic. Hegel thought, like Kant, that a complete list of all possible categories could be produced by the application of an *a priori* principle. But his attempt to carry out the programme has met with criticism even from his own supporters, and it is scarcely reasonable to suppose that where he failed others will succeed. If the Hegelian logic will not help, there is no short cut on the road to metaphysical truth.

§ 8. In the first chapter of this book[1] I discussed the reasons why a survey of the nature and extent of human knowledge, such as I was proposing to undertake, might be thought capable of defence even on utilitarian grounds. I pointed out that there were some philosophical problems dispute about which appeared to be interminable, and quoted from Hume and Kant to the effect that human reason could free itself of such tangles only if it undertook a survey of its own resources, with a view to determining what questions it could and what it could not answer. And I ended by suggesting that if we could show that philosophy has nothing positive to say about many of these traditional problems we should have arrived at a conclusion of negative value at least.

The reader may well be curious to know how this programme is to be squared with the contentions of the present chapter, and I will end with a few remarks on this point.

That philosophers (and metaphysicians in particular) have been engaged in the course of history in attempting to solve problems some of which they are intrinsically unfitted to tackle is a point which ought to emerge clearly from the discussions of the present book. Metaphysics as traditionally conceived, as an attempt to describe the nature of reality as such, where reality is taken to lie behind and beyond anything we know in sense-experience, is an altogether impossible project. It is altogether impossible because the human mind entirely lacks the intellectual resources which would enable it to transcend the given and penetrate to what Kant called the world of things in themselves. We could only know things in themselves by acquaintance if we had a power of intellectual intuition, by description if we could guarantee that certain of our intellectual concepts applied to them. But, as we have seen, neither condition can be fulfilled.

It follows that there is a whole range of traditional metaphysical questions—questions such as those of the ultimate substance of the universe, the immortality of the soul, and the proof of God's existence—on which the philosopher has nothing positive to say. His function is confined here to pointing out the assumptions which those who attempt to answer such questions make, and to

[1] Pp. 5–8 above.

indicating the fallacious character of their general point of view. But that does not mean that metaphysics is ruled out in all its forms. If it is taken as an attempt to give a unitary account of experience, by finding a set of ultimate concepts and principles in terms of which all sides of it are to be understood, it seems to be a perfectly legitimate inquiry: a conclusion which is confirmed by the fact that we can devise tests by which to judge the merits of rival metaphysical theories. And we must confess that in advocating the possibility of this sort of metaphysics we are claiming that philosophers can make a positive contribution to the solution of some traditional metaphysical disputes (the dispute between Science and Religion, for instance); and this is no doubt in formal contradiction with the sceptical suggestions of our first chapter.

But though we speak here of philosophers contributing to the solution of these problems, which continue to engage the interest of thoughtful persons despite the apparently interminable character of the disputes about them, it must not be thought that we (or anyone else) can promise any early pronouncement on the final validity of the contesting theories. Of all the branches of human learning, philosophy is the slowest to progress; and inside philosophy metaphysics is the part about which it is least possible to make quick decisions. But the spectacle of metaphysicians struggling with the same questions through the centuries need not prove wholly depressing. In the analytic parts of philosophy—in theory of knowledge at least—the patient work of generations of inquirers has resulted in the attainment of a standpoint which, if it does not enable us to resolve all our problems, at any rate makes us very much more their master than men were before the development started. And when philosophers turn, as turn they must and will, from preoccupation with the departmental questions of theory of knowledge, logic, and ethics to take up once more the attempt to attain a synoptic view of all experience and all knowledge, it is reasonable to hope they will be able to make progress of a not dissimilar kind.

INDEX

Absolute, the, 131, 169, 173, 174, 249.
Absolute Idea, Hegel's category of, 170–1.
Absolute presuppositions, 87, 126–9, 155, 185, 240; admission of, not decisive in favour of rationalism, 129 (cf. 240); expressed in prescriptive judgements, 137.
Abstract ideas, 32.
Adequacy, in metaphysical systems, 245–7, 250.
Aesthetic judgements, in Kant, 231.
Alexander, S., 194.
Analytic judgements, as understood by Kant, 37–8; redefined to meet criticism, 41; in what sense necessary, 42; not always trivial, 48–9; ought to be accepted by rationalists and empiricists alike, 49; Ayer's definition of, 96; tell us nothing of the structure of fact, 190.
Analytic)(synthetic judgements, distinction of, Kant's account, 37–8; not upset by idealist criticism, 39; nor by critics of subject-predicate logic, 39; nor by criticism of three laws of thought, 40; restated, 41; its importance for theory of knowledge, 48 ff.; neglected in Coherence Theory of Truth, 86 (cf. 183).
Appearance and reality, rationalist distinction between, 15, 131, 239.
Apperception, pure and empirical, 196, 201–2; transcendental unity of, 22, 140, 183, 198–201, 202, 211.
A priori, ambiguity of, as applied to analytic and synthetic judgements, 41 ff.
— and empirical thinking, 124, 132 ff., 178 ff.
— imagination, notion of an, 182, 184; Kant on, 164–5.
— principles, as presuppositions of experience, 29, 85–7, 110–12, 126–9, 160–2; their relation to experience, 188–9; alternative sets of, Chap. X.
Aristotle, on the hierarchy of sciences, 2; conception of scientific knowledge, 14, 53–4, 55–6, 98; on intellectual intuition, 31, 35–6, 53–6; on universals, 31, 54–6, 100–3; on the three laws of thought, 40, 97–8, 218; argument for self-evident truths, 53–4, 81; on matter and form, 54–6, 144; his categories, 108–9; on metaphysics, 130, 238; on substance, 143–4; on dialectic, 171.
Association of ideas, will not account for objective knowledge, 122–3.
Ayer, A. J., criticizes Kant on analytic judgements, 40 (cf. 96); on philosophy of Nature, 67; on logical propositions, 95 ff.; on the propositions of philosophy, 193; on self-consciousness, 201.

Baumgarten, A. G., 136.
Becoming, Hegelian category of, 174.
Being, pure, Hegelian category of, 170–1, 174.
Belief, Hume's theory of, 177, 180.
Bergson, H., 62–3.
Berkeley, G., on abstract ideas and universals, 32, 100–1; his theory of objects, 119–20; on self-knowledge, 193–5.
Bosanquet, B., 5, 20, 124.
Bradley, F. H., on thinking and sensing (feeling), 28, 61–2, 84, 221; on the ambiguity of 'idea', 32; his analytic judgement of sense, 39; and intellectual intuition, 61–2; on similarity, 101; denounces empiricism, 115; on 'redintegration', 122; on the criterion of historical truth, 127; attitude to dialectic, 172; attitude to the principle of contradiction, 174; on positivism, 238.
Butler, J., 173.

Categories, general history of the notion, 107–10; Kantian conception of, Chaps. VI, VII (particular categories recognized by Kant, 142); pure and schematized, 125, 133–5; can any limits be set to their use? 129–35, 160, 239;)(ideas of reason, 161–2; possibility of an empiricist doctrine of, 163, 176; rational or irrational? 163, 182–4, 189; in Hegel, 169 ff.; conflict between different sets of, 175, 189, 235–8 (and Chap. X generally); Hume's attitude to, 176 ff.; do they change in the course of history? 184 ff., 240–1; how far conventional, 185–9.
Causality (causal principle, causal relation), Hume's view of, 44–5, 148–51, 153–4, 177–9; Kant's account of, 148 ff., 165 (limits of Kantian treatment, 149); Leibniz on, 149; Locke on, 149–50; Clarke on, 150; Mill on, 151–2; Collingwood on, 154–5;

through the will, 154; mechanical and teleological, 162 (cf. 232 ff.); Hegelian category of, 170.
Certainty, 81–8.
Church, R. W., 174.
Clarke, S., 150.
Cogito, Descartes's, 21, 195, 200.
Coherence Theory of Truth, 33, 48, 82–7.
Collingwood, R. G., on absolute presuppositions, 87, 126, 128, 155, 185, 240; on substance, 148; on causation, 154–5; on the overlap of philosophical concepts, 173; on cosmological presuppositions, 188; on psychology and philosophy, 214–15; his *Speculum Mentis*, 223.
Common-sense thinking, in Hegel, 65.
Common world, 116–18, 140, 190.
Comprehensiveness, as a test of metaphysical systems, 243–5.
Comte, A., 238.
Concepts and intuitions, their relation in Kant, 132–5, 203–4.
Conceptualism, rejected by Plato and Aristotle, 56; defined, 99–100; on what basis defensible, 102–5.
'Consciousness in general', 118, 124.
Contradiction, principle of, in Hegel, 169 ff.; in Bradley, 174 (*see also* Laws of thought).
Convention, and logical laws, 96–7, 187, 208; and categorial thinking, 185–9, 240–1; and ethics, 188.
Couturat, L., 144.
Croce, B., 20, 63.

Dawes Hicks, G., 225.
Demonstrative)(moral reasoning, in Hume, 176, 182–3; Hegel's attitude to the contrast, 183.
Demonstrative reason not the source of the categories, 182.
Departmental character of human thinking, 2, 85.
Departmental studies, and theory of knowledge, 4–5; and metaphysics, 242.
Descartes, R., on scientific knowledge, 17, 27, 53–4, 78, 80–1; on self-knowledge, 20–1, 193, 195, 200; on inference, 54–7; on innate ideas, 109; on the external world, 119.
Determinant)(reflective judgement, in Kant, 162, 233.
Developed)(immediate experience, 114–15 (and Chap. VI generally), 152–3, 160, 178, 221–3; are there different kinds of? 229 ff.; metaphysics properly concerned with, 238.
Dialectic, in Hegel, 65, 169 ff., 248; different senses of, 170–1; Bradley's attitude to, 172.
Discursive understanding, characterized, 70, 103, 133; importance of universals for, 103–4; confronted with problem of separating objective from subjective, 123; its relation to different forms of sensibility, 133–4; categories involved in, according to Kant, 164; relation of logic to, 213.
Discursive view of human intellection, maintained by Kant, 47, 52; and knowledge of the individual, 59 ff., 76; Bradley on, 61–2; rejected by Hegel, 64 ff.; and the thing in itself, 70; and the problem of order, 72–5.

Eddington, A. S., 155.
Empiricism (empiricist), general contrast with rationalism, 12–20; and metaphysics, 15, 235; moderate and extreme, 18; and the self, 20–3, 201–2, 211–14; and different types of experience, 23, 222; and sense-experience, 24–5, 30–7, 115; not to be identified with sensationalism, 31, 37; should accept 'logical' function of intellect but reject 'real' use, 36–7; issues with rationalism specified, 52; interpretation of self-evidence, 81–2; and mathematics, 89, 91 ff.; and logic, 95 ff., 212–13; conception of scientific knowledge, 126–7; and *a priori* concepts, 163, 176, 186; how far acceptable, 190–1; and philosophical propositions, 211 ff.; and mysticism, 227.
Empiricists, philosophical and non-philosophical interests of, 18–19.
Essence, real and nominal, 145.
Ethical principles, and intellectual intuition, 47, 99; and convention, 188.
Ethics, Kantian, 205, 207, 231-2, 246; logical positivist, 245–6.
Evidence for metaphysical conclusions, 243–5.
Ewing, A. C., 57.
Existence, not a predicate, 76.
Experience, suggested different forms of, 23–4, Chap. X; mystical, 23–4, 69, 153, 223–9, 239; rationalist interpretation of, 24, 223, 248; Hegel's attitude to, 28–9, 66–9, 170–1, 175; and order, 72–5; as a 'rationalist fiction', 112–13; immediate and developed, 114–15 (and Chap. VI generally), 152–3, 160, 178, 221–3.
Experiences, correlation of different persons', 117–18.

Facts, test of conformity with, in Coherence Theory, 83; connexion with judgement, 83, 117; and fiction, 84–5; and metaphysics, 243–5.
Factual)(prescriptive judgements, 18, 48, 50–1, 88, 98–9, 137–9, 218.
Feeling, in Bradley, 28, 61–2, 84, 221.
— philosophies of, Hegel's antipathy to, 23.
Fichte, J. G., 202.
Form and matter, in Aristotle, 54–6, 144.
Formal logic, and transcendental logic, 5, 167–9, 170, 208; Kant's attitude to, 166–7, 207–8; judgement in, 168; Hegel's attitude to, 173.

Gentile, G., 20, 116, 195, 203.
Given, the, characterized, 13, 116; and the thing in itself, 64, 70–2; problem of finding order in, 72–5; known in feeling, 84; cannot be argued away, but needs interpretation, 84, 88, 244; its transformation into a world of experience, 103–4, 110–12 (and Chap. VI generally).
Green, T. H., 115.
Ground and consequent, 150–1, 154.

Hegel, G. W. F., on the utility of logic, 5–6; on theory of knowledge, 9–11; criticizes Kant's thing in itself, 10–11, 27, 64 ff.; conception of philosophy, 11, 28–9, 65–9, 75–6, 173–6; on self-knowledge, 22, 195, 203 ff.; his antipathy to philosophies of feeling, 23; contrasts understanding and reason, 24, 27–8, 173, 175–6, 183; treatment of sensation, 27–9, 65–6; on different levels of thought, 65; on philosophy of Nature, 67–9; on the 'impotence' of Nature, 68; truth in his view of the co-operation of thought and sensibility, 74–5; his conception of dialectic and the categories, 169–76; his personal conceit, 171–2 (cf. 248); attitude to formal logic, 173; and the principle of contradiction, 173–4; his attempt to devise a definitive metaphysics, 247 ff.; what we can learn from him, 249–51.
Herder, J. G., 232.
Historicism, 237.
History, empiricist attitude to, 18–19; differing rationalist attitudes to, 19–20; expelled from the body of knowledge by Descartes, 78; presuppositions of, 127 (cf. 85 and 232); Kant's attitude to, 231–2.
Hobbes, T., 149.
Homogeneity and specification, 74, 161.
Human nature, science of, 19.
Hume, D., on the pleasures of theory of knowledge, 6; on the need for theory of knowledge, 7; interests of, 19; on the science of Man, 19; on self-knowledge, 21, 71, 193, 201; on the presuppositions of experience, 29, 163, 176 ff.; on universals, 32, 37, 100–1; undue narrowness of his empiricism, 32, 37, 182; on logical necessity, 43; on psychological necessity, 44; on causality and the causal relation, 44–5, 148–50, 153–4, 177–9; on imagination, 45–6, 121–2, 146, 176 ff.; on 'experience', 112, 115; his theory of objects, 120–1; on substance, 145–6; on thinghood, 158, 179; distinguishes moral from demonstrative reasoning, 176; on belief, 177, 180; on probable reasoning, 177–8; his radical empiricist principle, 178, 214; needs to recognize something like synthetic *a priori* thinking, 179–80; distinguishes the Vulgar from Philosophers, 180; how far a Kantian, 181–2, 183–4; on the reason of animals, 183; on philosophy and psychology, 213–14.

'Idea', ambiguity of, 32.
Ideas, representative theory of, 116.
Ideas and impressions, in Hume, 178.
Ideas of reason, 140, 142, 161.
Imagination, as a possible source of *a priori* principles, 29, 45–6, 111, 129, 179–82; Hume's conception of the, 45–6, 121–2, 146, 176 ff.; its importance in sense-perception, 122; Kant's theory of, 164–6; notion of an *a priori*, 182, 184.
Immediate experience, 114–16, 152–3, 190, 221–3, 244; are there different forms of? 223 ff.
Individual, knowledge of the, 59 ff., 76.
Induction, 59, 74.
Inference, said to be synthetic, 46, 56–9; should be classed among the 'logical' functions of the intellect, 58–9; 'linear', 86.
Inge, W. R., 224.
Innate ideas, 109, 119.
Inner sense, 22, 192, 196 ff., 210.
Intellect, 'logical' and 'real' use of, Kant's statement of the distinction, 34; restatement in modern terms, 35–6; its importance for theory of knowledge, 36–7; acceptance of, makes empiricism more plausible, 37; both uses necessary for objective knowledge, 191.

Intellectual concepts, Kant's theory of, in the *Dissertation*, 130–1, 164, 171.
Intellectual intuition, four theories of distinguished, 52–7; theory that it is involved in inference, 57–9, 176; 'full-blooded' sense, 59 ff. (accepted by Spinoza, 60–1; by Bradley, 61–2; by Bergson, 62–3; Hegel's attitude to, 28–9, 64 ff., 203–4; Kant on, 69; problems raised by, 69–76); argument that it is needed to explain self-evident truths, 77 ff.; and mathematics, 88–9, 92; not necessary if modern philosophy of mathematics is accepted, 93; and logic, 95–9, 208, 218–19; and ethics, 99; and universals, 99–105; consequences of rejecting, 190; and theory of knowledge, 213, 219–20.
Introspection, empiricist account of, 21, 192–3; rationalist attitude to, 22, 193–5, 215 ff.; involves a subject- and an object-self, 21, 201, 209–10.
Intuitions and concepts, in Kant, 132–5, 203–4.

Jaeger, W., 130.
James, W., 227.
Johnson, W. E., 36, 157.
Joseph, H. W. B., 47, 72, 97–8.
Judgement, belongs to the 'logical' side of the intellect, 35, 58 (but cf. 168–9, 182); and facts, 83, 117; determinant and reflective (in Kant), 162, 233; and Kant's categories, 167–9; in formal logic, 168 (*see also* Analytic)(synthetic judgement, Prescriptive)(factual judgement).
Judgements of experience and perception (in Kant), 114.

Kant, I., *passim*.
Keynes, J. M. (Lord), 74.
Knowledge, questions asked about, 3 ff.; of the individual, 59 ff., 76; of relations of ideas)(of matters of fact, 176–7 (*see also under individual philosophers*).

Laws of thought, the three traditional, 40–1, 97–8.
Leibniz, G. W., on truths of reason)(truths of fact, 15–16, 136; on sensing and thinking, 16, 26, 31, 65; criticized by Kant, 26–7, 136; on logical necessity, 43; on the sphere of logic, 98, 213; his conception of substance, 144–5; on causality, 149; sources of his metaphysics, 249.
Lewis, C. I., on experience and order, 73; on the propositions of logic, 95 ff.; his theory of the *a priori*, 185–9, 240–1.
Limited independent variety, Keynes's law of, 74.
Locke, J., on theory of knowledge, 1, 4; on reflection (inner sense), 22, 192, 197, 206; on ideas, 32; on universals, 32, 103; on the nature and extent of knowledge, 78–81; on innate ideas, 109; his solution of the problem of objectivity, 119; on substance, 145, 158; rules out knowledge of the true substance of the self, 193.
Logic, compared with theory of knowledge, 4–5, 219; formal and transcendental, 5, 167–9, 170, 208; its supposed identity with mathematics, 94–5; modern empiricist account of, 95 ff., 212–13; derivation of Kant's categories from formal logic, 166 ff.; and self-knowledge, 207 ff.; its connexion with discursive consciousness, 213.
Logical laws, Mill on, 16; the criterion of analytic judgements, 41; appear to be synthetic *a priori*, 50, 95–9; attitude of Coherence Theory to, 86–7; define the possible, 98, 213, 218; expressed in prescriptive judgements, 99, 137, 218; how known, 218–19.
Logical necessity, 42–4, 69, 93–4.
Logical positivists, classed as moderate empiricists, 18; their undue suspicion of intellectual activities, 37; have no use for synthetic *a priori* thinking, 176; metaphysicians in disguise, 238, 245; their account of ethical and theological statements, 245–6.
'Logical' use of the intellect, generally characterized, 35; should be accepted by empiricists and rationalists alike, 36; includes processes of inference, 58–9 (cf. 176); Hume's failure to recognize it, 182, 183.
Logics, alternative, 96–7, 212–13.

McTaggart, J. M. E., 176.
Materialism, 175, 232, 237, 242, 243–4, 245, 250.
Materiate forms, 102.
Mathematical propositions, why it is absurd to deny, 93–4.
Mathematics, its importance for rationalists, 17, 77–8, 90, 187; traditional rationalist account of, 88–9; Mill on, 89; Kant on, 89–91, 137; modern empiricist view of, 91 ff.; its

supposed identity with logic, 94–5; its fascination for philosophers, 186–7.
Matter, and the Kantian category of substance, 147.
Matter and form, in Aristotle, 54–6, 144.
Mechanical and teleological principles, in Kant, 162, 232–4.
Metaphysical deduction of the categories, in Kant, 166–9; in Hegel, 169–76.
Metaphysics, human partiality to, 7; rationalist fondness and empiricist shyness of, 15; method of, according to Descartes and Spinoza, 78; and the categories, 129–35, 160, 189; traditional rationalist account of, 130, 160, 190, 238–9, 251; Kant's early attitude to, 130–2; Kant's later view of, 135, 207, 240; proper subject of, 189, 237, 241 (and Chap. X generally); origin of different metaphysical systems, 237; Collingwood on, 240; its relation to departmental studies, 242; criteria for choosing between different systems of, 243–7 (comprehensiveness, 243–5, adequacy, 245–7); Hegel's attitude to, 247 ff.; future prospects of, 252.
Mill, J. S., on logical laws, 16; on necessary truths, 16–17; on the science of human nature, 19; on mathematics, 89; on causation, 151–2.
Modality, Kant's categories of, 142, 248.
Moral)(demonstrative reasoning, in Hume, 176, 182–3; Hegel's attitude to, 183.
Moral judgement and experience, in Kant, 231–2; logical positivist account of, 245–6.
Mure, G. R. G., 56–7, 174.
Mystical experience, 23–4, 69, 153, 223–9, 239; a possible ambiguity in, 224–5; does it consist in having strange sensations? 226; a suggested test of its objectivity, 227–8; materialist attitude to, 244.
Mystics and non-mystics, 227.

Natura formaliter spectata)(*natura materialiter spectata*, 148 (cf. 113).
Nature, Hegelian theory of the 'impotence' of, 68; Kantian)(empiricist attitude to, 113 (cf. 124–5) (*see also* Philosophy of Nature).
Necessary truths, rationalist account of, 12, 14 ff., 77, 191; empiricist attitude to, 13, 16–17 (cf. Chap. V generally); ambiguity of, 42.
Necessity, four types of distinguished, 42–8 (logical necessity, 42–4, psychological, 44–6, synthetic or intuitive, 46–7, transcendental, 47–8); necessity the essence of objectivity, according to Kant, 122, 124–5; in Nature not logical necessity, 125; of the causal relation, 153.
Newton, I., 4, 90, 154–5, 229, 232.
Nominalism, 31–3, 99–101.
Notions, Berkeley's theory of, 32, 194.
Number, in Hume, 43; in Kant's *Dissertation*, 90.

Oakeshott, M. J., 223.
Objective, problem of, arises for discursive consciousness, 123; belief in, does not involve belief in separate things, 159.
Objects and the objective, knowledge of, 118 ff.; Descartes on, 119; Locke on, 119; Berkeley on, 119–20; Hume on, 120–1; Kant on, 121 ff. (and Chap. VI generally), 148, 152–3, 157, 159; Lewis on, 185–9.
Orderly character of experience, 72–5 (cf. 122–3) (order in general, 73–4, particular forms of order, 74–5).
Overlap of philosophical concepts, in Collingwood, 173.

Paton, H. J., 91, 135, 147.
Pepper, S. C., 242, 244.
Perception and conception, 33 (cf. 84, 115–18).
Perceptual experience, in Kant, 229, 232 ff.
Phenomenalism, 70–2, 119–21.
Philosophical and psychological knowledge of the self, 206 ff.
Philosophical propositions, status of, 206 ff.
Philosophies, notion of a hierarchy of, 174–5, 248, 250.
Philosophy, in what sense a unity, 1–3; Hegelian conception of, 11, 28–9, 65–9, 75–6, 173–6; and experience, 75–6; empiricist conception of, 193, 211 ff.; of mind and self-knowledge, 193, 209 ff.; Kantian view of, 206–7.
Philosophy of Nature, three theories of the function of, 66–7; Whitehead on, 67; Hegel's attitude to, 67–9.
Physics, Kant's attitude to, 197, 229–35.
Plato, his theory of Forms, 36, 56, 101–3; on the relation of mind to the object of knowledge, 56; on 'hypotheses', 87; familiar with the notion

of categories, 107–8, 129; on dialectic, 171.
Possibility, its connexion with discursive consciousness, 69, 213.
Possible experience, in Kant, 113–15.
Prescriptive)(factual judgements, 18, 48, 50–1, 88, 98–9, 137–9, 218; generally and specially prescriptive judgements, 138; in what sense are prescriptive judgements true? 138–9 (cf. 185 ff., 241).
Pre-Socratic conception of substance, 143, 148.
Price, H. H., 18, 35, 101, 105, 122.
Prichard, H. A., 9, 112, 115–18.
Probable reasoning, in Hume, 177–8.
Propositions, their status in empiricist theories, 212.
Psychological necessity, 44–6.
Psychology, rational, 21, 192–3, 198–9, 202, 210, 218; empiricist attitude to, 21, 192–3, 213–14; rationalist attitude to, 193–5, 204, 214 ff.; Kantian view of, 197; its relation to theory of knowledge, 213–14.
Purpose, concept of, 162, 233.

Quality, Kant's categories of, 142, 248.
Quantity, in Hume, 43; Kant's categories of, 142, 248.
Question and answer, their importance in thinking, 127–8.

Rational)(irrational belief, 180 ff.
Rational)(non-rational elements in the self, 215–16.
Rational science of Nature, 19, 64–5 (cf. 77–81).
Rationalism, general contrast with empiricism, 12–20 (main issues specified, 52); and self-knowledge, 20–3, 193–5, 202 ff., 214–16; and different types of experience, 23–4, 222–3; and sensation, 25–9 (cf. 64 ff.); direct arguments for, Chaps. IV, V; indirect arguments for, Chaps. VI–VIII; general nature of Kant's, 125–6, 160, 163–6, 183–4; and Lewis's theory of the *a priori*, 186; how far acceptable, 190–1.
Rationalists, moderate and extreme, 18; pre-Kantian and post-Kantian, 19; philosophical and non-philosophical interests of, 19–20; their claim that the intellect has a 'real' use crucial, 36.
'Real' use of the intellect, generally characterized, 35–6; crucial point for rationalists, 36; not established by reference to inference, 58–9; necessary for objective knowledge, 191.
Realism, as a theory of universals, 100 ff.; its two forms, 101–2.
Realist objection to Kant, 115–18.
'Reality', ambiguity of, 33, 116.
Reason,)(understanding, 24, 27–8, 160–1, 173, 175–6, 183 (cf. 64 ff.); and judgement, 161–2; and imagination, 176–84; practical and theoretical, in Kant, 231–2.
Reasoning, moral and demonstrative, 176, 182–3.
Reciprocity, Kantian category of, 156–7; Hegelian category of, 170.
Reflection, in Locke, 192, 206; its ambiguity, 205–6; rational, 211, 215, 217 ff.
Reflective)(determinant judgement, 162, 233.
Regulative)(constitutive principles, 162, 233.
Relation, Kant's categories of, 142 (and Chap. VII generally), 248.
Religion, Kant's treatment of, 246.
Religious experience, cf. Mystical experience.
Roth, L., 17.
Russell, B. A. W. (Earl Russell), interests of, 18–19; his view of the concepts of mathematics, 94–5; on imagination in sense-perception, 122; on Leibniz, 144, 149; on the self, 201.

Savages, principles governing their thinking, 187–8.
Schelling, F. W. J., 23.
Schematism (schematized categories), 125, 133–5, 164–5.
Science, descriptive theory of, 13–14; Aristotelian conception of, 14, 53–4, 55–6, 98; Cartesian view of, 17, 27, 53–4, 78, 80–1; Bergsonian theory of, 62–3; classical rationalist conception of, Chap. V; empiricist view of, 126–7.
Self as subject and object, 21–2, 194–5, 197–201, 204–5, 209–11; activity of, emphasized by rationalists, 194–5; and accepted by Kant, 197–8; can it be known as active? 199–200, 203–5; Kant's phenomenal and 'real' selves, 199, 205; rational)(non-rational elements in, 215–16.
Self-consciousness, rationalist stress on and interpretation of, 193, 195, 199, 201, 203; Ayer on, 201.
Self-evident truths, 53, 77 ff.; rationalist and empiricist interpretations of, 81–2; denied in Coherence Theory, 82–7; truth in theory of, 87–8.

Self-knowledge, 20–3, Chap. IX; empiricist difficulties with, 20–3, 192 ff.; Descartes on, 20–1, 193, 195, 200; Hume on, 21, 71, 193, 201; Kant on, 21–2, 196 ff.; Hegel on, 22, 195, 203 ff.; Locke on, 22, 192, 193, 197, 206; Berkeley on, 193–5; paradox of, 209–10; strength of empiricist interpretation of, 210; strength of rationalist interpretation of, 210–11; as provided by psychology and philosophy of mind, 211 ff.

Sensation, its passivity, 13, 25, 117; distinguished from sense-perception, 24–5, 30–7, 84, 110–12, 114, 117; rationalist treatment of, 25–9 (cf. 64 ff.); does not afford knowledge in itself, 35, 84, 114, 190; enables us to grasp things in their particularity, 76; identified with immediate experience (q.v.), 114.

Sensationalism, extreme form of empiricism, 18; wrongly identified with empiricism as such, 31, 37.

Sense-data, and sensibilia, 71; and concepts correlative terms, 73; correspondence between different persons', 192.

Sense-experience, cf. Sense-perception.

Sense-judgements never complete in themselves, 83–4.

Sense-perception, and sensation, 24–5, 30–7, 84, 110–12, 114, 117; Aristotle's account of, 56.

Sensing and thinking, Leibniz's account of, 16, 26, 31, 60, 65; Kant on, 26–7, 64, Chap. VI; Hegel on, 27–9, 65–6; Bradley on, 28, 61–2, 84, 221; Spinoza on, 60.

Smith, N. Kemp, 91, 166.

Space, original idea of, in Kant, 26.

Space and time, Kant's assertion of their importance in mathematics, 90–2; and the categories, 125, 134; as forms of human sensibility, 133–4.

Spinoza, B., and logical necessity, 43; on the three grades of knowledge, 60–1 (cf. 169); and the method of metaphysics, 78; his monism, 157; the fundamental experience behind his system, 249 (cf. 62).

Stace, W. T., 68.

Substance, 142 ff.; its ambiguity, 142–3; pre-Socratic notion of, 143; Aristotle's conception of, 143–4; Leibniz on, 144–5; Locke on, 145; Hume on, 145–6; Kant on, 146–8, 165; Collingwood on, 148; Spinoza on, 157; Hegelian category of, 170.

Substance and substances, 148, 157–9.

Sufficient reason, principle of, 16.

Synthesis, Kant's doctrine of, 121 ff., 132–3; intellectual and figurative, 125.

Synthetic *a priori* judgements, Kant's interest in, 38, 41; in what sense necessary? 42 ff.; importance of, for theory of knowledge, 49–50; not adequately dealt with in Coherence Theory, 86–7; Hume's attitude to, 176–82; denied by Lewis, 186.

Synthetic judgements, as defined by Kant, 38; redefined to meet criticisms, 41.

Synthetic or intuitive necessity, 46–7.

Tautologies, 17, 92 (cf. 185–9).

Teleological judgements, in Kant, 232 ff., 248.

Thales, 143.

Theory of knowledge (epistemology), main questions asked in, 3–4; its relation to other studies, 4–5; compared with logic, 4–5, 219; utility of, 5–8; two objections to, 8–11; its relation to psychology, 206 ff.; how are empiricists to explain knowledge of its propositions? 213–14; does it involve intellectual intuition? 213, 219–20; its ambiguous status, 220; progress in, 252.

Thing in itself, the, 10–11, 27, 29, 33, 64, 68, 69–72, 104, 116.

Thinghood, idea of, 157 ff., 179.

Thinking, and different kinds of experience, 24, 223; of savages and civilized men, 187–8 (*see also* Sensing and thinking).

Time, and substance, 147; and causality, 152, 154–5 (*see also* Space and time).

Transcendental logic, 5, 164, 167–9, 170, 208; necessity, 47–8; meaning of 'transcendental' in Kant, 48.

Truth, criterion of, empiricist and rationalist accounts of, 12 (and Chap. V) (*see also* Coherence Theory of Truth).

Truths of reason)(truths of fact, and main controversy between rationalism and empiricism, 15–18, 190–1; Kant's attitude to, 18, 125–6, 136–7; and the distinction between factual and prescriptive judgements, 138; law of causality a truth of reason, according to Leibniz, 149 (cf. 150).

Understanding)(reason, 24, 27–8, 160–1, 173, 175–6, 183 (cf. 64 ff.); nature of an intuitive, 52–3, 69, 203;)(imagination (in Kant), 164–6.

Universals, concrete and abstract, 28, 52–3, 68–9, 76, 175–6; empiricist errors about, 31–2; and intellectual intuition, 54–6, 99–105; their importance for discursive consciousness, 103–4; thinking in terms of a *pis aller*, 104 (*see also* Conceptualism, Nominalism, Realism).

Vleeschauwer, H. J. de, 112–13, 166, 167.
Vulgar, the (in Hume), 180.

Weldon, T. D., 201.
Whitehead, A. N., 67, 148.
Wilson, J. Cook, 9, 39, 77, 112.
Wolff, C., 16, 238–9.

PRINTED IN GREAT BRITAIN AT THE UNIVERSITY PRESS, OXFORD
BY CHARLES BATEY, PRINTER TO THE UNIVERSITY